T0214051

Lecture Notes in Computer Science   12814

More information about this subseries at http://www.springer.com/series/7409

Jamal Bentahar · Irfan Awan ·
Muhammad Younas · Tor-Morten Grønli (Eds.)

Mobile Web and Intelligent Information Systems

17th International Conference, MobiWIS 2021
Virtual Event, August 23–25, 2021
Proceedings

 Springer

Editors
Jamal Bentahar
Concordia University
Montreal, QC, Canada

Irfan Awan
University of Bradford
Bradford, UK

Muhammad Younas
Oxford Brookes University
Oxford, UK

Tor-Morten Grønli
Kristiania University College
Oslo, Norway

ISSN 0302-9743   ISSN 1611-3349 (electronic)
Lecture Notes in Computer Science
ISBN 978-3-030-83163-9   ISBN 978-3-030-83164-6 (eBook)
https://doi.org/10.1007/978-3-030-83164-6

LNCS Sublibrary: SL3 – Information Systems and Applications, incl. Internet/Web, and HCI

This Springer imprint is published by the registered company Springer Nature Switzerland AG
The registered company address is: Gewerbestrasse 11, 6330 Cham, Switzerland

Preface

Welcome to the proceedings of the 17th International Conference on Mobile Web and Intelligent Information Systems (MobiWis 2021), which was held online this year due to the ongoing COVID-19 pandemic. Organizing an online conference confronts a number of challenges for both participants and organizers due to the diversity of technological tools being used and different time zones across the globe, nevertheless we were hopeful that the conference would run smoothly without any major problems.

The Program Committee put together an interesting technical program which included papers covering emerging topics in the areas of mobile web and intelligent information systems. The area of mobile web has gained significant attention from users, researchers, developers, and technology providers due to the increasing use of machine learning and other artificial intelligence techniques for developing mobile web applications. This is evidenced through the enormous use of mobile devices such as smart phones, tablets, and wearable devices in businesses, public and health services, and various smart cities applications. The role of mobile web technology and intelligent applications during the current pandemic has already demonstrated their significance and inspired researchers to find innovative solutions for various challenges that have emerged.

Practitioners in the research and development community face enormous challenges as they attempt to gain insights from highly complex mobile web infrastructure and to design effective solutions that can benefit users as well as technology providers. The MobiWis conference therefore aims to advance mobile web, intelligent information systems, and related mobile technologies from both research and practical applications perspectives. It includes interesting and timely topics such as mobile web systems, recommender systems, security and authentication, context-awareness, advanced mobile web applications, cloud and IoT, mobility management, mobile and wireless networks, and mobile web practice and experience.

This year, MobiWis attracted many high-quality submissions from across the globe. All submitted papers were rigorously reviewed by members of the Technical Program Committee. Based on the reviews, 15 papers were accepted for the conference, which is around 37% of the total submissions. The accepted papers covered a range of topics related to the main theme of the conference, including mobile web and apps, networks and communication, security and privacy, cloud and IoT computing, web applications, and various mobile web technologies. They also included papers on practical applications of technologies in areas of healthcare, government, Bitcoin, education, and eco-computing.

Many people have contributed their time and efforts to the organization of MobiWis 2021. The success of this conference is truly attributed to all the people who invested serious efforts in its smooth running. We are sincerely grateful to the Program Committee who provided timely, constructive, and balanced feedback to the authors. We are also thankful to the authors for their contributions to the conference.

We sincerely thank the general co-chairs, Thanh Van Do and Stephan Böhm, and the local organizing chairs, Flora Amoto and Francesco Piccialli, for their help and support.

Our sincere thanks also go to the Springer LNCS team for their valuable support in the production of the conference proceedings.

August 2021

Jamal Bentahar
Irfan Awan
Muhammad Younas
Tor-Morten Grønli

Organization

General Co-chairs

Thanh Van Do   Telenor, Norway
Stephan Böhm   RheinMain University of Applied Sciences, Germany

Program Co-chairs

Jamal Bentahar   Concordia University, Canada
Tor-Morten Grønli   Kristiania University College, Norway

Local Organizing Co-chairs

Flora Amoto   University of Naples "Federico II", Italy
Francesco Piccialli   University of Naples "Federico II", Italy

Publication Chairs

Irfan Awan   University of Bradford, UK
Muhammad Younas   Oxford Brookes University, UK

Journal Special Issue Coordinator

Satish Narayana   University of Tartu, Estonia

Workshop Coordinator

Filipe Portela   University of Minho, Portugal

Publicity Chair

Nor Shahniza Kamal Bashah   Universiti Teknologi MARA, Malaysia

Program Committee

Abdel Lisser	Université Paris-Saclay, France
Agnis Stibe	ESLSCA Business School Paris, France
Andrea Omicini	University of Bologna, Italy
Aneta Poniszewska-Maranda	Lodz University of Technology, Poland
Carlos Calafate	Technical University of Valencia, Spain
Chi (Harold) Liu	Beijing Institute of Technology, China
Christophe Feltus	Luxembourg Institute of Science and Technology, Luxembourg
Dan Johansson	Umea University, Sweden
Do van Thuan	Linus AS, Norway
Fatma Abdennadher	National School of Engineering of Sfax, Tunisia
Florence Sedes	Université Paul Sabatier, France
Hiroaki Kikuchi	Meiji University, Japan
Ivan Demydov	Lviv Polytechnic National University, Ukraine
Jorge Sa Silva	University of Coimbra, Portugal
Jozef Juhar	Technical University of Košice, Slovakia
Jung-Chun Liu	Tunghai University, Taiwan
Katty Rohoden	Jaramillo Universidad Técnica Particular de Loja, Ecuador
Lianghuai Yang	Zhejiang University of Technology, China
Lidia Ogiela	Pedagogical University of Cracow, Poland
Lulwah AlSuwaidan	King Saud University, Saudi Arabia
Marek R. Ogiela	AGH University of Science and Technology, Poland
Masahiro Sasabe	Nara Institute of Science and Technology, Japan
Michal Gregus	Comenius University in Bratislava, Slovakia
Mikko Rissanen	Improvements, Malaysia
Muslim Elkotob	MB TDF Group, Germany
Nor Shahniza Kamal Bashah	Universiti Teknologi MARA, Malaysia
Norazlina Khamis	Universiti Malaysia Sabah, Malaysia
Novia Admodisastro	Universiti Putra Malaysia, Malaysia
Ondrej Krejcar	University of Hradec Kralove, Czech Republic
Pablo Adasme	University of Santiago de Chile, Chile
Paolo Nesi	University of Florence, Italy
Perin Unal	METU, Turkey
Philippe Roose	IUT de Bayonne, France
Pınar Kırcı	Istanbul University, Turkey
Riccardo Martoglia	University of Modena and Reggio Emilia, Italy
Sajad Khorsandroo	The University of Texas at San Antonio, USA
Sergio Ilarri	University of Zaragoza, Spain
Shinsaku Kiyomoto	KDDI R&D Laboratories Inc., Japan
Stephan Böhm	RheinMain University of Applied Sciences, Germany
Thanh Van Do	Telenor, Norway

Contents

Security and Privacy

A Secure 5G Eldercare Solution Using Millimeterwave Sensors

Boning Feng[1]([✉]), Akihiro Kajiwara[2], Van Thuan Do[1,3], Niels Jacot[3],
Bernardo Santos[1], Bruno Dzogovic[1], and Thanh van Do[1,4]

[1] Oslo Metropolitan University, Pilestredet 35, 0167 Oslo, Norway
{boning.feng,bersan,bruno.dzogovic}@oslomet.no
[2] University of Kitakyushu, 1-1 Hibiki, Wakamatsu-ku, Kitakyushu, Fukuoka 808-0135, Japan
kajiwara@kitakyu-u.ac.jp
[3] Wolffia AS, Haugerudveien. 40, 0673 Oslo, Norway
{vt.do,n.jacot}@wolffia.net
[4] Telenor ASA., Snarøyveien 30, 1331 Fornebu, Norway
thanh-van.do@telenor.com

Abstract. The world is ageing fast and the need of efficient digital solution enabling elderlies to age at home is getting urgent. Unfortunately there is so far no such a solution which is sufficiently efficient, customizable, secure and reliable. This paper presents a solution called Ageing@home which is efficient, easy to deploy, privacy preserving, unobtrusive and customizable by making use of millimeter wave sensors, 5G network slicing and open unifying IoT platform. The paper provides a detailed description of the advantageous use of the millimeter wave sensors and present the proposed 5G network slicing alternative. An open unifying IoT platform capable of bridging diverse heterogeneous IoT devices from different vendors is also introduced.

Keywords: 5G mobile networks · 5G network slicing · mmWave sensors · Unifying IoT platforms · Assisted living · Elderly care · Home based elderly care

1 Introduction

As the world population is getting older every day, challenges are increasing both for the elderly citizen but also for countries all over the world [1]. To meet these challenges multiple digital making use new technologies to provide necessary needs and assistance to senior citizen such that they can age comfortably, safely and securely at their home. This is by far the most economical and sustainable solution for the whole society. In Europe, the *Ambient Assisted Living (AAL) Programme* [2] has as objective the development and use of new technologies to allow elderly and disabled people to live comfortably at home, improving their autonomy, facilitating daily activities, ensuring better security, monitoring and treating sick people. Similarly, in the Nordic countries including Norway, *Welfare technologies* [3] have been proposed to provide better services for the elderly living at home but mostly at nursing homes. Unfortunately, although

© Springer Nature Switzerland AG 2021
J. Bentahar et al. (Eds.): MobiWIS 2021, LNCS 12814, pp. 3–15, 2021.
https://doi.org/10.1007/978-3-030-83164-6_1

promising all existing solutions are not adopted because of multiple weaknesses such as instability, configuration complexity, installation difficulties, fragmentation, lack of user centricity, and security and privacy issues. In this paper, we present Ageing@home, a welfare technology solution, which addresses the mentioned weaknesses by combining latest advances in three technology fields namely sensors, mobile communication and Internet of Things (IoT). The paper starts by a summary of the requirements on Ageing@home followed by a clarification of the limitation of current eldercare solution. Next is the conceptual architecture which enables a flexible and adaptable inclusion of welfare technologies and services based on individual needs. The main part of the paper consists of the detailed description of the three fundamental technology components of Ageing@home namely millimeter wave sensors, 5G network slicing and unifying IoT platform. A description of a partial proof-of-concept implemented at the Secure 5G4IoT lab at the Oslo Metropolitan University is also given to complete the presentation of our Ageing@home solution. The paper concludes with some suggestions of further works.

2   Requirements on the Ageing@home Solution

The majority of people want to live at home as long as possible because they will have the feeling of independence, comfort, safety, security, joy and happiness. In addition and quite importantly, by living at home, the seniors will put less pressure on the healthcare system at the same time as the incurred costs are by far lower than the ones at the nursing homes. However, in order to be successful Ageing@home must satisfy the following requirements:

- It shall ensure the security and safety of elderly people
- It shall ensure the privacy and dignity of elderly people
- It shall prioritize the well-being and individuality of elderly people
- It shall be affordable to the majority of elderly people

Although reasonable when taken for itself these requirements might be conflicting with others and make the realization of a good Home-based Elderly Care solution quite challenging. For example, to provide adequate security and safety protection might have negative consequences on privacy and well-being. The prioritization of the well-being and individuality of elderly people may raise the costs and make the Home-based Elderly Care solution not affordable to the majority.

3   Limitation of State-of-the Art Eldercare Solutions

There are currently many research activities both in EU and the Nordic countries. As umbrella programme there are Active & Assisted Living (AAL) programme, a European Innovation Partnership with 19 countries and Nordic Ambient Assisted Living coordinated by the Nordic Council of Ministers. In addition to numerous national projects in European countries there are also multiple COST and H2020 projects such as Sheld-on, Activage, Phara-on, Ghost-IoT, etc. Unfortunately, so far the AAL Digital solutions has still quite low uptake due to the following limitations:

- **Instability:** Most of solutions using Wireless LAN 802.11 experience occasional loss of connection due to interference, channel collision, coverage variation, etc.
- **Configuration complexity:** The usage of Wireless LAN requires also the configuration of several parameters for each installation, which is error prone. Further, security protection requires considerable knowledge and efforts.
- **Installation difficulties:** The installation of sensors and devices at the elderly home could be difficult due to the furniture, time consuming and hence annoying to the users.
- **Fragmentation:** The current digital solutions are "silos" applications that operating in isolation without interworking and interoperability with each other. Consequently, the introduction of additional services will require a full installation of hardware and software which incurs high cost and disturbance to the elderly
- **Lack of user centricity:** The current digital solutions are too much technology oriented [4] consisting of a bunch of technologies that are put together and offered to the elderly without sufficient considerations of the elderly user's preferences or the health personnel's opinions [5].
- **Security and Privacy issues:** Although it is necessary to collect data to provide effective services to the elderly these data are personal data which illegal access constitutes a privacy violation [6]. Unfortunately, the protection of personal data is currently not adequate. Further the use of video camera has been considered as obtrusive by elderly who feels watched.

4   Ageing@home Conceptual Architecture

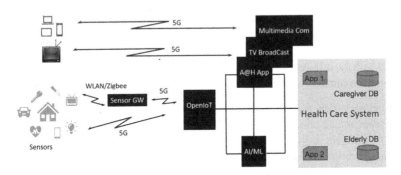

Fig. 1. The Ageing@Home conceptual model

To be able to accommodate all the improved welfare technologies described above in a customized, adaptable and scalable way the Ageing@Home end-to-end solution has an architecture represented by a conceptual model shown in Fig. 1.

Multiple heterogeneous sensors, both wearable aka on-body and ambient aka off-body with dedicated mission are connected to an open unifying cloud IoT platform (OpenIoT) directly via 5G or indirectly, first via certain Local Area technologies such as Wireless LAN IEEE 802.11x, Zigbee, Z-wave, etc., to a Sensor Gateway and then via

5G to the OpenIoT. The sensors collect data and upload to the OpenIoT, which can then forward the collected data depending on the need to the Ageing@Home applications (Ageing@Home Apps), the Artificial Intelligence/Machine Learning (AI/ML) Platform or the Health Care System (HCS), where they are consumed in various ways. At the AI/ML Platform they [the data] are in multiple analytic tasks, especially the elaboration of the elderly's profile, which allow for better understanding the elderly and to respond appropriately to their needs and mood. When necessary, the data can be anonymized before being forwarded and stored.

The AI/ML Platform has interfaces with the Ageing@Home Apps and the HCS, which are then enabled to invoke various analytic tasks. The interface between the Ageing@Home Apps and the HCS enables the Ageing@Home Apps to access the HCS user and caregiver database and also other functionality, while the HCS can control the Ageing@Home Apps. The Ageing@Home Apps are essential to the implementation and provision of the targeted welfare technologies such as Digital night vision, Entertainment, Event and vital sign monitoring and detection, etc. Two Ageing@Home Apps, Broadcasting of Physical exercises and Multimodal communication, as communication apps have direct connection with their devices, i.e. TV, PC, tablets, etc.

5   Millimeter Wave (mmWave) Sensors for Ageing@home

5.1   Brief About mmWave Sensors

As their name indicates, mmWave radar sensors or simply radar sensors are active sensors that transmit millimeter waves to detect objects and their changes in the environment such as heat, light, sound or motion, etc. Millimeter waves are electromagnetic radio waves typically defined to lie within the frequency range of 30–300 GHz.

5.2   Advantages with mmWave Sensors in Eldercare

Compared with the infrared or ultrasonic technology which are commonly used in ehealth applications the mmWave sensors demonstrate with the following advantages:

Higher Accuracy, Penetration and Reliability: By using wavelength in millimeters, mmWave sensors are able to achieve millimeter range accuracy and to penetrate materials such as plastic, drywall, clothing, etc. They are also generally less sensitive to ambient temperature and surrounding environment.

Better Privacy Protection: The use of mmWave sensors in the monitoring of events and accidents is perceived by elderlies as less intrusive than cameras that are rejected by most elderlies. The use of mmWave sensors in the monitoring of events and accidents is perceived by elderlies as less intrusive than cameras that are rejected by most elderlies.

More Freedom of Movement: So far most of the sensors used in ehealth are on-body or wearable sensors that although accurate and reliable have some limitations such as limiting physical movements, detaching and attaching at bath, falling down and loss, etc.

5.3 The Use of mmWave Sensors in Ageing@home

Ageing@home proposes to use mmWave sensors developed at the Kajiwara lab of the university of Kitakyushu to realise the following welfare services:

- *Health and stress monitoring in living*: includes the monitoring of blood pressure, blood glucose, heart rate, body temperature [7]
- *Health and accident prevention monitoring in bedrooms*: includes heart attack, fall accident, sleep apnea syndrome [8]
- *Accident prevention and early accident detection in bath and toilet room:* requires special sensors that fulfil the conditions of the bathroom e.g. temperature, humidity, pressure, etc. [9]

The wider available bandwidth of the mmWave sensors will offer high range resolution and allow smaller coverages suitable for the deployment at every room in the house as shown in Fig. 2. The mmWave sensors are mounted in all rooms and able to capture in a non-contact manner movement data and vital data which are sent to the open unifying cloud IoT platform a gateway via a gateway installed in the elderly home. The data allow not only the detection of vital anomalies upon occurrence but also their prediction prior to occurrence such that doctors can intervene earlier. A sensing algorithm has been developed at the Kajiwara lab.

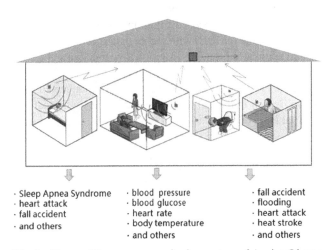

· Sleep Apnea Syndrome	· blood pressure	· fall accident
· heart attack	· blood glucose	· flooding
· fall accident	· heart rate	· heart attack
· and others	· body temperature	· heat stroke
	· and others	· and others

Fig. 2. The mmWave sensor monitoring system of Ageing@home

To ensure the reliability and accuracy of Ageing@home it is necessary to study and optimize both the location and number of the sensors for each home to accommodate their different layouts and structures. In addition, in order to cope with presence or absence of different caregivers in the house and also with the visit times which the care are given, it is necessary to consider and optimize the type of data to be collected and the operating hours of the sensors.

By performing these optimizations, it is possible to provide quick and appropriate response to abnormal situations, to prevent occurrence of abnormal situations and to reduce burden on caregivers. If an anomaly is detected, the health care system can be notified and assistance measures can be taken and deployed. There may be a need to consult the location information and the movement flow of elderly dementia who has exited their home and got lost.

Movement on the bed such as getting out of bed, moving, turning over, and vital information such as breathing, electrocardiography, and blood pressure can be continuously monitored without contact.

Accidents in the bathroom can be fatal to the elderly living alone at home. Each year around 17,000 people died from heat shock during bathing and minor accidents that lead to fatal consequences. It is hence necessary to detect accidents in the bathroom quickly but without invading privacy by using video camera. Again, mmWave sensors with high resolution range and humid resistance have proposed to monitor and collect data in the bathroom which are sent to the AI/ML platform for the estimation of various dangerous state or behavior using multiple ML algorithms.

6   Ageing@home 5G Network Slicing

6.1   Brief Introduction to 5G Network Slicing

The 5th generation mobile network or simply 5G [10] is well known for its superiority compared to 4G in terms of performance, coverage and quality of service and the promise of enhanced mobile broadband (eMBB) with higher data speed and the support of a wide range of services and application ranging from massive machine-type communications (mMTC) to ultra-reliable and low-latency communications (URLLC). Less known but not less important is the fact that 5G is a softwarized and virtualized network. Indeed, a 5G network is not made up of physical network elements as traditional mobile network but of software virtual Network Functions [11].

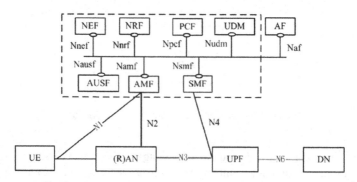

Fig. 3. The 5G Reference Architecture (Courtesy of 3GPP)

As shown in Fig. 3 the 5G Reference Architecture is composed of the following Network Functions:

On the User plane:

- **UE** (User Equipment): is the user's mobile phone.
- **(R)AN** (Radio Access Network): is the Access Network Function which provides connectivity to the mobile phone.
- **UPF** (User Plane Function): handles the user plane traffic, e.g., traffic routing & forwarding, traffic inspection and usage reporting. It can be deployed in various configurations and locations depending on the service type.
- **DN** (Data Network): represents operator services, Internet access or 3rd party services.

On the Control plane:

- **AMF** (Access and Mobility Management Function): performs access control, mobility control and transparent proxy for routing SMS (Short Message Service) messages.
- **AUSF** (Authentication Server Function): provides authentication functions.
- **UDM** (Unified Data Management): stores subscriber data and profiles. It has an equivalent role as HSS in 4G but will be used for both fixed and mobile access in 5G core.
- **SMF** (Session Management Function): sets up and manages the PDU session according to network policy.
- **NSSF** (Network Slice Selection Function): selects the *Network Slice Instance* (NSI), determines the allowed *network slice selection assistance information* (NSSAI) and AMF set to serve the UE.
- **NEF** (Network Exposure Function): exposes the services and capabilities provided by the 3GPP network functions.
- **NRF** (NF Repository Function): maintains NF profiles and supports service discovery.
- **PCF** (Policy Control function): provides a policy framework incorporating network slicing, roaming and mobility management and has an equivalent role as PCRF in 4G.
- **AF** (Application Function): interacts with the 3GPP Core Network (CN) to provide services

The software nature of the 5G network enables the realisation of the network slicing concept which can be defined as by the 5G Infrastructure Public Private Partnership (5G PPP) as *"network slice is a composition of adequately configured network functions, net-work applications, and the underlying cloud infrastructure (physical, virtual or even emulated resources, RAN resources etc.), that are bundled together to meet the requirements of a specific use case, e.g., bandwidth, latency, processing, and resiliency, coupled with a business purpose"* [10].

6.2 The Ageing@home Network Slicing

In order to provide a connection which provides adequate protection of security and privacy at an acceptable level of reliability a dedicated and isolated end-to-end network slice will be established. This healthcare network slice is a logical network realised by dedicated vNFs (Virtual Network Functions) [12] for both access network and core network as shown by Fig. 3. Only devices equipped with SIM cards own by the hospital can be authorised to connect to this healthcare network slice. While IoT devices are in general not allowed to some smartphones may be permitted to have simultaneous connection to the public network slice depending on the security policy of the hospital (Fig. 4).

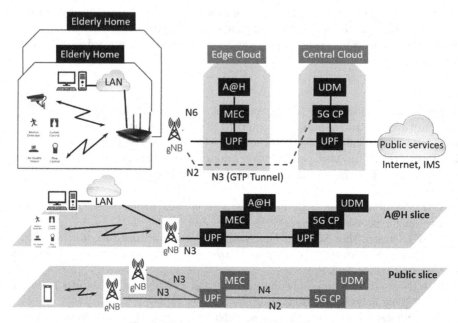

Fig. 4. Network slicing for Ageing@home

As shown in Fig. 3, the Ageing@Home solution consisting of OUIP (open unifying IoT platform), AI/ML platform and a variety of Ageing@Home applications are hosted on a MEC (Multi-access Edge Computing) host, which is located on Edge Cloud. Since the Edge Cloud is in the same area as the elderly home, very low latency can be achieved making this deployment option quite suitable for Welfare technologies, such as Broadcasting of physical exercises and mobility sessions technology. Further, both the security and privacy are considerably enhanced because communications between sensors and the Ageing@home do not have to traverse the entire mobile network, but only a short path between the gNBs and the Edge Cloud.

7   An Open Unifying Cloud IoT Gateway

Current IoT applications such as eHealth, Smart Home, Smart Living, security, etc. are mostly vertical applications that are not able to communicate with each other. The Ageing@home solution shall include an open unifying cloud based IoT platform capable of incorporating heterogeneous devices and sensors from different manufacturers and also capable of interacting with other IoT platforms. The interoperability between

IoT platforms is achieved by developing a data integration framework, focusing on the implementation of a data exchange architecture, application interfaces and identity management that enable data to be accessed and shared appropriately and securely across the complete spectrum of care, within all applicable settings and with relevant stakeholders, including by the individual senior citizen. Last but not least, the Ageing@home open IoT platform is able to interact with existing IoT systems at the elderly home such as security system, consumer electronics, energy, etc. which enable re-use and integration of existing infrastructure (Fig. 5).

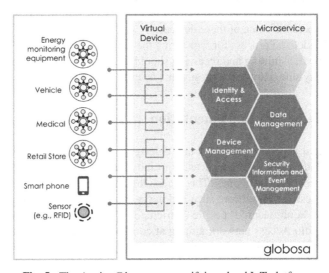

Fig. 5. The Ageing@home open unifying cloud IoT platform

To address those challenges, we propose a user-centric privacy-aware framework that handles data of different devices and components from various vendors to efficiently integrate smart objects into IoT solutions. The framework will ensure that consumers' personal data will only be shared with consumers' consent, unless required and limited for the use of product features.

A further development has been the disassociation of data from the architectures. In IoT architectures, data continues to be managed and processed for primary applications (the applications for which the architectures were originally designed). However, enterprises have recognized that data sets from one IoT architecture may in fact add value to other IoT architectures and applications. By disassociating data from IoT architectures, or making it accessible for other applications, a range of opportunities has opened to design and develop new services based on aggregation of data sets and federation of information from different sources, potentially delivering unparalleled insights.

Given the dynamism of deployment and scalability expectations which comes with IoT, microservice-based architecture is an important part of the overall IoT strategy. Microservice-based architecture offers a way of scaling the infrastructure both horizontally and vertically giving long term benefits to the IoT application systems. Each of the services as shown in Figure can scale based on the needs.

In IoT, the role of Identity Management is expanding [13]. It is no longer just about identifying people and managing their access to various online services and to different types of data (i.e. sensitive data, non-sensitive data, personal data, device data, etc.). Identity Management must now be able to identify devices, sensors, monitors, and manage their access to sensitive and non-sensitive data. Our open user-centric privacy-aware framework must include methods for managing device identity and be able to do some of the following:

- Establish a naming system for IoT devices.
- Determine an identity lifecycle for IoT devices, making sure it can be modified to meet the projected lifetime of these devices.
- Create a well-defined process for registering the IoT devices; the type of data that the device will be transmitting and receiving should shape the registration process.
- Define security safeguards for data streams from IoT devices.

8   Proof-of-Concept Implementation

To prevent illegal access to resources and elderly data the Healthcare slice has to be completely isolated from the other slices, especially the public enhanced Mobile Broadband slice for regular smartphones. This means that regular mobile subscribers will be prevented to access the Healthcare slice and the resources and services associated to it.

To fulfil the requirement, a specific restricted network policy has to be established in the Cloud Radio Access network aiming at constraining access to specific network resources and allowing only authorised traffic.

As shown in Fig. 6, the 5G4IoT lab has established an early 5G network consisting of a Cloud Radio Access Network (C-RAN), connected to a cloudified OpenAirInterface [14] EPC (Evolved Core Network). The infrastructure is deployed using functional split between a Baseband Unit and the Remote Radio Head, with the NGFI (Next Generation Fronthaul Interface). In order to achieve network slicing, the User Equipment with SIM_1 is associated with the Mobility Management Entity MME_1 instance running in the core network, as well as the IoT device with SIM_2 correlated with the MME_2. Both MME instances are virtualized into container environment using the Docker technology. The same applies to the other constituents of the core network, including two instances of HSS (Home Subscriber Server) databases, specifically HSS_1 and HSS_2 related to MME_1 and MME_2 instances correspondingly. The Docker container networking interface (CNI) should thus disallow the two databases to communicate with each other and allow only their corresponding MME instances to perform DIAMETER authentication in their own network domain. By establishing tunnel within a VPN network, the IoT devices with SIM_2 can also securely access their own slice to the SGW (Serving Gateway) and PGW (Packet data network Gateway), initiating a route to the corresponding MME_2 with a private network broadcast domain. For the purpose of establishing appropriate routes, the S/PGW are set to create virtual GTP-U (GPRS Tunneling Protocol User data tunneling) tunnels between the virtual interface of the instance to the corresponding virtual interface of the MME_1 and MME_2 subsequently, with different IP domains.

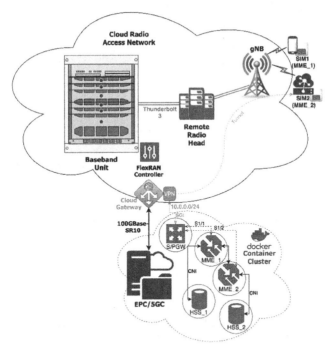

Fig. 6. 5G4IoT lab Cloud Radio Access Network slicing concept

In order to associate an explicit user to the matching database, the FlexRAN controller conjoins the equivalent IMSI (International Mobile Subscriber Identity) values of the device to the ones in the conforming HSS_2 database. This way, the User Equipment (mobile phones) are incapable of reaching the registered devices in the HSS_2 database, since their IMSI values are meticulously canalised into the HSS_1 and their traffic routed explicitly within that route.

Allied to the described network, an identity provisioning and management system (IDMS) [13] has been implemented as shown in Fig. 6, as a way to strengthen as well as simplify the authentication process for users (e.g. caregivers) and devices using the network by offering a single sign-on mechanism across the network and the application layers. More precisely, we inherit existing components from the network that can provide a secure way to identify a device and used it a unified way between layers.

To achieve a consensus on which parameters can be used as identifiers, i.e. identity federation, an API was also developed [15] to bridge between the IDMS and the network. After issuing the identities for the desired caregivers/devices, a module is created and given to the healthcare center, so that when a verification request has to occur, the healthcare center will confirm with the system as if one is eligible to provide support to an elderly person.

This identity management system is created by using an instance of the Gluu Server [16] that provides a combination of the provisioning and management tools, as well the option of deploying OpenID clients for integrations with third-party applications (Fig. 7).

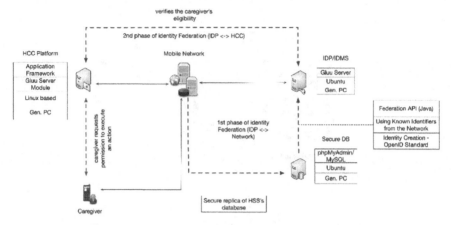

Fig. 7. Implementation of the identity management system

9 Conclusion

In this paper we have presented Ageing@home, a welfare solution which enables elderly to age comfortable, safely and securely at their home by making use of three major technologies namely mmWave sensors, 5G network slicing and open unifying IoT platform. Although these technologies have been tested and successfully validated separately at the Secure 5G4IoT lab and the Kajiwara lab, a fully integrated prototype has not been done. Further, it is necessary to carry out proper validation with real users [17, 18]. For that it is required to run a field trial at with a limited number of elderlies living in a municipality in Norway or Japan. Findings from the field trial will be used to improve and optimize the sensors, the 5G network slice, the IoT platform and also the AI/ML algorithms used in the detection and prediction of anomalies. As longer-term continuation works, innovative welfare technologies and services are envisaged to be included and deployed in Ageing@home. The ultimate goal is naturally the successful commercial deployment and the wide adoption of Ageing@home in Norway, Japan and all over the world.

Acknowledgement. This paper is a result of the H2020 CONCORDIA project (https://www.concordia-h2020.eu) which has received funding from the EU H2020 programme under grant agreement No 830927. The CONCORDIA consortium includes 23 partners from industry and other organizations such as Telenor, Telefonica, Telecom Italia, Ericsson, Siemens, Airbus, etc. and 23 partners from academia such as CODE, university of Twente, OsloMet, etc.

References

1. United Nations, Department of Economic and Social Affairs, Population Division (2017). World Population Ageing 2017 (ST/ESA/SER.A/408)
2. http://www.aal-europe.eu/

3. Velferdsteknologi. https://www.helsedirektoratet.no/rapporter/implementering-av-velfer
   dsteknologi-i-de-kommunale-helse-og-omsorgstjenestene-2013-2030/Implementering%
   20av%20velferdsteknologi%20i%20de%20kommunale%20helse-og%20omsorgstjenes
   tene%202013-2030.pdf/_/attachment/inline/cf340308-0cb8-4a88-a6d7-4754ef126db9:6f3
   a196c2d353a9ef04c772f7cc0a2cb9d955087/Implementering%20av%20velferdsteknologi%
   20i%20de%20kommunale%20helse-og%20omsorgstjenestene%202013-2030.pdf
4. Memon, M., Wagner, S.R., Pedersen, C.F., Beevi, F.H.A., Hansen, F.O.: Ambient assisted
   living healthcare frameworks, platforms, standards, and quality attributes. Sensors (Basel)
   14(3), 4312–4341 (2014). https://doi.org/10.3390/s140304312
5. van Heek, J.O., Ziefle, M.: They don't care about us! Care personnel's perspectives on ambient
   assisted living technology usage: scenario-based survey study. JMIR Rehabil. Assist. Technol.
   5(2), e10424 (2018). https://doi.org/10.2196/10424
6. Muñoz, D., Gutierrez, F.J., Ochoa, S.F.: Introducing ambient assisted living technology at the
   home of the elderly: challenges and lessons learned. In: Cleland, I., Guerrero, L., Bravo, J.
   (eds.) IWAAL 2015. LNCS, vol. 9455, pp. 125–136. Springer, Cham (2015). https://doi.org/
   10.1007/978-3-319-26410-3_12
7. Morimatsu, A., Matsuguma, S., Kajiwara, A.: Heart rate estimation of a moving person using
   79GHz-Band UWB radar. In: 2019 IEEE Sensors Applications Symposium (SAS), Sophia
   Antipolis, France, pp. 1–5 (2019). https://doi.org/10.1109/SAS.2019.8706073
8. Tsuchiyama, K., Kajiwara, A.: Accident detection and health-monitoring UWB sensor in
   toilet. In: 2019 IEEE Topical Conference on Wireless Sensors and Sensor Networks (WiSNet),
   Orlando, FL, USA, pp. 1–4 (2019). https://doi.org/10.1109/WISNET.2019.8711812
9. Kashima, K., Nakamura, R., Kajiwara, A.: Bathroom movements monitoring UWB sensor with feature extraction algorithm. In: 2013 IEEE Sensors Applications Symposium
   Proceedings, pp. 118–122 (2013)
10. 5G Infrastructure Public Private Partnership (5G PPP): View on 5G Architecture (Version
    2.0), 5G PPP Architecture Working Group, 18 July 2017
11. ETSI: GS NFV 002 Network Functions Virtualization (NFV); Architectural Framework,
    v.1.1.1, October 2013
12. Dzogovic, B., Santos, B., Noll, J., Do, V.T., Feng, B., Van Do, T.: Enabling smart home
    with 5G network slicing. In: Proceedings of the 2019 IEEE 4th International Conference on
    Computer and Communication Systems ICCCS 2019, IEEE Catalog Number CFP19D48-
    USB, Conference, Chair Yang Xiao, Singapore, 23–25 February 2019, pp. 543–548 (2019).
    ISBN 978-1-7281-1321-0
13. Santos, B., Do, V.T., Feng, B., van Do, T.: Identity federation for cellular Internet of Things. In:
    Proceedings of the 2018 7th International Conference on Software and Computer Applications
    - ICSCA 2018, pp. 223–228 (2018)
14. OpenAirInterface Software Alliance (OSA): a non-profit consortium fostering a community of
    industrial as well as research contributors for open source software and hardware development
    for the core network (EPC), access network and user equipment (EUTRAN) of 3GPP cellular
    networks. https://www.openairinterface.org/
15. Santos, B., Do, V.T., Feng, B., van Do, T.: Towards a standardized identity federation for
    Internet of Things in 5G networks. In: 2018 IEEE SmartWorld 2018 Proceedings, pp. 2082–
    2088 (2018)
16. Gluu Server. https://www.gluu.org/. Accessed May 2019
17. Lawton, M.P., Brody, E.M.: Assessment of older people: self-maintaining and instrumental
    activities of daily living. Gerontologist **9**(3), 179–186 (1969)
18. https://www.rand.org/health/surveys_tools/mos/36-item-short-form.html

A Framework for Investigating GDPR Compliance Through the Lens of Security

Angelica Marotta[1]([envelope]) [iD] and Stuart Madnick[2] [iD]

[1] MIT Sloan School of Management, 245 First Street, Cambridge, MA 02142, USA
amarotta@mit.edu
[2] MIT Sloan School of Management, 100 Main Street, Cambridge, MA 02142, USA
smadnick@mit.edu

Abstract. The General Data Protection Regulation (GDPR) was widely seen as a significant step towards enhancing data protection and privacy. Unlike previous legislation, adherence to GDPR required organizations to assume greater responsibility for cybersecurity with respect to data processing. This shift represented a profound transformation in how businesses retain, use, manage, and protect data. However, despite these innovative aspects, the actual implementation of the GDPR security side poses some challenges. This paper attempts to identify positive and negative aspects of GDPR requirements and presents a new framework for analyzing them from a security point of view. Firstly, it provides an overview of the most significant scholarly perspectives on GDPR and cybersecurity. Secondly, it presents a systematic roadmap analysis and discussion of the requirements of GDPR in relation to cybersecurity. Results show that some of the GDPR security controls, such as the Data Protection Impact Assessments (DPIA), records on processing, and the appointment of a Data Protection Officer (DPO), are some of the most critical from a security viewpoint. Finally, it provides recommendations for tackling these challenges in the evolving compliance landscape.

Keywords: GDPR · Cybersecurity · Compliance · Regulations · Risk management

1 Introduction

Today, every organization has a "digital footprint." Every time employees communicate, engage with customers through the Internet, use a device, or simply advertise their business, they are leaving a data trail behind them. The more data they share, the more their digital footprint grows. With the large volume of information that must be handled, it is challenging to keep track of which digital assets need to be secured. As a result, data protection is now a major area of focus in the field of compliance and security. The introduction of the General Data Protection Regulation (GDPR), which came into effect in the European Union on 25 May 2018, was widely seen as a significant step towards enhancing data protection and privacy [1]. The Regulation was designed to allow individuals to control their data and require organizations to better handle data processing.

© Springer Nature Switzerland AG 2021
J. Bentahar et al. (Eds.): MobiWIS 2021, LNCS 12814, pp. 16–31, 2021.
https://doi.org/10.1007/978-3-030-83164-6_2

Individuals and regulators were presented with new regulatory mechanisms, including administrative fines and an extension of the requirements' scope. In this context, the new security requirements under the GDPR benefitted from the lessons learned from data protection authorities' past experience and a more conscious conception of the digital environment in which companies operate. The GDPR specifically explains what risks data processing may pose, such as identity fraud, professional secrecy issues, data disclosure, etc. Figure 1 shows the main security aims of the GDPR [2].

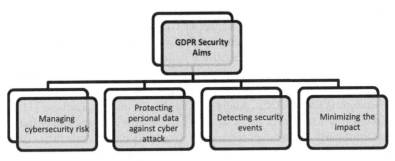

Fig. 1. GDPR security aims

However, despite these innovative aspects, there is some confusion regarding the actual implementation of the GDPR's security side. Some argue that GDPR provides a solid security structure to operate by, but the reality is more complicated. GDPR is primarily data privacy legislation whose main pillars are privacy, policy, and cybersecurity. Organizations need to implement all three pillars to successfully comply with the strict requirements of the GDPR and be secure. Marotta and Madnick [3–5] investigated this issue in an extensive way. In particular, the authors argue that compliance is not black and white but rather a combination of factors, which may either have a positive or negative impact on cybersecurity. In this paper, this concept is further extended to explore the impact of GDPR "through the sense of security." More specifically, the study examines each GDPR requirement with particular attention to security to identify controls that are likely to increase or reduce the general level of cybersecurity in an organization. The work provides the following contributions to the study of cybersecurity compliance. Firstly, it offers a review of the main scholarly viewpoints on GDPR and cybersecurity. Secondly, it presents a systematic analysis and discussion of the requirements of GDPR with respect to cybersecurity. Thirdly, it provides recommendations and future perspectives on the evolving compliance landscape.

2 Literature Review and Background

In today's changing threat landscape, businesses are required to perform two essential and intertwined tasks: proactively addressing cyber risks and maintaining compliance with laws and regulations. However, as shown in the comparative compliance analysis conducted in a previous study [6], several issues prevent companies from pursuing these objectives and achieving an effective balance between compliance and cybersecurity.

Some of them depend on the industry in which a company operates. For example, in the healthcare sector, regulatory language may make it difficult for health operators and patients to comprehend and interpret regulations. These considerations apply to almost every enforcement setting, but they are particularly pertinent in the context of GDPR [7]. For example, Huth and Matthes (2019) argued that GDPR poses challenges regarding the integration of privacy concerns in software development processes. Tsohou et al. [8] also agreed that data controllers face difficulties complying with the GDPR and proposed mechanisms and tools to assist organizations in adhering to the requirement. Conversely, other authors who conducted analyses on this topic found positive results [9]. For example, Horák et al. [10] discussed the impact of GDPR on cyber-security software and operations. In particular, they conducted a DPIA assessment to investigate risks related to information sharing in cybersecurity. Their findings indicated that the risks were not high and that the DPIA aided in a better understanding of risks and their management. They also pointed out that this assessment provides a solid ground for information sharing in cybersecurity under GDPR. Along with this line of thought, Lachaud [11] argued that the GDPR (particularly Article 42 and 43) "encourages data controllers and processors to use third-party certification schemes to voluntarily demonstrate their conformity with the GDPR." According to the author, this "endorsement" represents a new type of "regulation instrument" whose flexibility helps fill the gap between self-regulation and regulation. Another research trend observed in the literature is the use of comparative analysis to investigate whether the security principles outlined in the GDPR are consistent with other frameworks. Saqib et al. [12] performed a comparison between the security requirements of the GDPR and the Directive on security of network and information systems (NISD). More specifically, the author studied how GDPR influences the NISD. This mapping provided interesting results regarding possible difficulties that businesses may experience while implementing compliance with GDPR and NISD. Other scholars conducted a similar investigation to compare the controls provisioned in ISO standards (e.g., ISO/IEC 27001:2013 and ISO/IEC 27002:2013) and the data protection requirements set by the GDPR [13–15]. These studies agree in assessing the importance of integrating GDPR with other frameworks and evaluating multiple factors that have an impact on security.

2.1 Brexit and the UK Version of GDPR

According to Marotta and Madnick [6] an essential factor influencing the relationship between compliance and security is the geographical aspect surrounding compliance. According to the authors [6], "regulations uniquely impact organizations and the global actors connected to their operations." As shown in a case study[1] conducted by the same authors [6], this aspect is particularly evident in Europe due to the high level of interdependencies among the Member States. For example, according to Chivot and Castro [16], the European Commission stated that one year after the introduction of the GDPR, some Member States, such as Greece, Portugal, and Slovenia, still had not completely adopted national legislation to adhere to the GDPR. Therefore, Member

---

[1] Case Study #5: Understanding the Compliance Forces that Influence Cybersecurity in the Banking Sector, especially in the UK.

States struggled to homogeneously implement the Regulation across Europe. Following Brexit (the UK's exit from the EU), this issue became more pronounced because the UK is no longer regulated domestically by the GDPR. Instead, the UK now has incorporated the GDPR into its data protection law; it created its own version (known as the UK-GDPR), which took effect on 31 January 2020 [17]. UK organizations are now required to amend their GDPR documentation to align it with the new regulatory criteria. The UK-GDPR security aims remained conceptually the same (outlined above in Fig. 1) [2]. However, in the context of the UK-GDPR, these aims need to be adapted to the new scope of the Regulation and reflect the independent jurisdiction of the UK. To make this transition easier, the EU established a period of six months (lasting until June 2021) to ensure the unrestricted flow of data between the UK and the EU. Nevertheless, for some companies, this transitional phase means that there are still two different GDPR laws they have to deal with – one that applies if they have users from inside the EU, the other if they have users from inside the UK. This situation further complicates the processing of data and the consequent security implications.

3   Analysis of GDPR Requirements

The GDPR is intended to protect EU citizens from privacy or data breaches [1]. A personal data breach can be generally defined as a security incident that has affected the confidentiality, integrity, or availability of personal data. In the context of GDPR [1], a personal data breach is defined in Article 4(12) as:

> *"a breach of security leading to the accidental or unlawful destruction, loss, alteration, unauthorised disclosure of, or access to, personal data transmitted, stored or otherwise processed."*

This definition comprehensively describes a security breach; it shows the descriptive nature of the Regulation. Although the GDPR requires an analysis of the organizations' data processing activities and an evaluation of the necessary control measures, it is not intended to prescribe which requirements controllers are required to undertake. Its focus is on EU citizens' rights in relation to their personal data, and data security is just one aspect of that. Unlike other regulations, such as Payment Card Industry – Data Security Standard (PCI-DSS) and other standards with a specific list of security requirements, the GDPR covers security only at a very high-level. Thus, the GDPR gives companies the freedom to develop and define their control measures and meet their security goals. However, with greater flexibility comes greater responsibility which often many organizations tend to underestimate. This factor means that implementing the controls outlined by the GDPR does not guarantee that organizations are fully safeguarded from cyberattacks or that an employee does not mistakenly or purposefully disclose confidential data. The following analysis shows the positive and negative effects of the descriptive nature of GDPR.

3.1   Framework for Cybersecurity Compliance

The GDPR is divided into 99 Articles (and 173 Recitals). These Articles regulate the GDPR requirements that must be followed to be compliant and are explicit in terms of what is required from enterprises in relation to the collection and management of personal data. Subsections of the Articles are divided into Paragraphs, which are, in turn, divided into Points. Articles and Paragraphs are numbered sequentially throughout the Regulation document, while Points are sorted alphabetically. Paragraphs and Points of the Articles contain all explanatory notes of the Articles. Table 1 maps the main requirements (identified by the corresponding Articles, Paragraphs, and Points) that directly influence the implementation of security. For each of them, it provides an evaluation of the related security goals and compliance elements that may help (advantages) or hinders (disadvantages) the development of efficient cybersecurity strategies.

This analysis was performed through the *mapping methodology*[2] to identify the associations between compliance requirements and security impacts (each requirement of GDPR mentioned has both a positive and a negative aspect) [18]. Each requirement was also put in relation with its ideal security goal[3]. The included requirements were used to develop a greater understanding of security concepts and identify evidence for compliance-relevant issues and gaps. The resulting elements of this analysis are explained in the section below.

4   Discussion of Results

Table 1 revealed that GDPR introduced several security controls that potentially provide both advantages and disadvantages in relation to the initial security goal established by the GDPR. However, the degree to which a requirement is more or less advantageous (or disadvantageous) from a cybersecurity viewpoint is given by the relationship between the level of relevance attributed by the GDPR to a specific requirement in terms of security (indicated as "security goal" in Table 1) and the actual impact of that requirement on the overall organizational cybersecurity infrastructure[4]. Table 2 shows the values of these two variables[5] for each requirement (Articles).

The values indicated in Table 2 are visually presented in Fig. 2. The left-right (horizontal) direction represents the level of relevance of the security goal for a requirement; the up-down (vertical) direction represents the actual impact of the requirement. The correspondence between impact and relevance determines whether a requirement (Article) is advantageous or disadvantageous in terms of security. Articles located above the diagonal line are considered disadvantageous, while those located below the diagonal line are considered advantageous. All Articles located on the diagonal line are equally advantageous and disadvantageous.

Results show that the most critical security area of GDPR is that concerning security controls in relation to data protection (defined in the Regulation as "security of

---

[2] The mapping methodology is a research-based method for recording qualitative information, analyzing its distribution, and prioritizing relevant information in relation to a specific topic or research issue.

[3] The desirable compliance goal of a GDPR requirement established by the Regulation.

[4] Real impact of a GDPR requirement on cybersecurity practices, processes, and behaviors in an organization.

[5] The variables can assume the following values: Low = 1, Medium = 2, High = 3, Very High = 4.

Table 1. GDPR compliance framework

Article	Paragraph	Point	Requirement	Security goal	Advantages	Disadvantages
5 - Principles relating to processing of personal data	1	(f)	"…data shall be processed in a manner that ensures appropriate security of the personal data…"	Integrate security into personal data processing	Flexibility in forming cybersecurity programs	High level of uncertainty for organizations
	2	–	"The controller shall be responsible for, and be able to demonstrate compliance with, paragraph 1 ('accountability')."	Keep the controller (organization) accountable for security	Increase detection of bad behaviors, and customer trust	Employee liability is not covered
24 - Responsibility of the controller	1	–	"… the controller shall implement appropriate technical and organisational measures…"	Establish transparency over security procedures	Ensure the existence of data protection policies procedures	It does not provide an exhaustive list of all the obligations of the controller
25 - Data protection by design and by default	2	–	"…such measures shall ensure that by default personal data are not made accessible without the individual's intervention to an indefinite number of natural persons."	Limit data availability	Ensure that personal data access is restricted to selected users	Hard to define the scope of data access

(continued)

Table 1. (*continued*)

Article	Paragraph	Point	Requirement	Security goal	Advantages	Disadvantages
30 - Records of processing activities	1	–	"Each controller and, where applicable, the controller's representative, shall maintain a record of processing activities under its responsibility"	Ensure data availability for controllers	Reduce data storage costs and keep security information organized	No guidance on how to securely store information
32 - Security of processing	1	(a)	"…pseudonymisation and encryption of personal data."	Implement data protection by design	Increase security of data	Abstract and insufficient ways to protect data (e.g. the use of encryption)
		(b)	"ability to ensure the ongoing confidentiality, integrity, availability and resilience of processing systems and services;"	Implement the CIA Triad	Ensure basic security goals	Provide broad, generic framework
		(c)	"…ability to restore the availability and access to personal data in a timely manner in the event of a physical or technical incident;	Restore the availability	Greater trust between data subjects and organizations	Lack of guidance regarding restoring measures

(*continued*)

Table 1. (*continued*)

Article	Paragraph	Point	Requirement	Security goal	Advantages	Disadvantages
		(d)	"…process for regularly testing, assessing and evaluating the effectiveness of technical and organisational measures for ensuring the security of the processing."	Test and evaluate the effectiveness of security measures	Minimize the risk of a data breach and protect reputation	Lack of specification regarding the frequency
	2		"In assessing the appropriate level of security account shall be taken in particular of the risks that are presented by processing…"	Consider security risks in the data processing	Make security an integral part of organizational procedures	Subjective risk-based approach to security
33 - Notification of a personal data breach to the supervisory authority	1		"In the case of a personal data breach, the controller shall without undue delay and, where feasible, not later than 72 h after having become aware of it, notify the personal data breach to the supervisory authority competent"	Report breaches	Promote incentives to strengthen data security	Subjective judgement of whether or not the breach represents an actual risk

(*continued*)

Table 1. (*continued*)

Article	Paragraph	Point	Requirement	Security goal	Advantages	Disadvantages
	3	(d)	"…. describe the measures taken or proposed to be taken by the controller to address the personal data breach, including, where appropriate, measures to mitigate its possible adverse effects."	Document reporting procedures	Encourage mitigation measures and reflection on the efforts taken to mitigate the attacks	The requirement is vague about definition of "measures"
35 - Data protection impact assessment	1	–	"…the controller shall, prior to the processing, carry out an assessment of the impact of the envisaged processing operations on the protection of personal data…"	Identify and minimize risks resulting from data processing	Lower likelihood of data breach events	The context in which the DPIA is carried out is not strictly defined
37 - Designation of the data protection officer	1	–	"…The controller and the processor shall designate a data protection office…"	Provide general consultancy on security-related matters	Maintain an adequate security level across the organization	Delay internal security procedures

Table 2. Values of impact and security relevance

Article	Paragraph	Point	Cybersecurity impact	Relevance of security goal
5 - Principles relating to processing of personal data	1	(f)	3	4
	2	–	3	1
24 - Responsibility of the controller	1	–	4	1
25 - Data protection by design and by default	2	–	4	2
30 - Records of processing activities	1	–	4	2
32 - Security of processing	1	(a) - (d)	4	4
	2	–	3	4
33 - Notification of a personal data breach to the supervisory authority	1	–	2	4
35 - Data protection impact assessment	2	–	2	3
	1	–	4	3
37 – Designation of the data protection officer	1	–	1	1

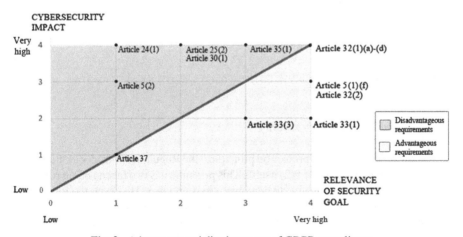

Fig. 2. Advantages and disadvantages of GDPR compliance

processing"). Such controls are addressed in the GDPR in the form of technical and organizational measures (Article 24 and 32, data protection impact assessments (DPIAs) (Article 35), records on processing (Article 30), data protection by design and by default techniques (Article 25) and the appointment of a Data Protection Officer (DPO) (Article 37). More advantageous controls appear in the GDPR's Article 5(1)(f),

> *"Personal data shall be processed in a manner that ensures appropriate security of the personal data, including protection against unauthorised or unlawful processing and against accidental loss, destruction or damage, using appropriate technical or organisational measures."*

The objective of this requirement is to ensure that personal data processing is performed considering integrity and confidentiality. However, not all organizations require the same degree of cybersecurity protection, which is why regulators purposefully left this requirement vague. On the one hand, this openness enables organizations to form their cybersecurity programs in a flexible manner; on the other hand, it leaves them with uncertainty about how to process data in "a manner that ensures appropriate security." The previously mentioned controls are also characterized by a certain degree of generality. The introduction of the DPIA as a means to identify high risks in relation to data processing is defined in a way that does not provide a clear picture of the procedure's contents. Some organizations already perform similar assessments (e.g., PIAs), and having a more accurate description of what DPIAs involve could help them get more uniform assessments. Article 5(2) is a requirement that has a significant impact on cybersecurity, although not directly (low level of security relevance from the standpoint of GDPR). It requires data controllers (in this context, "data controller" does not refer to one single individual within an organization but to the organization itself) to be responsible for and be able to demonstrate compliance with the GDPR's data protection principles defined in paragraph 1:

- Lawfulness, fairness, and transparency
- Purpose limitation
- Data minimization
- Accuracy
- Storage limitation
- Integrity and confidentiality security

In addition to the six data protection principles, the Regulation introduces the principle of *accountability* in Article 5(2) itself[6]. This principle has two facets: being responsible for compliance and being able to demonstrate compliance. However, the Regulation specifies that the responsibility to demonstrate compliance with this principle rests with the controller [1]. While this aspect is a fundamental part of an effective cybersecurity program, it may limit the scope of security responsibility of those involved in data processing security. Therefore, if an organization acts as the controller of its customers' data and employs inadequate security measures that result in unauthorized data access, the

---

[6] The GDPR ensures the implementation of three principles of the "CIA triad" (confidentiality, integrity, and availability).

organization is subject to GDPR penalties. However, the organization's cybersecurity manager responsible for guaranteeing personal data security would not have any types of regulatory "punishments." Another stakeholder who has no direct accountability for security is the DPO (Article 37). However, this regulatory figure has a significant role in implementing the Regulation and the consequent maintenance of an adequate security level. According to an October 2018 survey, a majority of companies (52%) that have appointed a DPO said they established one for compliance reasons only, and that the role did generate business benefits, including better security [19]. The DPO is an expert who has a predominantly legal profile, although he or she possesses some expertise in IT and risk management[7]. Its primary function is to provide supervision, evaluation, and regulatory consultancy regarding personal data processing management within a company. This professional figure is one of the first to be consulted when a data breach or other incident occurs. Apart from this instance, the GDPR does not indicate when consultation with the DPO is necessary or at least recommended. The lack of guidance regarding this aspect may delay internal security procedures or lead organizations to considering the DPO's role irrelevant. Furthermore, while the DPO is supposedly prepared enough to interact and communicate effectively with cybersecurity, the limitation of expertise on the topic can lead to decision-making issues. These characteristics make this requirement equally advantageous and disadvantageous from a security perspective (although not particularly determinant). Technical and organizational measures are further explained in Article 32, which requires implementing "appropriate technical and organizational measures to ensure a level of security appropriate to the risk." For example, a well-balanced requirement is Article 32 (1), which mandates the assessment of the security of processing, which also must consider "the state of art." The use of this very generic word is presumably a deliberate decision of regulators, which may be based on lessons learned from past experiences. The advantage of having "open" formulations is providing flexibility to the law and permitting its adaptation to different contexts and cases. Additionally, considering the rapid development of technology, it would prevent organizations from implementing outdated measures. However, in the absence of a more restrictive rule, organizations need to refer to common practice or other frameworks to perform security analyses and assess risk. Article 32, therefore, limits cybersecurity programs to a subjective risk-based approach to security, which may leave room for inaccurate interpretations. Finally, one controversial requirement of the GDPR is Article 33(1) that provides that, "in the case of a personal data breach, the controller shall without undue delay and, where feasible, not later than 72 h after having become aware of it, notify the personal data breach to the supervisory authority." Article 33 also specifies that if the organization can establish that the breach did not cause risks[8] for the data subjects or other individuals, then it has no obligations. The introduction of this rule (a new requirement under the GDPR) has positively impacted cybersecurity by emphasizing the focus on detection and reporting of cybersecurity incidents. One of

---

[7] According to Article 39, the DPO "shall in the performance of his or her tasks have due regard to the risk associated with processing operations," including security risk.

[8] For example, loss of sensitive personal data, such as medical records, email address, IP address or images.

the most immediate benefits of this obligation is the increased proactiveness; organizations are incentivized to protect both customers and the brand's reputation. A study performed by Neto et al. [20] compared reporting statistics in Europe and North America in a period between 2018 and 2019. They found that the number of reported attacks in North America increased by 38%, but by 80% in Europe, which is likely the consequence of the introduction of the GDPR. This output has also been formulated by the UK's independent authority (ICO). According to the ICO, the number of reports from all data controllers quadrupled following this requirement's implementation. However, the ICO also observed that more than 82% of the reported data breaches required no action from the organization [21]. Organizations are obliged to disclose personal data breaches to data protection authorities, but the way they manage their implications is subjective. This aspect leaves room for negligence, resulting in issues not being properly handled. In light of these considerations, it is clear that GDPR has a twofold effect on cybersecurity. On the one hand, it is important to note that it encourages organizations to have some form of cybersecurity strategy. The GDPR provides the opportunity to implement new or updated data protection and cybersecurity policies, processes, practices, and technical controls, including measures to secure data and data processing procedures. On the other hand, the analysis suggests that organizations may also report negative impacts because of the GDPR. For example, organizations may need to invest significantly in measures that are not sufficient to ensure security, including encryption. Subjectivity is also another negative factor, which may lead organizations to losing control over their cybersecurity goals. Therefore, while GDPR may provide an incentive and a guarantee for companies to strengthen data security, it is not intended to create an explicit duty to protect data, leaving companies vulnerable. As a result, the most considerable risk of GDPR is focusing excessively on the protection of data to the detriment of cybersecurity aspects. This swings the balance toward the assumption that GDPR might not be a key cybersecurity catalyst for organizations. However, an in-depth analysis of this hypothesis might be necessary to determine which aspects dominate in real-life settings and under what circumstances.

5 Recommendations and Future Perspectives

The inherent subjectivity of GDPR provides an interesting perspective to consider when evaluating GDPR requirements in terms of security. Despite having appropriate security measures in place and reporting breaches when necessary under the GDPR, an organization may still fail from a security point of view. It is, therefore, essential to be mindful of the main security goal of the GDPR, which is not to prevent data breaches but to ensure an appropriate security level. As a result, businesses are forced to plan for various situations. Some have also established GDPR task forces in the event that initial compliance decisions produce a different interpretation of the Regulation.

5.1 Recommendations: Organizational and International Contexts.

The organization's IT side needs to have an active role in advising the rest of the organization on what measures (both technical and organizational) are appropriate to minimize the risk of data breaches. For example, an organization may need assistance in implementing disaster recovery and business continuity plans and ensuring that the control measures remain in place and are effective [22]. In particular, the essential areas where the IT team can assist with GDPR compliance include those related to the requirements that are considered "disadvantageous" in Fig. 2 (e.g., accountability, data retention, DPIAs, and breach containment). From an international perspective, IT teams can also assist in determining whether and how data are being transferred to territories outside of the Economic European Area (EEA). However, to get the right and most relevant guidance towards security requirements, everyone in the company must take responsibility for keeping data handling activities secure and communicating with the IT team.

5.2 Future Perspectives

The first years of the GDPR were not as expected, but it is also true that a lot has happened since the GDPR's introduction. When the GDPR came into force in 2018, the world could never have foreseen the security complexities and implications of Brexit or the unprecedented Coronavirus pandemic. Consequently, there has been a greater emphasis on increasing data protection and has resulted in an enhancement of privacy legislation at a global level. Compliance with global security rules is becoming a larger concern for businesses around the world. The GDPR is not the only EU privacy regulation on policymakers' and companies' minds. The ePrivacy Regulation (ePR), intended to replace the 2002 ePrivacy Directive, deserves particular consideration as it is noteworthy in the European context of cybersecurity and the protection of information [23]. Alongside the GDPR, the new privacy regulation is set to introduce harmonized rules on the processing of data by electronic communications service providers (now extended to include WhatsApp and Facebook Messenger). As the GDPR matures and similar regulations take shape, the future of cybersecurity compliance is certainly more encouraging than it has been previously in terms of security. European organizations now have the opportunity to strengthen their data security policies and adapt to GDPR standards in a more targeted way. However, it is also necessary to consider that data protection relies on awareness and proactive measures to handle cybersecurity risks and ensure privacy effectively. Research on cybersecurity compliance has the potential to help in many critical areas related to GDPR security. For example, it is important to develop frameworks and methods to investigate how organizational culture and specific national dynamics influence the implementation and compliance of the GDPR and explore how regulators can improve and simplify the rules related to data processing security.

6 Conclusion

The adoption of GDPR has had a strong effect on privacy and protection practices while implicitly encouraging companies to strengthen and improve their information security policies, thus limiting possible data violations. It has dramatically increased European companies' understanding of cybercrime data breaches and the need for security. GDPR has given cybersecurity more weight by providing awareness on the concrete implications of cybercrime. However, while steps of progress have been taken in improving cybersecurity through GDPR, it cannot be assumed that the requirements imposed by the legislation are enough to handle cybersecurity in the context of privacy. Following scandals such as Cambridge Analytica and Facebook in recent years, as well as a high number of severe data breaches, concerns about the use and security of data have started to rise [24]. It has, therefore, become clear that the approach to addressing cybersecurity lies as much with mandatory regulatory requirements as it does with integrative measures.

Acknowledgements. The research reported herein was supported in part by the Cybersecurity at MIT Sloan initiative, which is funded by a consortium of organizations, and a gift from C6 bank.

References

1. The European Parliament and the Council of the European Union: Regulation (EU) 2016/679 of the European Parliament and of the Council of 27 April 2016 on the protection of natural persons with regard to the processing of personal data and on the free movement of such data (2016)
2. ICO Security outcomes | ICO. In: ico.org.uk. https://ico.org.uk/for-organisations/security-outcomes/. Accessed 25 Mar 2021
3. Madnick, S.E., Marotta, A., Novaes Neto, N., Powers, K.: Research Plan to Analyze the Role of Compliance in Influencing Cybersecurity in Organizations (2020)
4. Marotta, A., Madnick, S.E.: Analyzing the interplay between regulatory compliance and cybersecurity (revised). SSRN Electron. J. (2020). https://doi.org/10.2139/ssrn.3569902
5. Marotta, A., Madnick, S.: Perspectives on the relationship between compliance and cybersecurity. J. Inf. Syst. Secur. **16**, 27 (2021)
6. Marotta, A., Madnick, S.: Issues in information systems convergence and divergence of regulatory compliance and cybersecurity. **22**, 10–50 (2021). https://doi.org/10.48009/1_iis_2021_10-50
7. Zerlang, J.: GDPR: a milestone in convergence for cyber-security and compliance. Netw. Secur. **2017**, 8–11 (2017). https://doi.org/10.1016/S1353-4858(17)30060-0
8. Tsohou, A., Magkos, E., Mouratidis, H., et al.: Privacy, security, legal and technology acceptance elicited and consolidated requirements for a GDPR compliance platform. Inf. Comput. Secur. **28**, 531–553 (2020). https://doi.org/10.1108/ICS-01-2020-0002
9. Poritskiy, N., Oliveira, F., Almeida, F.: The benefits and challenges of general data protection regulation for the information technology sector. Digit. Policy Regul. Gov. **21**, 510–524 (2019). https://doi.org/10.1108/DPRG-05-2019-0039
10. Horák, M., Stupka, V., Husák, M.: GDPR compliance in cybersecurity software: a case study of DPIA in information sharing platform. In: ACM International Conference Proceeding Series, pp. 1–8. Association for Computing Machinery, New York (2019)
11. Lachaud, E.: The General Data Protection Regulation and the rise of certification as a regulatory instrument (2018)
12. Saqib, N., Germanos, V., Zeng, W., Maglaras, L.: Mapping of the security requirements of GDPR and NISD. ICST Trans. Secur. Saf. **166283** (2018). https://doi.org/10.4108/eai.30-6-2020.166283
13. Diamantopoulou, V., Tsohou, A., Karyda, M.: General Data protection regulation and ISO/IEC 27001:2013: synergies of activities towards organisations' compliance. In: Gritzalis, S., Weippl, E.R., Katsikas, S.K., Anderst-Kotsis, G., Tjoa, A.M., Khalil, I. (eds.) TrustBus 2019. LNCS, vol. 11711, pp. 94–109. Springer, Cham (2019). https://doi.org/10.1007/978-3-030-27813-7_7

14. Diamantopoulou, V., Tsohou, A., Karyda, M.: From ISO/IEC 27002:2013 information security controls to personal data protection controls: guidelines for GDPR compliance. In: Katsikas, S., et al. (eds.) CyberICPS. LNCS, vol. 11980, pp. 238–257. Springer, Cham (2020). https://doi.org/10.1007/978-3-030-42048-2_16
15. Lopes, I.M., Guarda, T., Oliveira, P.: How ISO 27001 can help achieve GDPR compliance. In: Iberian Conference on Information Systems and Technologies, CISTI. IEEE Computer Society (2019)
16. Chivot, E., Castro, D.: What the Evidence Shows About the Impact of the GDPR After One Year. Cent. DATA Innov (2019). http://www2.datainnovation.org/2019-gdpr-one-year.pdf. Accessed 25 Mar 2021
17. GOV.UK. Data protection - GOV.UK. Gov.uk (2014). https://www.gov.uk/data-protection/the-data-protection-act. Accessed 25 Mar 2021
18. Sutherland, S., Katz, S.: Concept mapping methodology: a catalyst for organizational learning. Eval. Program. Plan. **28**, 257–269 (2005). https://doi.org/10.1016/j.evalprogplan.2005.04.017
19. IAPP, Ernst, Young: IAPP-EY Annual Governance Report 2019 (2019)
20. Neto, N.N., Madnick, S., Paula, A.M.G.D., Borges, N.M.: Developing a global data breach database and the challenges encountered. J. Data Inf. Qual. **13**, 1–33 (2021). https://doi.org/10.1145/3439873
21. ICO. Information Commissioner's Annual Report and Financial Statements. ICO (2019)
22. Marotta, A., Martinelli, F.: GDPR survey: an analysis of the tools used for assessing GDPR compliance. Technical report (IIT B4-05/2020) - IIT CNR (2020)
23. Vinet, L., Zhedanov, A.: A "missing" family of classical orthogonal polynomials (2011)
24. Isaak, J., Hanna, M.J.: User data privacy: Facebook, Cambridge analytica, and privacy protection. Comput. (Long Beach Calif.) **51**, 56–59 (2018). https://doi.org/10.1109/MC.2018.3191268

Information Security Education
and Self-perception of Privacy Protection Risk
in Mobile Web in Obstetrics Students from Peru

Augusto Felix Olaza-Maguiña(✉) ⓘ and Yuliana Mercedes De La Cruz-Ramirez ⓘ

Universidad Nacional Santiago Antúnez de Mayolo, Centenario 200, Huaraz 02002, Peru
{aolazam,ydelacruzr}@unasam.edu.pe

Abstract. The objective of the study was to determine the information security education topics developed in the training of obstetrics students and their relationship with the self-perception of privacy protection risk in mobile web during the COVID-19 pandemic at the Santiago Antúnez of Mayolo National University (UNASAM) (Huaraz-Peru). A correlational cross-sectional investigation was developed, with 164 obstetric students. The information was collected through a questionnaire applied online between November and December 2020, having determined its validity and reliability. The Chi squared statistical test ($p < 0.05$) was used, while the information processing was carried out using the SPSS program. It was determined that 61.6% of obstetric students perceived a high risk in the protection of their privacy in mobile web during the development of their activities in the academic cycle 2020-I. Likewise, it was evidenced that the majority of students stated that they had not developed the topics consulted with regard to information security education during their virtual studies in obstetric, especially with regard to the recommendations for the use of passwords (83.5%), privacy protection strategies (81.1%) and data management through the creation of backups (79.9%), showing a statistically significant relationship with the self-perception of privacy protection risk in mobile web ($p < 0.05$). It was concluded that the low development of information security education topics in the training of obstetric students is related to the self-perception of high risk in the privacy protection in mobile web during the COVID-19 pandemic.

Keywords: Information security education · Privacy protection · Mobile web · Obstetrics · COVID-19

1 Introduction

Information security is an issue that has reached notable importance in recent decades [1], due to the increasingly common use of the Internet and applications in mobile web, a situation that has increased at the same time the insecurity and risk of loss of valuable information in various aspects of human life, such as the economy, commerce and the financial system [2, 3].

In this sense, in order to prevent and/or reduce the risk of insecurity, an aspect that is extremely important is information security education, which can not only be

J. Bentahar et al. (Eds.): MobiWIS 2021, LNCS 12814, pp. 32–43, 2021.
https://doi.org/10.1007/978-3-030-83164-6_3

applied in the training of professional specialists in this area [1, 4], but also as a tool for disseminating information to the entire population in general, including university students [3], who permanently develop their academic activities through the use of digital tools based on the use of mobile web, through which they also have interaction with their teachers and classmates, accessing different platforms, applications and websites, in which if they do not take due care and caution, they can be exposed to the loss of important data, both in the academic and personal aspect [2].

In recent years, the results of research related to information security education and the protection of privacy in university students have been published [2–4], in which the creation and application of secure software and systems stands out, characterized by a permanent updating of the curricula based on dynamic and attractive content for young university students [4], with few studies in health sciences students [5–7], who are also exposed to the same risks of students of other professional careers; but whose preparation with respect to information security acquires an even more marked character, if it is taken into account that with the application of technology to the patient care process, it is relevant for students to have the necessary skills that guarantee cybersecurity [8, 9] and protection of the privacy of user data [5] in mobile web, for example during the application of electronic medical records [10] or during the development of telemedicine [9], activities that form part of the job profile of obstetric professionals.

On the other hand, it is important to highlight that despite the relevance of information security education and the advances reported by researchers in various countries [1, 3], this aspect has not yet been treated and included with sufficient emphasis. in the training of university students who use virtual education in Peru [11], which until before the arrival of the COVID-19 pandemic, was still very limited to a few university institutions, practically leaving aside the training of human resources in health, who, unlike students of other careers, have had access to mobile web without a thorough knowledge of what information security really means; having been forced to carry out their classes in a totally virtual way with the declaration of the health emergency in said country since March 2020, where there is no research on the situation of information security education and the protection of privacy in mobile web in obstetrics students, such as those currently trained for 5 years equivalent to 10 academic cycles at the Santiago Antúnez de Mayolo National University (UNASAM), which is a state-run institution located in a remote place in Peru (Huaraz, 3,052 m.a.s.l.), whose obstetric students are mostly in a situation of social and economic vulnerability [12].

In this sense, due to the considerations expressed in the preceding paragraphs, the present investigation was carried out with the aim of determining the topics of information security education developed in the training of obstetric students and their relationship with self-perception of privacy protection risk in mobile web during the COVID-19 pandemic at UNASAM, for which the present paper has been written, where information related to the methodology, results, discussion, conclusions and future steps to be followed by other researchers has been considered.

2 Methodology

2.1 Research Design and Population Under Study

A correlational cross-sectional research was carried out, for which it was considered to work with the entire population of 189 obstetric students enrolled in the 2020-I academic cycle at UNASAM, considering as inclusion criteria being over 18 years of age, develop their study activities exclusively through the use of mobile web and have virtual assistance greater than 70%; while the exclusion criteria taken into account were withdrawal from the academic cycle and student absenteeism.

On the other hand, it is important to clarify that of the entire population under study (189) with which it was decided to work, 20 students agreed to collaborate with a pilot test aimed at evaluating the reliability of the data collection instrument, 164 students voluntarily accepted participate in the research, who met the inclusion and exclusion criteria mentioned above, showing only the refusal of 5 students, who did not accept and/or did not respond to the request for collaboration with the study.

2.2 Variables

Sociodemographic Characteristics. Age (18–24 years ≥25 years), sex (female, male), origin (rural area, urban area) and academic cycle (I–III cycle, IV–VI cycle, VII–X cycle).

Topics of Information Security Education. Taking as reference theoretical background [3] and previous studies carried out with university students [2–7], it was considered as first general topic in the training of obstetric students, to the information security fundamentals that they might have been taught regarding basic information security terminology (yes, no), importance of information protection (yes, no), privacy protection strategies (yes, no), and responsible use of social networks (yes, no). The second general topic was password security about the rules for establishing strong passwords (yes, no) and general recommendations for the use and management of passwords (yes, no). The third general topic of information security education was referred to the email security standards that obstetric students may have learned during their virtual studies in mobile web, considering the email management suggestions (yes, no) and handling attachments from unknown sources including spam (yes, no). The fourth general topic addressed the data management that could have been taught to students for the security of their information, referring to storage (yes, no), backups (yes, no) and recovery of lost data (yes, no).

Self-perception of Privacy Protection Risk. To evaluate this self-perception of obstetric students during the COVID-19 pandemic, the opinion of the students was respected based on their own experience during their virtual studies in mobile web corresponding to the 2020-I academic cycle (low risk, medium risk and high risk).

2.3 Data Collection Procedure

A questionnaire composed of 16 questions was developed and applied, of which the first 4 questions were referred to the sociodemographic characteristics of the obstetric students. The following 11 questions corresponded to the information security education topics that could have been developed in the training of obstetric students during their virtual studies in the 2020-I academic cycle. Finally, regarding the self-perception of privacy protection risk of obstetric students in mobile web during the COVID-19 pandemic, 1 question was asked about said self-perception.

In order to ensure the validity of the data collection instrument, the content of the questionnaire was evaluated through expert judgment, the results of which were applied Kendall's concordance test, through which the validity of said questionnaire was determined, with a significance level of 0.001. In the same way, a pilot test was carried out with 20 obstetric students, as a result of which the reliability of the instrument could be determined through the application of Cronbach's alpha index, obtaining a value of 0.891. After the procedures described above, the questionnaire was applied completely online between November and December 2020, for which a virtual form was prepared, which was sent to the institutional email of each of the students.

2.4 Statistical Analysis

The information processing was carried out using the SPSS program, version 22.0 for Windows. Regarding the statistical analysis, a descriptive analysis based on the presentation of absolute frequencies and percentages was performed first; followed by the application of the Chi square test with a significance level of $p < 0.05$, in order to determine the relationship of the information security education topics developed in the training of obstetric students with the self-perception of privacy protection risk in mobile web during the COVID-19 pandemic.

2.5 Ethical Considerations

In order to guarantee the privacy and confidentiality of the information made known to the study authors, an informed consent form was sent to the institutional mail of obstetric students, requesting their voluntary participation, in accordance with the provisions of the World Medical Association and the Declaration of Helsinki [13]. Similarly, it was complied with presenting the corresponding research protocol to the Ethics Committee of UNASAM, who approved and authorized the execution of the study.

3 Results

The sociodemographic characteristics of the 164 obstetric students who agreed to participate in the research and completed the questionnaire by filling in the respective virtual form, are shown in Table 1, highlighting a predominance of female students (88.4%) under the age of 25 years (85.4%).

Table 1. Sociodemographic characteristics of students.

Characteristic	n	%
Age		
- 18–24 years	140	85.4
- ≥25 years	24	14.6
Sex		
- Woman	145	88.4
- Man	19	11.6
Origin		
- Rural area	79	48.2
- Urban area	85	51.8
Academic cycle		
- I–III cycle	91	55.5
- IV–VI cycle	60	36.6
- VII–X cycle	13	7.9

The majority of obstetric students perceived a high risk in protecting their privacy in mobile web during the development of their activities in the academic cycle 2020-I (61.6%) (Table 2), of which the largest proportion denied having developed during their virtual studies some content regarding the information security fundamentals, such as basic terminology (56.1%), importance of information protection (54.9%), privacy protection strategies (56.7%) and responsible use of social networks (55.5%); evidencing that the non-development of all the aforementioned contents had a statistically significant relationship with the self-perception of privacy protection risk of obstetric students in mobile web ($p < 0.05$) during the COVID-19 pandemic.

Table 2. Information security fundamentals according to the self-perception of privacy protection risk in mobile web.

Fundamentals	Self-perception of risk						Total		p-value[a]
	Low risk		Medium risk		High risk				
	n	%	n	%	n	%	n	%	
Basic terminology									
- Yes	14	8.5	12	7.3	9	5.5	35	21.3	<0.001
- No	5	3.1	32	19.5	92	56.1	129	78.7	
Importance of information protection									
- Yes	16	9.8	13	7.9	11	6.7	40	24.4	<0.001
- No	3	1.8	31	18.9	90	54.9	124	75.6	

(continued)

Table 2. (*continued*)

Fundamentals	Self-perception of risk						Total		p-value[a]
	Low risk		Medium risk		High risk				
	n	%	n	%	n	%	n	%	
Privacy protection strategies									
- Yes	13	7.9	10	6.1	8	4.9	31	18.9	<0.001
- No	6	3.7	34	20.7	93	56.7	133	81.1	
Responsible use of social networks									
- Yes	17	10.4	15	9.1	10	6.1	42	25.6	<0.001
- No	2	1.2	29	17.7	91	55.5	122	74.4	
Total	19	11.6	44	26.8	101	61.6	164	100	

[a]Chi square test.

Regarding password security (Table 3), which became the second topic of information security education that could have been developed in the training of obstetric students during their virtual studies in the academic cycle 2020-I, the majority of students who perceived a high risk in protecting their privacy in mobile web, stated that they had not developed any content referring to the rules for establishing secure passwords in the different applications they used (54.3%), as well as the general recommendations for the use and administration of their passwords (57.9%), finding that the non-development of said topics presented a statistically significant relationship with the self-perception of privacy protection risk of obstetric students in mobile web ($p < 0.05$).

Table 3. Password security according to the self-perception of privacy protection risk in mobile web.

Password security	Self-perception of risk						Total		p-value[a]
	Low risk		Medium risk		High risk				
	n	%	n	%	n	%	n	%	
Rules for establishing strong passwords									
- Yes	15	9.2	14	8.5	12	7.3	41	25.0	<0.001
- No	4	2.4	30	18.3	89	54.3	123	75.0	
Recommendations for the use of passwords									
- Yes	12	7.3	9	5.5	6	3.7	27	16.5	<0.001
- No	7	4.3	35	21.3	95	57.9	137	83.5	
Total	19	11.6	44	26.8	101	61.6	164	100	

[a]Chi square test.

The third topic of information security education that was consulted was the security with respect to email (Table 4), observing that the highest proportion of students who perceived a high risk in the protection of their privacy in mobile web, denied have developed during their studies some content on email management suggestions (53.1%) and the handling of attachments from unknown sources including spam (55.5%), evidencing that in all the aforementioned cases it was found a statistically significant relationship with the self-perception of privacy protection risk of obstetric students in mobile web (p < 0.05).

Table 4. Email security according to the self-perception of privacy protection risk in mobile web.

Email security	Self-perception of risk						Total		p-value[a]
	Low risk		Medium risk		High risk				
	n	%	n	%	n	%	n	%	
Email management suggestions									
- Yes	18	11.0	15	9.2	14	8.5	47	28.7	< 0.001
- No	1	0.6	29	17.6	87	53.1	117	71.3	
Handling attachments from unknown sources									
- Yes	17	10.4	13	7.9	10	6.1	40	24.4	< 0.001
- No	2	1.2	31	18.9	91	55.5	124	75.6	
Total	19	11.6	44	26.8	101	61.6	164	100	

[a]Chi square test.

In Table 5, it is revealed that with respect to the fourth topic of information security education that could have been developed in the training of obstetric students, concerning data management, it could be determined that the majority of students who perceived a high risk in protecting their privacy in mobile web, declared not having received guidance on storage (56.1%), backups (56.7%) and recovery of lost data (55.5%); observing that the non-development of all the previously mentioned sections had a statistically significant relationship with the self-perception of privacy protection risk of the students in mobile web (p < 0.05) during the COVID-19 pandemic.

Table 5. Data management according to the self-perception of privacy protection risk in mobile web.

Data management	Self-perception of risk						Total		p-value[a]
	Low risk		Medium risk		High risk				
	n	%	n	%	n	%	n	%	
Storage									
- Yes	16	9.8	12	7.3	9	5.5	37	22.6	< 0.001
- No	3	1.8	32	19.5	92	56.1	127	77.4	

(*continued*)

Table 5. (*continued*)

Data management	Self-perception of risk						Total		p-value[a]
	Low risk		Medium risk		High risk				
	n	%	n	%	n	%	n	%	
Backups									
- Yes	14	8.5	11	6.7	8	4.9	33	20.1	< 0.001
- No	5	3.1	33	20.1	93	56.7	131	79.9	
Recovery of lost data									
- Yes	15	9.2	14	8.5	10	6.1	39	23.8	< 0.001
- No	4	2.4	30	18.3	91	55.5	125	76.2	
Total	19	11.6	44	26.8	101	61.6	164	100	

[a]Chi square test.

4 Discussion

The results evidenced in this research, regarding the high percentage of obstetric students who denied having developed the different topics consulted on information security education, are similar to those found in other studies [3, 14], where it was possible to show that the training of university students on information security is deficient [15], especially in those professional careers that, due to their nature and field of action, prioritize the contents directly related to their professional profile, forgetting that information security education is a cross-cutting issue of great importance for all areas of knowledge, especially if the use of digital equipment and tools in mobile web that students apply for the development of their academic activities is taken into account [2, 3]; especially during the COVID-19 pandemic [16].

The aforementioned deficiencies in the information security education of obstetric students would be explained not only in the non-consideration of said subject in the current curriculum, but also in the little knowledge that teachers have about computer security, for example, in the fundamentals of this area with respect to the basic terminology of information security, importance of information protection, privacy protection strategies and responsible use of social networks, determining in this research that all these aspects were scarcely addressed by the teachers during the teaching-learning sessions; probably due to the fact that within the teaching staff that participate in the training of obstetric students, the collaboration of professionals specializing in cybersecurity is not taken into account.

Another aspect that would explains the deficiencies evidenced in information security education would be that topics related to bioinformatics are not being developed, a reality that has also been evidenced in other studies [2, 3, 5], which highlights the little importance attributed to the protection of information [6, 7, 10, 17] and privacy of students in mobile web [15], emphasizing the ignorance they have of the dangers and threats to which they can be exposed if they do not take sufficient care and precaution, a situation that could be improved if information security education began from primary and secondary education institutions [18, 19].

In relation to the findings regarding password security education, these findings were also similar to those reported by other researchers [20–22], who also concluded that not it is provided enough education to the general population, with emphasis on the student population, on the rules for the establishment of secure passwords and the proper use and administration of them, having increased the theft of information as a result of the violation of passwords in which personal data is considered, the same that are of easy identification by other people, mainly due to the lack of training of mobile web users [20].

Another aspect, related to what was disclosed in the preceding paragraph, is the issue of email security education, which was also identified as an information security issue very little addressed in the training of obstetric students, a reality that according to other research carried out in other countries [14, 23, 24], also shows deficiencies with respect to the few suggestions that are given to people on the proper administration of their email and management attachments from unknown sources in mobile web, including spam, having a feeling of false security and therefore little control and care of the information that can be sent and/or receive through said mean [25, 26], especially during the COVID-19 pandemic, in which the dissemination of unreliable information has increased [16].

Similar to the aforementioned findings, education in data management was also insufficient, mainly with respect to the storage, backups and recovery of lost data, being this aspect highlighted in other studies [27, 28] as the most affectation due to the little education that exists in this regard, being frequent the loss of important data both in the academic and personal fields, which in the case of students, can seriously affect the efficient fulfillment of the assigned activities [27].

On the other hand, a finding of this research that deserves special attention is the high-risk self-perception that obstetric students have regarding the protection of their privacy in mobile web during the COVID-19 pandemic, a self-perception that was related to the lack of development of information security education issues, a situation that coincides with what has been reported in other scientific publications [2, 15, 29], where the feeling of risk in the privacy in mobile web [30], has been further increased during the pandemic [31, 32], especially in those nations with problems of scarce computer literacy as Peru, a reality that has also affected students of health sciences careers such as obstetrics, whose teaching-learning process and minimal participation in information security education, places them in a particularly vulnerable situation.

However, despite the aforementioned findings, it is important to recognize the existence of several limitations in the present research, such as the lack of precision of more details related to the development of information security education and the privacy protection risk of obstetric students in mobile web, which could allow knowing other important aspects that were not only based on the students' point of view, but also on the participation of other actors such as teachers, also constituting the cross-sectional design applied in the study an important limitation, which does not allow us to carry out a long-term evaluation with respect to the subjects under study, especially in relation to proposals to improve information security education in health sciences students, limitations directly related to the complicated situation in which online university education is currently being carried out in Peru, as a result of the health emergency caused by COVID-19.

5   Conclusions and Future Steps

5.1   Conclusions

In this sense, it is concluded that the scarce development of information security education issues in the training of obstetric students is related to the self-perception of high risk in the privacy protection in mobile web during the COVID-19 pandemic at UNASAM, reason for which actions should be carried out, with the aim not only of improving information security education for students in this and other professional careers, but also at improving the content of the curriculum in university higher education, aspects on which the contribution of this paper is based, as it serves as a reference especially in health sciences students.

5.2   Future Steps

Based on the conclusions, it is suggested to carry out future research aimed at validating the relevance of the topics related to information security education and the protection of privacy in mobile web in the curriculum of the career of obstetrics, in which could be considered the issues addressed in the present research, as well as other aspects directly related to the professional profile and patient care.

Likewise, the training of teachers in general on the subject of information security in mobile web should be considered, with the interdisciplinary collaboration of specialists, which in turn would allow complementing the findings made known in the present investigation regarding the situation of the information security education in obstetric students from a Peruvian state-run university in the midst of a pandemic; information that could be compared with students of other medical specialties and/or professional careers in general.

Financing. The authors have fully financed the execution of this research.

Conflict of Interest. The authors declare that they have no conflict of interest.

Acknowledgements. Our most sincere thanks to the obstetrics students of UNASAM, for their collaboration in the development of this study, as well as to the authorities of the research units of UNASAM, for their support in the corresponding administrative process.

References

1. Trabelsi, Z., Zeidan, S., Saleous, H.: Teaching emerging DDoS attacks on firewalls: a case study of the blacknurse attack. In: 2019 IEEE Global Engineering Education Conference (EDUCON), Dubai, pp. 977–985. IEEE (2019). https://doi.org/10.1109/EDUCON.2019.872 5133

2. Guan, S., Zhang, H., Cao, G., Wang, X., Han, X.: The practice of the college students' network security quality education. In: Deng, K., Yu, Z., Patnaik, S., Wang, J. (eds.) ICMIR 2018. AISC, vol. 856, pp. 110–114. Springer, Cham (2019). https://doi.org/10.1007/978-3-030-00214-5_14

3. Wang, S., Qu, Y., Zheng, L., Xiao, Y., Shi, H.: Exploration of information security education of university students. In: Xhafa, F., Patnaik, S., Zomaya, A.Y. (eds.) IISA 2017. AISC, vol. 686, pp. 476–480. Springer, Cham (2018). https://doi.org/10.1007/978-3-319-69096-4_66

4. Løvgren, D., Li, J., Oyetoyan, T.: A data-driven security game to facilitate information security education. In: 2019 IEEE/ACM 41st International Conference on Software Engineering: Companion Proceedings (ICSE-Companion), Montreal, pp. 256–257. IEEE (2019). https://doi.org/10.1109/ICSE-Companion.2019.00102

5. Lin, K.-Y.: Application of a blended assessment strategy to enhance student interest and effectiveness in learning: case study with information security literacy. Comput. Inform. Nurs. **38**(10), 508–514 (2020). https://doi.org/10.1097/CIN.0000000000000665

6. Park, E., Kim, J., Wile, L., Park, Y.: Factors affecting intention to disclose patients' health information. Comput. Secur. **87**, 101340 (2019). https://doi.org/10.1016/j.cose.2018.05.003

7. Adawiyah, R., Hidayanto, A., Chandra, I., Samik, R.: Identification of how health information security awareness (HISA) influence in patient' health information protection awareness (PHIPA). In: 2019 5th International Conference on Computing Engineering and Design (ICCED), Singapore, pp. 1–6. IEEE (2019). https://doi.org/10.1109/ICCED46541.2019.9161123

8. Song, Y., et al.: Revision of the measurement tool for patients' health information protection awareness. Healthc. Inf. Res. **22**(3), 206–216 (2016). https://doi.org/10.4258/hir.2016.22.3.206

9. Kumar, R., et al.: Fuzzy-based symmetrical multi-criteria decision-making procedure for evaluating the impact of harmful factors of healthcare information security. Symmetry **12**(4), 664 (2020). https://doi.org/10.3390/SYM12040664

10. Park, E., Kim, J., Park, Y.: The role of information security learning. Comput. Secur. **65**, 64–76 (2017). https://doi.org/10.1016/j.cose.2016.10.011

11. Espíritu, W., Machuca, C., Subauste, D.: Reference model for health data security management supported in a blockchain platform. In: VI Iberoamerican Conference of Computer Human Interaction, HCI 2020, Arequipa, pp. 185–193. CEUR-WS (2020)

12. Instituto Nacional de Estadística e Informática: Encuesta nacional de hogares. INEI, Lima (2018)

13. World Medical Association. Declaration of Helsinki – Ethical principles for medical research involving human subjects. https://www.wma.net/policies-post/wma-declaration-of-helsinki-ethical-principles-for-medical-research-involving-human-subjects/. Accessed 9 Jan 2021

14. Song, O., Connie, T., Sayeed, M.: Security and Authentication: Perspectives, Management and Challenges. Nova Science Publishers Inc., Melaka (2017)

15. Qian, J.: Practice path and security mechanism of "Internet + Education" in the era of artificial intelligence. In: Atiquzzaman, M., Yen, N., Zheng, Xu. (eds.) Big Data Analytics for Cyber-Physical System in Smart City: BDCPS 2020, 28–29 December 2020, Shanghai, China, pp. 1002–1011. Springer, Singapore (2021). https://doi.org/10.1007/978-981-33-4572-0_144

16. Maserat, E., Jafari, F., Mohammadzadeh, Z., Alizadeh, M., Torkamannia, A.: COVID-19 & an NGO and university developed interactive portal: a perspective from Iran. Heal. Technol. **10**(6), 1421–1426 (2020). https://doi.org/10.1007/s12553-020-00470-1

17. Cha, K., Song, Y.: Factors associated with practice of health information protection among nursing students. J. Korean Acad. Fundam. Nurs. **27**(1), 73–80 (2020). https://doi.org/10.7739/jkafn.2020.27.1.73

18. Bocharov, M., Simonova, I., Mogarov, M.: The effect of systematically teaching information security on the children's anxiety level. Perspektivy Nauki i Obrazovania **40**(4), 169–182 (2019). https://doi.org/10.32744/pse.2019.4.14
19. Bocharov, M., Simonova, I., Bocharova, T., Zaika, A.: Information security education system in secondary school and assessment of the level of anxiety of schoolchildren. In: 17th International Conference on Cognition and Exploratory Learning in Digital Age, CELDA 2020, Lisbon, pp. 11–18. IADIS Press (2020)
20. Hanyu, L.: Research on data confidentiality and security of computer network password. J. Phys. Conf. Ser. **1648**, 022078 (2020). https://doi.org/10.1088/1742-6596/1648/2/022078
21. He, S., Fu, J., Chen, C., Guo, Z.: Research on password cracking technology based on improved transformer. J. Phys. Conf. Ser. **1631**, 012161 (2020). https://doi.org/10.1088/1742-6596/1631/1/012161
22. Walia, K., Shenoy, S., Cheng, Y.: An empirical analysis on the usability and security of passwords. In: 2020 IEEE 21st International Conference on Information Reuse and Integration for Data Science (IRI), Las Vegas, pp. 1–8. IEEE (2020). https://doi.org/10.1109/IRI49571.2020.00009
23. Zhang, J., Li, W., Gong, L., Gu, Z., Wu, J.: Targeted malicious email detection using hypervisor-based dynamic analysis and ensemble learning. In: 2019 IEEE Global Communications Conference (GLOBECOM), Waikoloa, pp. 1–6. IEEE (2019). https://doi.org/10.1109/GLOBECOM38437.2019.9014069
24. Suresh, S., Mohan, M., Thyagarajan, C., Kedar, R.: Detection of ransomware in emails through anomaly based detection. In: Hemanth, D.J., Kumar, V.D.A., Malathi, S., Castillo, O., Patrut, B. (eds.) COMET 2019. LNDECT, vol. 35, pp. 604–613. Springer, Cham (2020). https://doi.org/10.1007/978-3-030-32150-5_59
25. Liginlal, D.: HIPAA and human error: the role of enhanced situation awareness in protecting health information. In: Gkoulalas-Divanis, A., Loukides, G. (eds.) Medical Data Privacy Handbook, pp. 679–696. Springer, Cham (2015). https://doi.org/10.1007/978-3-319-23633-9_25
26. Mohamed, A., Chen, L.: Data privacy protection: a study on students awareness of personal data privacy protection in an e-health environment. Adv. Sci. Lett. **23**(6), 5299–5303 (2017). https://doi.org/10.1166/asl.2017.7363
27. Peng, Z., Feng, X., Tang, L., Zhai, M.: A data recovery method for NTFS files system. In: Niu, W., et al. (eds.) ATIS 2015. CCIS, vol. 557, pp. 379–386. Springer, Heidelberg (2015). https://doi.org/10.1007/978-3-662-48683-2_34
28. Gaidamakin, N., Gibilinda, R., Sinadskiy, N.: File operations information collecting software package used in the information security incidents investigation. In: 2020 Ural Symposium on Biomedical Engineering, Radioelectronics and Information Technology (USBEREIT), Yekaterinburg, pp. 559–562. IEEE (2020). https://doi.org/10.1109/USBEREIT48449.2020.9117671.
29. Chen, Y., Wen, C.: Taiwanese university students' smartphone use and the privacy paradox. Comunicar **27**(60), 61–70 (2019). https://doi.org/10.3916/C60-2019-06
30. Dogruel, L., Jöckel, S.: Risk perception and privacy regulation preferences from a cross-cultural perspective. A qualitative study among German and U.S. smartphone users. Int. J. Commun. **13**, 1764–1783 (2019)
31. Bai, Y., Gao, C., Goda, B.: Lessons learned from teaching cybersecurity courses during Covid-19. In: Proceedings of the 21st Annual Conference on Information Technology Education, SIGITE 2020, New York, pp. 308–313. Association for Computing Machinery (2020). https://doi.org/10.1145/3368308.3415394
32. Parthasarathy, S., Murugesan, S.: Overnight transformation to online education due to the COVID-19 pandemic: lessons learned. eLearn **9**(1) (2020). https://doi.org/10.1145/3424971.3421471

Web and Mobile Applications

Measuring and Evaluation of the Results of UI-Re-engineering in the Nursing Field

Sergio Staab[✉], Johannes Luderschmidt, and Ludger Martin

RheinMain University of Applied Sciences, Wiesbaden, Germany
{sergio.staab,johannes.luderschmidt,ludger.martin}@hs-rm.de

Abstract. Since all systems and services are ultimately aimed at human users, it is essential to address the interaction between humans and machines. A disproportionately growing number of care recipients and the associated avalanche of data in all areas of modern care continuously increases the need for more efficient, higher-quality and at the same time more cost saving options for care and its networking of relatives, doctors and nurses. As part of a project to digitize dementia residential communities, an information platform called INFODOQ was developed. The system serves as a transparent information, coordination and communication platform for various dementia residential communities to optimize the daily care and nursing routine. After completion, the system underwent several analytical and empirical evaluations in which nursing teams were involved. The subject of the work presented here is the presentation of the evaluation results, the subsequent reengineering process of nursing documentation and the presentation of a specially developed analysis tool. We discuss the requirements and problems arising from the interaction of nursing staff with digital nursing documentation. Present analysis procedures regarding acceptance and usability for software development. Aiming at improvements in the interaction between caregivers and software through a new guideline for the development of care documentation. The principle of "ambient freedom of objects", i.e., the proportionality of each individual object in the context of the granularity of the user interface. Characteristics include self-localization, clarity and simplicity.

Keywords: Re-engineering · Health informatics · Interface development · User experience and usability

1 Introduction

Demographic change and the associated improvement in medical care and nutrition as well as changes in housing conditions have a lasting impact on the life expectancy of generations. In addition, reduced birth rates and the resulting ageing of society are leading to a decline in the population and a massive increase in people in need of care. This results in a large shortage of junior care staff. Forecasts by the German Federal Statistical Office [1] show that in the next 15 years more than 66,000 skilled workers will be lacking in outpatient nursing alone. The shortage of nursing staff will result in a loss of value added and overall losses of 35 billion euros by 2030 due to vacant

© Springer Nature Switzerland AG 2021
J. Bentahar et al. (Eds.): MobiWIS 2021, LNCS 12814, pp. 47–61, 2021.
https://doi.org/10.1007/978-3-030-83164-6_4

positions. On average, the healthcare sector is growing more than one percent faster than the entire German economy per year and at the same time, it is one of the least digitized sectors. According to Haefker and Tielking [2], only 20% of clinics work with electronic nursing documentation. Based on such figures, the question arises as to why information science is so little accepted in this sector in particular. On the one hand, the basis of this scientific work rests on the problem of the increasing number of people in need of long-term care. With this work we want to investigate this issue. We analyze the nursing software INFODOQ which is currently being actively used by two dementia residential communities. Furthermore, we establish metrics regarding acceptance and usability for the correct software development of nursing systems and re-examine them using the newly designed software. The following questions are fundamental for this work: Which requirements and problems arise during the interaction of nurses with digital nursing documentation? How can the user-friendliness of interfaces in nursing documentation be increased in the context of these points? The paper contains the following contributions:

- Presentation of an information platform developed in the context of the digitalization of dementia residential communities
- Discussion of requirements and problems arising from the interaction of nursing staff with digital nursing documentation as well as investigation of these requirements and problems by means of analytical and empirical evaluations
- Revision of the existing software in consideration of the evaluations
- Establishment of analysis procedures regarding acceptance and usability for software development of maintenance systems
- Comparison of the initial and revised nursing documentation by means of analysis procedures
- Demonstration of improvements in the interaction between nurses and software through our work as well as derivation of guidelines for the development of User Interfaces (UI) in the field of nursing documentation

In Sect. 2, this paper starts with an insight into opinions on acceptance criteria that generally exist for interactions with software in medical care settings. Section 3 describes the implemented nursing software INFODOQ. In Sect. 4 empirical and analytical evaluations based on INFODOQ are presented. Section 5 describes the functionality of the analysis tool and the re-engineering measures for the transformation of the nursing documentation. The analysis of the initial and revised versions of the nursing documentation interfaces follows in Sect. 6. Section 7 contains the conclusion and guidelines for the development of software in the nursing sector.

2 Related Work

In the medical field, central administrative activities and services can be supported almost seamlessly by IT systems. According to Haefker and Tielking [2], the entry of information science into the narrower field of medical treatment and care is more difficult due to ethical, social and technical reasons.Many works in the field of software development are based on the heuristics for the design of interfaces formulated by Nielsen and Molich [3].

These include visibility of system status, correspondence between system and reality, user control and freedom, stability, flexibility and efficiency, an aesthetic and minimalist design as well as assistance in recognizing, evaluating and correcting mistakes. As part of the project UCARE (Gräfe and Rahner [4]) from 2017, a usability competence center was developed to support small and medium-sized software manufacturers in the care industry. Nielsen's ten heuristics are also taken up here and extended by the subjective perception of the viewer of a software.

In the work by Hielscher, Kirchen-Peters and Sowinski [5], the topic of the acceptance of nursing staff is addressed as follows: A decisive factor for the positive acceptance of the IT-supported documentation is the individual self-confidence in the direct handling of computers as well as the acceptance of the care process mapped in the documentation system. In addition, the social context of the group of colleagues and their acceptance of the technology represent a considerable factor, since nursing staff within work teams or shifts have a significant influence on the willingness to use the technology. It should be noted that technical settings should not be regarded as static variables. They can change during the introduction of IT systems and with increasing service life. The administration of the maintenance process is shifted "into the system" by digitizing the documents, away from management and specialists. This tends to reduce the scope for consideration and negotiation processes regarding the correctness or execution variants of the individual maintenance steps. Deviations are still possible, but automatically become justifiable and directly transparent for management. In this context, the obligation to provide reasons is to be regarded as very important.

Wechsler [6] describes possible contextual challenges within the development of a mobile health-related application on the basis of a mobile health project from 2015. She emphasizes that software designers have to adapt flexibly to the respective needs of nurses. In order to avoid discrepancies between the ideas of nurses and those of designers regarding the application, it should be ensured at the beginning of development that nurses understand that the design process requires their participation in order to achieve the best possible results. A possible way to do this would be to educate them about the value of design research activities in advance. The transfer of knowledge between nurses and designers should be made efficient. Both sides should commit themselves in advance to participate in the respective design process.

3   INFODOQ

INFODOQ [7] is a web-based information platform for use in outpatient residential care groups. The system was developed in response to the desire for a transparent information, coordination and communication platform for various dementia residential communities to optimize day-to-day care and nursing. A decisive factor for the digitalization of the documentation, which until now has only been available in analog form, is the enormous increase in performance. In addition to the reduction of redundant or incorrectly addressed information and communication channels and the simultaneous reduction of bureaucratic and administrative effort, the system ensures effective and efficient care and maintenance. Furthermore, the information platform offers a transparent way for the mobile use of information as well as for the coordination and scheduling of relatives, nurses and assistants. INFODOQ can be roughly divided into the front end, which is responsible for the display and direct interaction with the user, and the back end, which is responsible for the operating logic, persistence and provision of data and its security.

4 Evaluation

In the following the different analytical and empirical usability evaluations as well as the focus group of the investigations are described. The different needs and expectations of the nurse staff pose a particular challenge to the design and development of the software in the following project. A structure of the personas which are presented as fictitious users of the application with their characteristics and abilities follows. Nurses are persons who actively deal with the information platform in order to optimize digitization, transparency to other user groups and, above all, the performance increase of their work. Nurses interact with the information platform on a daily basis; they log the activities and behavioral characteristics of the residents and any changes they make. The following persona represent members of the nurse staff:

Sahra:

- Experience: is familiar with the use of technical devices, uses various management apps such as notes and calendars, registered on various online platforms, has experience with account management
- Procedures: systematically examines applications to learn more about their functions, uses full-featured applications and is not afraid of new functions
- Targets: creation and editing of documents, addition of people to activities, filtering and printing of documents

4.1 Test Execution

Various summative (i.e., the evaluation of a system towards the end of the development process) and formative (i.e., the evaluations accompanying the development) usability evaluations were carried out within the framework of the INFODOQ project to scale the usability as well as the acceptance analysis.

In order to eliminate trivial quality errors and to ensure low resource consumption, the system was first examined using heuristic evaluation. A group of evaluators with expertise in the area of the domain to be tested categorised usability problems in ten heuristics on behalf of later users. These heuristics are listed below: Visibility of system status, correspondence between system and real world, user control and freedom, consistency and standards, avoidance of errors, recognition before remembrance, flexibility and efficient use, aesthetic and minimalistic design, support in recognizing, understanding and processing errors and help and documentation. Subsequently, the system was examined for heuristics. Furthermore, fundamental design and functional errors were eliminated. Afterwards, empirical methods such as interviews and observing actual users were carried out. A description of the empirical questionnaire method with handwritten notes in which ten active nurses were involved in the evaluation of the INFODOQ project follows. Before each test was started, the tests were pre-tested with two independent persons (so-called pre-tests) to ensure that the questions and tasks asked were understandable and that the required equipment was well-functioning. The pre-test was conducted under the same conditions as the actual test in order to test the approach.

The usability tests were carried out at two locations in different care communities directly on site. The advantage of on-site testing is that the participants are in their natural environment and can use their devices such as computer, mouse, and keyboard. This means that the focus can be placed solely on the application. Moreover, the test subjects are not influenced by the periphery. Several methods have been used for the tests. At first, the nurses were given tasks to work on. Meanwhile, the test leader logged the observations. This procedure has the advantage that the nurses get to know the functionalities of the application. They can also ask the test manager for help if they are stuck with a task. Following the completion of the task, remaining ambiguities were clarified in a discussion. Parallel to the processing of the questions, the test leader also took notes on the observations. It was recorded whether the task was successfully completed, whether problems occurred and assistance from the test leader was required or whether there were interventions by the test leader.

4.2   Observations

The three youngest test subjects, aged 25 and 26, managed to complete the tasks well. They were able to carry out all tasks independently, confident, and needed no help. In addition, they completed the tasks faster as the other participants. The required duration was between 15 and 20 min. As soon as they could not complete a task directly, for example because they did not know under which subpage they could find the functionality, the participants independently familiarized themselves with the other subpages of the application and looked for a suitable solution mechanism. The described scenario occurred in task 12. In this task, the participants were asked to create a new info message. In order to be able to do this, the item "Note" had to be selected in the navigation.

In contrast, five of the seven older test had difficulties in completing the tasks. They dared to try less and did not want to make any mistakes. These five participants needed 25 to 65 min to complete the tasks. The fourth participant was noticeably nervous during the execution of the tasks. It took her over an hour to complete the tasks. In addition, she was not trained in operating a computer; for example, she often pressed the right mouse button instead of the left one. The participant also needed more time, as she was disturbed by a person during the performance of the seventh task, asking her why she needed so much time. After that, she was even more nervous and had even more concerns about doing something wrong. This made her ask questions in advance for the following tasks to speed up the test. The participant was motivated by the test leader to try to complete the tasks independently. Furthermore, she was reminded that the results would be treated anonymously and that she could not cause any irreparable damage to the system.

5   Re-engineering and Analysis

5.1   Nursing Documentation

The functionality of nursing documentation is divided into the documentation of nursing services and nursing reports. Nursing services are displayed in a matrix of all activities of the patients in a shift. The activities range from helping with cooking and handicraft lessons to training of everyday skills and day structures. A day in the shared flats consists of three shifts, each with different nursing staff. Figure 1 shows an activity matrix in which nurses enter the respective activities as a binary decision with their name abbreviation. The header contains information about the respective shift. Below that the patients are shown visually and by name. This is followed by the nursing documentation matrix in which activities are assigned to residents.

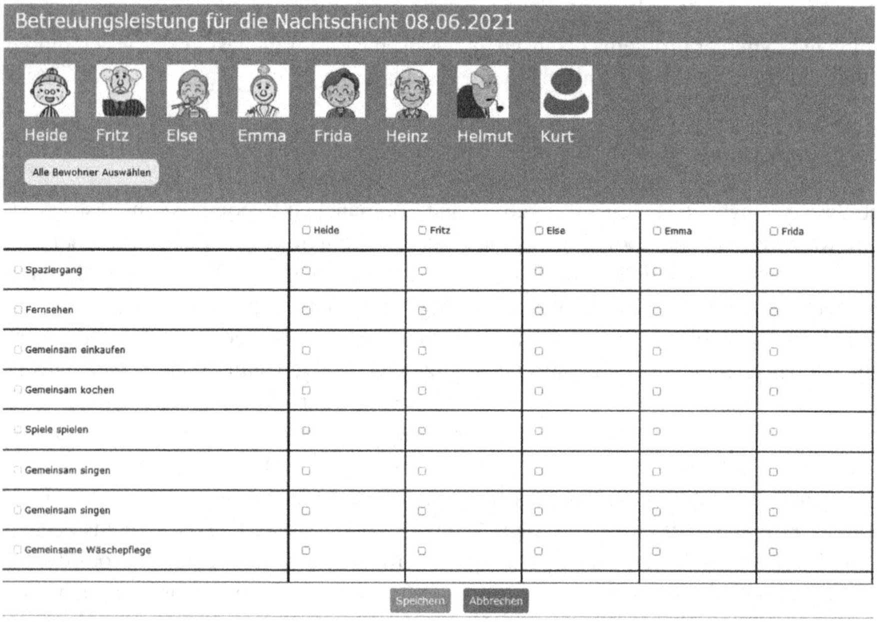

Fig. 1. Overview of a nursing service as a matrix: activities vertically and patients horizontally as table structure (Interface 1).

According to the evaluations, two user irritations occurred during the interaction of nurses with the nursing documentation: Column and row slippage and high physical effort by scrolling and clicking. Thereupon the nursing documentation was simplified in several steps; based on empirical studies of Tractinsky [8], Masaaki and Kashimuar [9]. Figure 2 shows the new design of the nursing documentation (in the following also called Interface 2). It is considerably narrower than the previous design. Columns and rows were masked by the hover effect which improves clarity and prevents slippage. The selection of all residents is integrated into the table. The image of an inhabitant changes by mouse interaction with the respective inhabitant name in the listing or the table header. The space savings offer the user significantly more content in the documentation matrix. The documentation can now be closed using the two icons which are marked in color in the upper right-hand header area. The differences between the interaction of the nurses with the old user interface (Interface 1) and the new user interface (Interface 2) were investigated in the next step using a specially developed analysis tool. With this tool, user behavior, performance, characteristics, competence, regularity, learning success, user irritation and the handling of different interfaces of one or more users can be compared and analyzed.

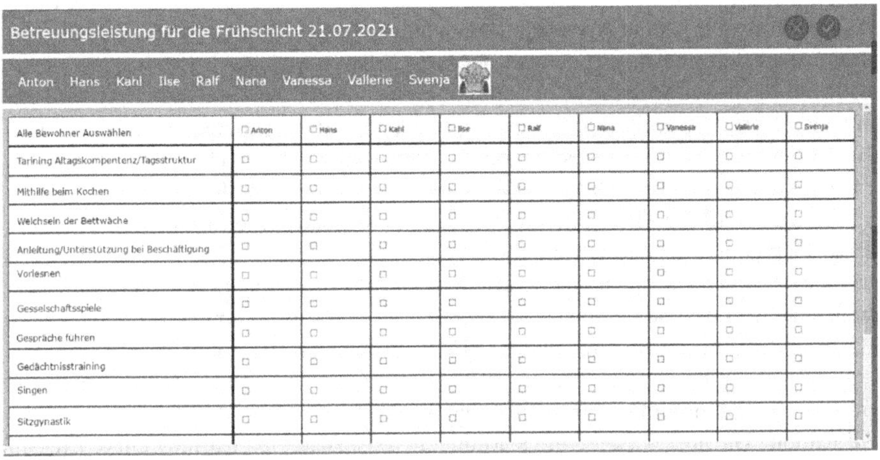

Fig. 2. Overview of a nursing service as matrix, version 2: activities vertically and patients horizontally as table structure (Interface 2).

For this purpose, analysis procedures and performance metrics such as time on task, task success, efficiency, learnability as well as an effort based and psychological reaction analysis are used (more on this in the following).

5.2 Analysis Procedures

The analysis tool is based on four different analysis methods, which are described below.

Interaction of the Users. Atterer and Schmidt [10] describe a solution for detailed logging of user interactions with AJAX-based web applications. They generate protocol data via an intermediate proxy. This approach reaches far beyond the field of usability tests. The following user actions can be logged on HTML pages: Mouse movements (pixel coordinates, ID and HTML DOM tree positions of the elements over which the mouse pointer is moved), scrolling (pixel offset), clicks, ID and DOM tree position of the clicked element, selection of drop-down menu entries, keystrokes (displayed modification keys such as Shift/Alt/Ctrl), text selection in form fields and resizing of the browser window. In summary, various interaction events can be logged from the metadata of mouse interactions, scroll strokes, clicks, keystrokes and dwell time.

Performance Analysis. Tullis and Albert [11] describe in their book the calculation of performance indicators based on certain user behavior, scenarios or tasks. Regardless of the technology, users interact with a system in some way. These behaviors form the cornerstone of performance metrics. Performance metrics are among the most valuable tools for any usability professional. Tullis and Albert describe the following types of performance metrics as Performance Metrics: Task Success, Time on Task, Errors, Efficiency and Learning Ability.

Effort-Based Analysis. In their work, Tamir, Komogortsev and Mueller [12] put forward the hypothesis that usability is a function of effort and time. The use of effort to measure usability assumes that the less effort it takes to achieve a certain goal, the more usable the software is. One approach to an analysis could be to set a set of goals and measure the effort and time a subject needs to achieve each goal. If developers estimate the effort and time required, it is possible to compare the observed effort with the estimated effort. If the observed effort is greater than the estimated effort, a problem arises that requires further investigation. One approach is to execute the task n times per user to determine the learning curve of the user himself. The fewer task executions are necessary until the effort curve per user E(u) stagnates, the faster the user seems to have adapted to the interface and the task structure. The calculation of the effort (E) determines the physical and temporal effort of a user per modification within a task execution. This includes the number of all mouse clicks (MCall), number of double clicks (MCD), number of mouse movements (MM) and number of scrolled pixels (SM). To analyze the usability, the average effort of all users has to be measured on an expert ideal line, i.e., the minimum effort E(e) that an expert would need to process the same modification. The area between the learning curve E(u) and the learning curve E(e) up to the point at which the slope of the effort E(u) is zero is to be regarded as the learning phase. The difference between curves E(u) and E(e) represents the comprehensibility of the interaction with regard to the task/the interface underlying the task. The greater the difference, the more difficult it seems to be to handle the software optimally. Figure 3 shows the average effort of user E(u) and expert E(e).

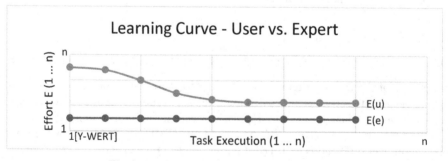

Fig. 3. Learning curve of user versus expert [11].

The line chart shows a series of data points connected by interpolated straight line segments. The horizontal axis counts up the task executions. The vertical axis describes the effort.

Psychological Reaction Analysis. Freeman and Ambady [13] present the real-time processing of their mouse tracking method for task evaluation in their work. Motor responses can be considered as the final result of a feed-forward pipeline of perception, cognition and action. Conclusions can be drawn about the temporal course of perceptual cognitive processing. This is done as follows: A trajectory is the measurement of a movement from a starting point in the context of a task to a target point over a distance. During each trajectory, three pieces of information are recorded: time (how many milliseconds have elapsed), the x-coordinate of the mouse (in pixels), and the y-coordinate of the mouse (in pixels). The distance covered by each competitor is calculated as the "mean trajectory". This can be done by the number of competitors or by the number of attempts of a single competitor. Based on this basic data, analyses can now be carried out in many different ways, for example by measuring the spatial attraction. First, an idealized response trajectory (a straight line between the start and end point of each trajectory) is calculated. The following example is based on an attempt to calculate a trajectory with one start point and two destinations (trivial answers) #1 and #2, where answer #2 is correct. The MD (Maximum deviation) of a trajectory is then calculated as the largest vertical deviation between the actual and its idealized trajectory from all time steps. The higher the MD, the more the trajectory deviates in the direction of the unselected alternative. The AUC (Area Under the Curve) of a trajectory is calculated as the geometric area between the actual trajectory and the idealized trajectory. Figure 4 shows an exemplary trajectory that leads to the right to the selected answer (#2).

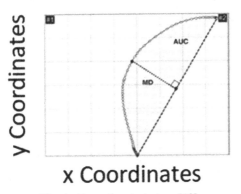

Fig. 4. Exemplary trajectory [13].

The amount of spatial attraction to an unselected answer (#1) is calculated. In addition, an idealized reaction trajectory (straight line) is displayed, which is used to calculate the MD and AUC.

5.3 Analysis Tool

Figure 5 shows the dashboard and different analysis areas. The header area contains general data about tasks (one interaction with documentation per user), the number of users and interfaces.

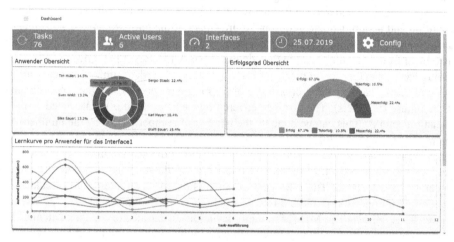

Fig. 5. Analysis dashboard.

The user overview shows all active users, i.e., all users of the system who have run through a task at least once. The distribution of the number of tasks, repetitions per user and their successes are represented by two nested pie charts, one as a percentage and one as an actual number. The success rate overview provides a semi-circular donut diagram that shows the total success rate, both as a percentage and as an actual number, across all users and interfaces. The learning success analysis is based on calculations of the effort and the concept of learning success. The learning curve of the expert is marked as a continuous effort line in green, the learning curve of the users in different colors.

Specific Analysis of a User. The "Active Users" section opens the modal of the user analysis. The analysis regarding the users shows different interactions, characteristics and efforts of a user as well as the comparison of all users regarding the mentioned points. Data about time, effort and the results are displayed. Figure 6 shows the analysis of the average time and physical effort of a modification per user, averaged over the number of task executions of each user.

Outliers can be quickly identified and specifically analyzed. For example, it would now be the task of the usability analyst to find out why Mr. Mayer needs about twice as much time to process a modification as all other users. In contrast, his effort to execute modifications seems to be similar to that of other users. Figure 7 shows the number of executions and the percentage of completion for each user. Mr. Mayer's 12 executions are in the average; the non-routine handling of the system will therefore not be the reason.

Figure 8 shows a view of the usability analyst on the user analysis of Mr. Mayer.

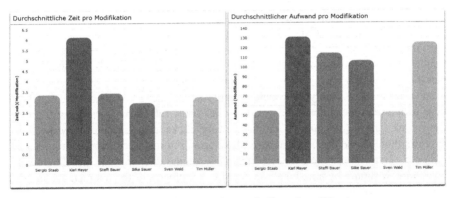

Fig. 6. Analysis of average time and effort of modifications.

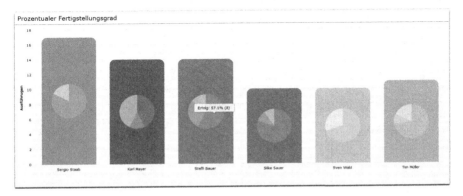

Fig. 7. Percentage of completion per user.

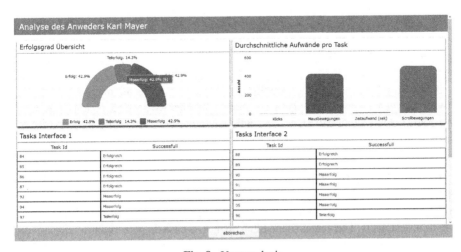

Fig. 8. User analysis.

This modal visualizes all interactions of a user. In the header area, the user's executions as well as the associated successes, partial successes and failures, the effort of clicks, mouse movements, scroll movements and the time required are compared. All executions/tasks of the user can be viewed down to the data level. This is followed by two tables that list the user's tasks in Interface 1 and Interface 2. The tasks can be selected per line and open the Task Analysis Module. Figure 9 shows the task analysis modal and the mouse path analysis contained therein. The click array (all click interactions of a user during a task) shows all x and y coordinates of the clicks from the table analysis_clicks and draws them as red dots. The Mouse Move array returns the x and y coordinates of the mouse cursor. These are connected from coordinate to coordinate and drawn with a black line. It should be noted that the x and y coordinates of the interactions and the background image are scaled at runtime using the display sizes. Thus, the mouse interactions and the mouse path analysis can be displayed in a normalized way across any window size. In addition, the raw data for each task and the learning curve described above can be displayed for each user per interface.

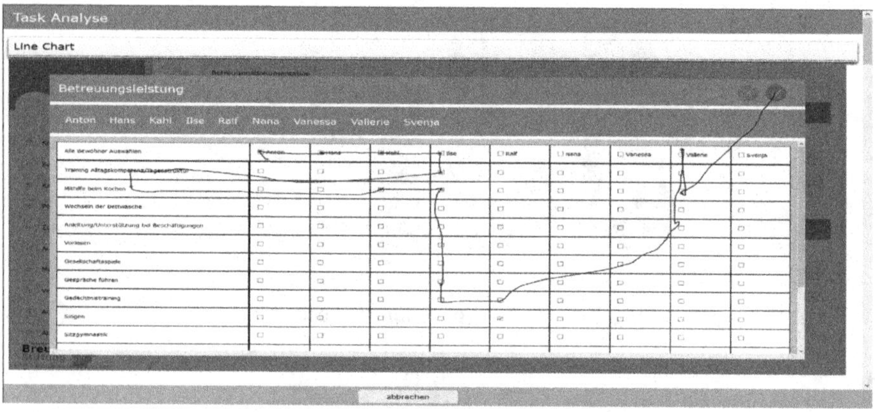

Fig. 9. Mouse path analysis.

If Mr. Mayer's mouse paths would show complex or even fluctuating trajectories between the respectively selected objects, there would be two possible conclusions: One user would not have understood the distribution of the objects, with several users a bad or misunderstood distribution of the objects on the respective interface could be concluded.

6   Evaluation of the Interfaces

Three computer science students and three nurses are involved in the execution of the tasks as test subjects. The goal is (depending on the use case) to perform different activity manipulations with the same 16 activities. The respondent is thus offered a matrix of 9×16 selection options with checkboxes in the documentation matrix. The tests are logged and monitored by a test leader in the background. This ensures that the three use cases with different logging objectives are adhered to. After each test, the tracked data is recreated and logged. It is also ensured that the interaction data is correctly stored and further processed. In the following, the results of the previous evaluation are described. Interface 1 seems to be easier to understand, especially for laymen. Both the click effort and the scrolling movements are relatively high, but the time required, and the help needed is on average higher compared to the use cases of Interface 2. It seems as if Interface 1 is more inviting in the first learning steps and offers an easier way of arranging objects. As expected, the learning curve of the three – in relation to the computer – experienced users decreases much faster. For them, the user interface of Interface 2 seems to be more performant after multiple use; especially the effort of mouse and scroll movements is significantly reduced.

7 Conclusions

On the basis of the evaluations described in the previous chapter, this chapter focuses on the digitization of transparent nursing documentation which is necessary but hardly articulated. The findings of the summative empirical methodology for evaluating the interaction of nurses with the INFODOQ system underpin various of the problems addressed. Even if the heuristics described by Nielsen [3] had previously been ana-lytically identified by usability experts and integrated into the system, the requirements and problems of the nurses before and during the interaction are not only ensured by the design and function optimization. The subjective reference of each individual user turns out to be an important point. This includes perceptual characteristics such as hearing and sight as well as behavioral characteristics such as experience, motivation, individual preferences, abilities and knowledge. It should be noted that age generally represents a strong point of reference to the subjective limits described above. An interface from the point of view of a younger or older user does not seem to be pertinent for both. It can be assumed that users of a certain age on average no longer possess the same background knowledge in dealing with computer-aided systems as younger users. Their motivation to deal with new systems also decreases with increasing age. If individual self-confidence in the direct use of the computer is not strengthened, even small tasks such as regis-tration seem to pose major obstacles. In the beginning, any design irritation is directly related to the acceptance of the entire system. Frequently, if a manager or a colleague is not immediately available for advice when problems arise, the hurdle seems insur-mountable. After consultation with nurses, it turned out that the desired transparency of all interactions is rather perceived as the external management of the original care work. This diminishes the undisputed advantages of the system and puts the actual added value in the background. In the introductory phase of nursing documentation software, the stress for nurses due to additional work and time expenditure is significantly higher than the actual added value of the system. In particular, many older nurses do not have the pertinence and relevance to use nursing documentation software in addition to their experienced use of computers.

The actual work facilitation simply cannot be experienced. Decisions suddenly have to be substantiated; in addition, interactions can be perceived as external management of the original care work. Based on the evaluations from the INFODQ project, inter-faces must meet the following requirements in the direction of user-friendly interaction between nurses: Be simple. In this context, simple means that a person from the addressed target group has enough basic pertinence to be able to record and carry out the process without user irritations Gast [14]. Another requirement: Be emotional. This means that a person from the addressed target group sees a fundamental usefulness with regard to the relevance of the subjective point of view. It should be noted that the knowledge contained in information is to be classified as relevant if it objectively serves to prepare a decision or to close a knowledge gap. If the system is simple and emotional, then a certain motivation arises which exceeds the threshold potential of the nerve cells of a user and thus allows the objective information to be processed. It should be noted that nursing documentation software must be designed to be brain-friendly by means of user experience and usability. This means objective knowledge must be prepared in the context of the internal reference of the target groups addressed and processes must be reduced to the essentials.

Objective knowledge must be enriched with emotional values in the context of the internal reference of the target groups addressed. It turns out that experienced computer users have a significantly higher competence. For them, user interfaces are much quicker to become functionally apparent and pertinent. Their perception process is much more pronounced through interaction with other systems. The structure of the system and the respective interfaces are more paramount. In addition, these users focus much more on usability and user experience, but also here the heuristics do not provide holistic user satisfaction. In everyday life, nurses must be able to access desired information much more quickly and easily. The heuristic of minimalism is a decisive approach that must be pursued in combination with user experience and usability measures. How can the user-friendliness of interfaces in nursing documentation be increased in the context of these points? User experience and usability measures can be understood as the simplification of objective knowledge by refining emotions that build fictional relevance. This means that objective knowledge must be designed in a way that is acceptable to the subject as a person (usability). During the process of information transfer, the user should be given an emotional part that builds up subjective relevance (experience). In order to support the development and commissioning of nursing documentation software, we extend the concept of dialogue design of usable systems by the principle of the ambience freedom of objects, i.e., the proportionality (benefit - user irritation) of each individual object. This means that the result of the use must be in the context of the granularity of the nursing documentation software in order to keep the previously described user irritation as low as possible. In this context, self-localization, clarity and simplicity are the characteristics of nursing documentation.

References

1. Sarodnick, F., Brau, H.: Methoden der Usability Evaluation – Wissenschaftliche Grundlagen und praktische Anwendung 3. Auflage. Hogrefe Verlag, Bern (2016)
2. Haefker, M., Tielking, L.: Altern, Gesundheit, Partizipation: Alternative Wohn- und Versorgungsformen im Zeichen des demografischen Wandels. Springer Fachmedien Wiesbaden, (2017). https://doi.org/10.1007/978-3-658-16801-8
3. Nielsen, J.: Usability Engineering. Kaufmann, San Francisco (1993). ISBN 0-12-518406-9

4. Gräfe, B., Rahner, S., Root, E., Timmermanns, E.: Entwicklung eines Usability-Kompetenzzentrums zur Unterstützung von klein- und mittelständischen Softwareherstellern in der Pflegebranche (2017)
5. Hielscher, V., Kirchen-Peters, S., Sowinski, C.: Wissenschaftlicher Diskurs und Praxisentwicklungen in der stationären und ambulanten Langzeitpflege (2015)
6. Wechsler, J.: HCD Mobile Health Project: Post Collaboration Reflection of Researcher and Designer (2015). https://doi.org/10.1145/2846439.2846442
7. Bundesweites Journal für Wohn- Pflege- Gemeinschaften: Wissenschaft und Praxis zur Weiterentwicklung In Wohn-Pflege-Gemeinschaften 2018 (2018). https://www.kvjs.de/fileamin/dateien/soziales/fawo/wohn-pflege-journal_7–2018.pdf
8. Tractinsky, N.: Aesthetics and apparent usability: empirically assessing cultural and methodological issues. ACM: 0-89791-802-9/97/03 (1997)
9. Kiurosu, M. Kashirnuma, K.: Apparent usability vs. inherent usability experimental analysis on the determinants of the apparent usability. ACM: 0-89791-755-3/95/0005 (1995)
10. Atterer, R., Schmidt, A.: Tracking the Interaction of Users with AJAX Applications for Usability Testing (2007). ISBN 978-1-59593-593-9. https://doi.org/10.1145/1240624.1240828
11. Tullis, T., Albert, W.: Measuring the User Experience - Collecting, Analyzing, and Presenting Usability Metrics (2013). ISBN 978-0-12-415781-1
12. Feldman, L., Mueller, C.J., Komogortsev, O.V., Tamir, D.: Usability testing with total-effort metrics (2009).https://doi.org/10.1109/ESEM.2009.5316022
13. Freeman, J.B., Ambady, N.: MouseTracker: software for studying real-time mental processing using a computer mouse-tracking method. Behav. Res. Meth. **42**, 226–241 (2010). https://doi.org/10.3758/BRM.42.1.226
14. Gast, O.: User Experience im E-Commerce. Springer Fachmedien Wiesbaden (2018).https://doi.org/10.1007/978-3-658-22484-4

Investigating the Usability of Government Applications for Elderlies in the Kingdom of Saudi Arabia

Arwa AlMuaybid[✉] and Lulwah AlSuwaidan[✉]

College of Computer and Information Sciences, Imam Mohammad Ibn Saud Islamic University, Riyadh, Kingdom of Saudi Arabia
amuaybid@sm.imamu.edu.sa, lnsuwaidan@imamu.edu.sa

Abstract. There will be relatively more older adults worldwide than there were in the past in the twenty-first century. Saudi Arabia is a nation where the elderlies are increasing. Also, technology will expand and grow in this era at an unprecedented rate. Mobile applications could help elderly individuals, but they need to be usable and personalized to adopt. The study will aim to investigate the usability of mobile government applications popular in Saudi Arabia. First by a structured questionnaire with Saudi older adults to assist the user experience. The usability attributes also will be evaluated and tested in the research methodology, such as effectiveness, efficiency, satisfaction. The general basis for this study will be to enable the elderly to access better the benefits of using smartphones and applications, as this has positive effects on mental performance and the adoption of healthier lifestyles by improving access to health information and applications and supporting more independence. The result will highlight the need to develop government application interfaces to meet older adults' usability attributes in Saudi Arabia.

Keywords: Older people · Usability · User experience · Smartphones · Government applications

1 Introduction

Recently, smartphone applications have been used exponentially in Saudi Arabia. This has been shown because of the increasing power of computers and the increase in information technologies which allow a wide range of information applications and services. In fact, the cellular phone was developed for calls-only purposes, but due to the capabilities of a smartphone with modern technology, it becomes a powerful platform for various services, including real-time ones especially and the ability to run many applications simultaneously [1]. In 2019, the number of smartphone users in Saudi Arabia reached 28.8 million, and this number has increased steadily in the past two years and is expected to reach 36.17 by 2025 [2]. Additionally, the number of older people using a smartphone is growing, not only for communication purposes but also for its help as assistive technology through mobile applications [3].

© Springer Nature Switzerland AG 2021
J. Bentahar et al. (Eds.): MobiWIS 2021, LNCS 12814, pp. 62–73, 2021.
https://doi.org/10.1007/978-3-030-83164-6_5

Nowadays, most services are available online to limit barriers such as location, cost, and time. Using applications and services such as social security systems, health care, and community services has become a demand, and most older people must use them. Therefore, if the elderly in Saudi Arabia can use applications, the economic and social burdens of families, communities, and the country may be significantly reduced. In addition, the financial responsibility of caring for the elderly population must be reduced to be sustainable. Research shows that keeping the elderly self-sufficient in their own homes is the best way to manage this [4]. Other studies have found that mobile phones play an essential role in collectivist societies such as Saudi Arabia because they enable people to stay in frequent communication [5].

User experience (UX) design is the process that design teams use to create meaningful and relevant user experiences; this involves designing the entire process of acquiring and integrating the product, including branding, design, usability, and function [6]. The user experience is enhanced through the usability of the applications. Therefore, it can play a significant part in mobile apps' success [7]. In the last decade, mobile applications' usability has increased enormously, as did the quality challenges. In this way, the structures' continuous improvement moves toward quality assurance [8].

This research investigates smartphone applications and the use of the elderly, significantly increasing their usability to use government applications. The data collection was a quantitative method consisting of a questionnaire of older people in Saudi Arabia. Questionnaires are among the most widely used strategies adopted for gathering information and are an easy way to gain users' experience rapidly. The questionnaire was conducted using an online survey via google forms based on a User Experience Questionnaire (UEQ). This framework allows a fast evaluation of the UX of interactive products. It measures pragmatic aspects like efficiency, perspicuity, dependability, and hedonic aspects like stimulation or originality [9]. It was adopted to measure the primary elements of usability and applied with Saudi older adults.

The rest of the article is organized as follows. Section 2 presents an overview of the related work of this research. Section 3 discusses the research methodology. Section 4 presents a proposed prototype of this research. Finally, Sect. 5 concludes the article and shows the future works.

2   Related Work

A review of previous studies demonstrates that smartphone applications' usability and the question of human-computer interaction (HCI) have been addressed in many theoretical and applied studies as subjects of interest to information specialists.

2.1   Usability Definition

Usability can be defined as a Multidimensional feature for any product. International Standards Organization (ISO) standard 9241–11 defines usability as the "extent to which specified users can use a product to achieve specific goals with effectiveness, efficiency, and satisfaction in a specified context of use" [10]. In 2011, 9241–11 was replaced by ISO/IEC 25010. This form includes a software quality model that portrays usability as the degree to which a satisfied user can efficiently and effectively attain individual goals under specific conditions. However, there is a more recent revision of 2018 that includes several new approaches and definitions, such as user experience, which means user perception, including emotions, beliefs, preferences, perceptions, comfort, behaviors, and achievements, related to the system, product, or service that can occur before, during, and after use [11].

Usability measures the extent to which a specific user in each context can use a product or design to achieve a particular goal with effectiveness, efficiency, and satisfaction. "Usability is about human behavior. It recognizes that humans are lazy, get emotional, are not interested in putting much effort into, say, getting a credit card and generally prefer things that are easy to do vs. those that are hard to do." [12].

2.2 The User Experience of Older Peoples' Proportion

The worldwide population is aging at a fast pace. By 2050, according to World Population Prospects 2019 [13], 1 in 6 people in the world will be over the age of 65, up from 1 in 11 in 2019. One of the most detailed smartphones use studies among older adults was conducted in Spain [14]. In their study, the behaviors of a sample of smartphone users aged 20 to 76 were tracked for one month, and follow-up focus groups were conducted with participants aged between 55 and 81. The researchers concluded that older adults are increasingly using smartphones, but the overall extent of smartphone application usage declines with age. This research [15] found that 47.8% of respondents aged 75 or older belong to the "Apathetic" category of users and concluded that this is mainly due to their difficulties in dealing with technological devices and their limited need for social networking and communications.

Several studies show that older adults show substantial barriers to the use of smartphones, such as subjective barriers, technological barriers, and situational barriers. Subjective barriers are related to individuals' attitudes and abilities, such as the lack of know-how on using the smartphone, which may be related to a decline in both mental and physical ability due to old age. Technological barriers are mainly related to interface and usability concerns. Finally, situational barriers include economic costs, which are also significant obstacles to smartphone adoption [16].

On the other hand, Preeyanont [17] conducted a study to investigate how LINE applications' user interface affects the elderly when using smartphones. Their study involved 38 elderly participants (60–69 years) who performed eight different mobile phone tasks. Results showed that due to a decline in physical health, the elderly group had difficulty viewing content on-screen, leading to more errors.

Several studies have revealed how low smartphone usage levels among older adults result from multiple and often interacting factors. One of the qualitative research findings with older mobile phone users in South Africa was the inability to use mobile phone features, which were perceived as too complex. For some, this even included basic features such as making calls. There were also low levels of interest and negative attitudes towards mobile phones among this group because of their perceived complexity and a tendency to use them for minimal purposes such as making calls to family and friends. The study also revealed an increased sense of dependency among these older mobile phone users. They often needed to turn to their children or grandchildren to use their phones [18].

There are studies concerning older adults' use of technology. For example, the user-test research of three different smartphone applications showed the importance of using colors, easy navigation, and enhanced and simplified data visualizations [19]. The Elderly face problems such as understanding, vision, hearing, understanding the menu and navigation links, social contact, and mobile application infrastructure. Most of the time, elderly open apps face problems going back to the previous state or face problems closing the app; some applications put the back button at the top of the page. Other applications put the button at the bottom of the page [20].

Because of older people's age-related changes, many have recognized the importance of designing age-friendly products. Therefore, there is a need for the development of effective usability testing and evaluation for elderly users. A comprehensive guide to developing examples regarding cognitive issues in older users and how to apply them to a mobile or Ambient Assisted Living environment is needed for practical applications as new technology expands to fill these entities' needs [21]. Guidelines along with heuristic evaluation are considered efficient tools for assessing product design. Therefore, enormous research has been carried out to develop design and usability guidelines for older people explicitly. This study [22] reviewed the published design guidelines and checklist for older people's mobile phones. Additionally, there is a wide variety of research-based work [23] trying to develop a set of guidelines that allow designing usable and accessible mobile interfaces for the aging population. However, there are challenges those elderly users experience with familiar user interfaces that a younger person would not experience either because of aging.

The author in [20] tries to identify fundamental usage problems while interacting with a mobile phone. To improve the interface, a guiding framework called SMASH has been proposed. It consists of 12 usability cases. Five experts participated in this evaluation. The study showed that 27 indicative violations were encountered. Thus, this study shows some critical points which need to improve for a better Elderly and Low-literate user experience.

Previous studies were concerned with evaluating or testing the usability of smartphone applications. However, these studies were conducted in diverse academic environments; they emphasized the importance of smartphone applications' usability as a requirement for designing these practical applications' interfaces. Thus, this research will be justified by many of the previous studies' recommendations to the effect that evaluation of smartphones should focus on the usability criterion.

Few previous studies talked about government application interfaces and how to facilitate them to be used by the elderly, especially in Saudi Arabia's culture. Therefore, there is a need to investigate mobile app's usability for the government with older people in Saudi Arabia. Furthermore, investigating government applications' usability can affect government performance in improving public services to the public, especially the older people.

3   Research Methodology

More research is needed to investigate government applications among the elderly in Saudi Arabia based on the related works. This leads to the main question: How to improve smartphone government applications' usability to help elderly users in Saudi Arabia?

The research will evaluate government applications' usability and then develop usability guidelines designed for government application interfaces to investigate the above question. Based on these guidelines, a prototype will be created. This question opens more questions to be explored in this research as follow:

– What types of difficulties do older people in Saudi Arabia experience when using smartphones?
– What needs and requirements can be identified for the government applications for older people?
– What be design solutions for an app interface." developed to meet government applications for older people?

According to the research questions, the research objectives are as follows: To understand the users and motivations, deliver services that fulfill users' needs, and identify user behaviors. Additionally, determine where it will be possible to have an impact to improve the value of the service, and to redesign a new functioning, easy-to-use user interface, also to design a concept of an interface based on the preliminary study, moreover, to provide a unique experience for the users.

The conceptual research framework starts with specifying government applications and collecting data from a quantitative survey to identify user usability. Next, more information will appear using the evaluation, and a usability test will be presented in the research. A literature study of the problem domain has also been conducted. (See Fig. 1).

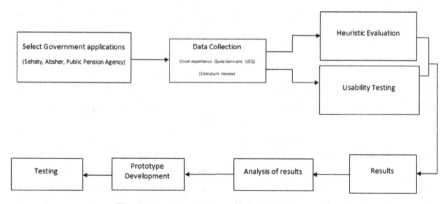

Fig. 1. Conceptual framework of the research.

The overarching strategy will be applied research. This paper presents methodology on how government apps can be improved towards better usability. The research starts with the preliminary study, where data is collected using the standard questionnaire UEQ [9] to specify and understand the research problem. In this phase, the emphasis is put on understanding the users and their usability situation.

The questionnaire was applied to three government applications ("Sehaty," "Absher," and "Public Pension Agency" [24]) in the Arabic language. (See Fig. 2, Fig. 3, and Fig. 4).

Fig. 2. Screenshots of "Sehaty" application

Fig. 3. Screenshot of "Absher" application

These applications were chosen considering that their use is essential, especially for the elderly. "Sehaty" application selected because it provides health services to individuals in Saudi Arabia and allows the user to access health information and obtain several health services offered by various bodies in the health sector, including assistance to update and follow up vital checks, track dispensed medicines, review and share sick leave, develop a healthy lifestyle, and calculate steps from Through integration with

Fig. 4. Screenshots of "Public Pension Agency."

the health program built into Apple's Health-Kit devices, and other services related to individual and family health, and increased health awareness. "Absher" application serves 19 million subscribers, provides more than 200 e-services, and provides users with multiple electronic services [25]. There is a link between government and private sectors, and it helps conduct users' private transactions smoothly and efficiently. It also enables users to view alerts in personal data. Finally, "Public Pension Agency" was selected because it gives users the ability to benefit from the Public Pension Agency's services, the retirement pension account. It also allows reviewing the benefits and offers and communicating with the institution by giving inquiries and suggestions.

The sample's responses are from the elderlies in Saudi Arabia. The current population of Saudi Arabia is 35,295,803 based on Worldometer elaboration of the latest United Nations data. The latest statistics of the Department of Statistics indicate that the number of elderlies is close to one million and three thousand, which is 5% of the total population. The age of responses is 50 years or above from male and female who use one of the selected government applications. The questionnaire uses a seven-stage scale. First, the data analyzed using the UEQ [9] data analysis tool by entering the data information that has been collected and rescales the data to the range −3 to 3 and calculates the scale values for pragmatic quality aspects (Perspicuity, Efficiency, and Dependability) and hedonic quality aspects (Stimulation and Novelty) per person and the scale means and standard deviation per item are calculated.

The benchmark shows how good the evaluated product is compared to the products in the benchmark data set. A graphic show for each scale how the results are related to the products in the benchmark data set and found that government applications' user experience compared to the benchmark has an insufficient user experience level (see Fig. 5, Fig. 6, and Fig. 7). The results of the questionnaire show in the determining using a questionnaire that government applications for the elderly need to be improved, and the experience of elderly users' needs to be developed.

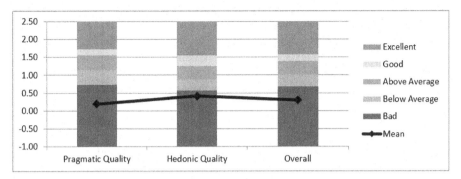

Fig. 5. Absher application benchmark

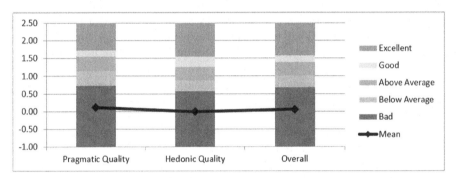

Fig. 6. Public pension agency application benchmark

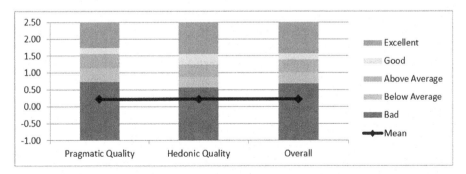

Fig. 7. Sehaty application benchmark

Based on the results and after determining the usability attribute issue using the general UEQ questionnaire, more information and results will appear using the evaluation. Finally, a usability test will be presented in the research.

4 Proposed Prototype

Generally, a new prototype will be developed to present the design based on the principles and test it to see how it is suitable by observing the older people. However, for now, and based on the literature review, it will consider some principal points when developing the prototype, such as screen brightness, size of the fonts, clear contrast, easy-to-read buttons, avoid using flashing texts, and generous spacing between items interfaces with reducing the number of buttons.

Based on the UEQ [9], and when focusing on the usability pragmatic quality aspects (Perspicuity, Efficiency, and Dependability), it shows that all these aspects of usability need to be improved. The current government application interfaces that have been selected ("Sehaty", "Absher," "Public Pension Agency") for now have some difficulties such as errors messages contain words that are incomprehensible to elderlies, for example: "There is a problem with the server." Lack of clarity and distinction more than what is required of entering the passcode or code sent on the mobile. The applications do not contain direct help methods like Chatbots. All these issues affected usability.

So, the proposed preliminary low-fidelity prototype will avoid the previous issues in the application's usability and have been tested by the questionnaire. In addition, the." proposed prototype will have the following user experience and user interface design guidelines pre recommendation to improve the usability attributes for the elderlies:

- Larger graphics, buttons, icons, and other clickable targets make it easy to understand how to use the application and that the elderly can click it without any error.
- Use the black and bigger size of the text.
- Use soft colors because the colors make users pleased to use the application.
- Design in a simple layout and removed unnecessary functions because too many parts will make confuse the elderly.
- Limit options to give a strong information scent on an uncluttered display to shows essential information for completing tasks.
- Offer more explicit information with simple words feedbacks about system status, such as writing terms in the Saudi colloquial dialect.
- Make tasks easier to complete by adding other login methods to save the password and re-enter it every time.
- The applications should contain direct help methods like Chatbots or virtual video calls.
- Present some elements and icons with 3d dimensions to make it a clear view for the elderly.
- Interaction with voice user interfaces has become one of the UX trends again due to its widespread adoption in UX/UI design. That will help elderlies to find the services easier by voice when trying to search.
- Improve the help section by adding learning videos of how to get each service to apply.

Personalization is one of the most important features that help to improve user interfaces. So, the proposed prototype's basic idea in this research is to make user interfaces age customized, including the design guidelines recommended to prevent usability issues in current applications.

To apply the personalization feature, the application will ask the user to create an account to enter the date of birth. Then, when the user is in the elderly's category (age from 60 or more), the personalized interfaces for elderlies and their attributes will appear. When the application asking the elderly to create an account, only the user needs to enter the ID number without any extra information, and based on that, all the information of the user will be imported from the central government database's user data. Also, it is proposed to add more extra options to let users access more easily through fingerprint or face recognition for sign-in. The following part of the proposed prototype is for the main interface and create an account and Sign-in user interfaces. (See Fig. 8).

Fig. 8. Proposed prototype.

5   Conclusion

This paper presents an empirical investigation on improving mobile application-oriented for older people. This paper aims to evaluate and improve the usability of government applications for the elderly in Saudi Arabia. This paper highlights the importance of enhancing the usability of mobile apps by presenting extensive related works. This research will also answer the following research question: How to improve smartphone government apps usability to help elderly users in Saudi Arabia? To answer the question, typical applications identified, the data collection findings concluded, including a preliminary study and concept development phase.

The paper has presented the methodology and the procedures for testing the government applications. The work will include performing a qualitative study to determine how to improve usability and formulate domain-specific design principles that focus on older people when using government applications to enhance user interfaces' existing designs and enhance user experience. It will include concept development, where a solution to the problem will be developed.

To use qualitative data, this study intends to evaluate the usability of government applications across the elderly in Saudi Arabia using a heuristic evaluation approach and usability testing on smart mobile phones to provide a comprehensive view of user interactions and satisfaction. Usability testing is an observational approach that allows an application to be evaluated by employing users to perform specific tasks. Data will be collected during the usability testing sessions while observing the participants performing developed task scenarios. Based on these guidelines, an app interface designed for older people in Saudi Arabia will be created. The consideration will be made as one of the government application's current interfaces will act as a starting point in this study. Better application usability would help keep these individuals motivated to make necessary changes and involvement in life.

References

1. Asyraf, R.A., Cagadas, R.: Usage, trend, attitude, likes, and dislikes of elderly on new technology smartphones. Qual. Quant. Res. Rev. **3**(2462–1978) (2018)
2. The number of smartphone users in Saudi Arabia from 2017 to 2025 (in millions) (2020). Retrieved 6 Mar 2021. https://www.statista.com/statistics/494616/smartphone-users-in-saudi-arabia/
3. Anderson, M., Perrin, A.: Tech Adoption Climbs Among Older Adults (2017). Retrieved 6 Mar 2021. https://www.pewresearch.org/internet/2017/05/17/tech-adoption-climbs-among-older-adults/
4. Queirós, A., Silva, A., Alvarelhão, J., Rocha, N.P., Teixeira, A.: Usability, accessibility and ambient-assisted living: a systematic literature review. Univ. Access Inf. Soc. **14**(1), 57–66 (2013). https://doi.org/10.1007/s10209-013-0328-x
5. Aldhaban, F., Unsal Daim, T., Harmon, R.: Exploring the adoption and use of smartphone technology in emerging regions: a literature review and hypotheses development. In: 2015 Proceedings of PICMET 2015: Management of The Technology Age (2015)
6. What is User Experience (UX) Design? (2020). Retrieved 29 Mar 2021. https://www.interactiondesign.org/literature/topics/ux-design
7. Costa, I., et al.: An empirical study to evaluate the feasibility of a UX and usability inspection technique for mobile applications. In: SEKE (2016)
8. Aggarwal, P., Grover, P., Ahuja, L.: Locating usability critical factors for mobile applications using ELECTRE-TRI method. In: 2019 9th International Conference on Cloud Computing, Data Science & Engineering (Confluence) (2019). https://doi.org/10.1109/confluence.2019.8776975
9. Díaz-Oreiro, I., López, G., Quesada, L., Guerrero, L.A.: Standardized questionnaires for user experience evaluation: a systematic literature review. Proceedings **31**(1), 14 (2019). https://doi.org/10.3390/proceedings2019031014
10. ISO 9241–11:1998. (1998). Retrieved 31 Mar 2021. https://www.iso.org/standard/16883.html
11. Ergonomics of human-system interaction—Part 11: Usability: Definitions and concepts (2018). Retrieved 31 Mar 2021. https://www.iso.org/obp/ui/#!iso:std:63500:en
12. What is Usability? (2021). Retrieved 7 Mar 2021. https://www.interaction-design.org/literature/topics/usability
13. United Nations: World Population Ageing 2019 [eBook]. New York (2019). Retrieved https://www.un.org/en/development/desa/population/publications/pdf/ageing/WorldPopulationAgeing2019-Highlights.pdf
14. Rosales, A., Fernández-Ardèvol, M.: Beyond WhatsApp: older people and smartphones. Rom. J. Commun. Public Relat. 18 1 27 (2016).https://doi.org/10.21018/rjcpr.2016.1.200

15. Vicente, P., Lopes, I.: Attitudes of older mobile phone users towards mobile phones. Communications, **41**(1) (2016). https://doi.org/10.1515/commun-2015-0026
16. Pang, N., Vu, S., Zhang, X., Foo, S.: Older adults and the appropriation and disappropriation of smartphones. In: Zhou, J., Salvendy, G. (eds.) ITAP 2015. LNCS, vol. 9193, pp. 484–495. Springer, Cham (2015). https://doi.org/10.1007/978-3-319-20892-3_47
17. Preeyanont, S.: User interface on smartphone for elderly users. Int. J. Autom. Smart Technol. **7**(4), 147–155 (2017). https://doi.org/10.5875/ausmt.v7i4.1339
18. Leburu, K., Grobler, H., Bohman, D.: Older people's competence to use mobile phones: an exploratory study in a South African context. Gerontechnology **17**(3), 174–180 (2018). https://doi.org/10.4017/gt.2018.17.3.005.00
19. Morey, S., Stuck, R., Chong, A., Barg-Walkow, L., Mitzner, T., Rogers, W.: Mobile health apps: improving usability for older adult users. Ergon. Des. Q. Hum. Factors Appl. **27**(4), 4–13 (2019). https://doi.org/10.1177/1064804619840731
20. Salman, H., Wan Ahmad, W., Sulaiman, S.: Usability evaluation of the smartphone user interface in supporting elderly users from experts' perspective. IEEE Access **6**, 22578–22591 (2018). https://doi.org/10.1109/access.2018.2827358
21. Dodd, C., Athauda, R., Adam, M.: Designing user interfaces for the elderly: a systematic literature review. Association for Information Systems (2017)
22. Petrovčič, A., Taipale, S., Rogelj, A., Dolničar, V.: Design of mobile phones for older adults: an empirical analysis of design guidelines and checklists for feature phones and smartphones. Int. J. Hum. Comput. Interact. **34**(3), 251–264 (2017). https://doi.org/10.1080/10447318.2017.1345142
23. Garcia-Sanjuan, F., Jaen, J., Nacher, V.: Tangibot: a tangible-mediated robot to support cognitive games for aging people—a usability study. Pervasive Mob. Comput. **34**, 91–105 (2017).https://doi.org/10.1016/j.pmcj.2016.08.007
24. Government Mobile Applications. (2021). Retrieved 9 Apr 2021. https://www.my.gov.sa/wps/portal/snp/content/mobileGovernment/!ut/p/z1/04_Sj9CPykssy0xPLMnMz0vMAfIjo8zivQIsTAwdDQz9LSw8XQ0CnT0s3JxDfA0MHA30w8EK_AxdDTwMTQz9DUyM3AwCXVwc_UxDDL0Mw8z0o4jRD1fgb2zqBFTga-7vGBxmaGBgSpx-AxwAqICg_iiwEnw-QDUDixPBCvC4ITg1T78gNzQ0wiAzIN1RUREAn_mKfw!!/dz/d5/L0lHSkovd0RNQUZrQUVnQSEhLzROVkUvYXI!/
25. Absher (application) - Wikipedia (2020). Retrieved 5 Apr 2021. https://en.wikipedia.org/wiki/Absher_(application)

Online Application for Bitcoin Price Visualization

Aleš Berger[✉], Milan Košt'ák, and Bruno Ježek

Faculty of Informatics and Management, University of Hradec Kralove, Hradec Kralove,
Czech Republic
{ales.berger,milan.kostak,bruno.jezek}@uhk.cz

Abstract. This paper presents a solution for the simple visualization of Bitcoin price. Current applications are often complex and include an amount of information that might be useful to some people. However, if someone is only interested in knowing the price, then these applications are needlessly complicated. Our proposed solution aims to display only a simple and clear visualization of price in a selected period and comparison to historical data. In the paper, we describe how to acquire data from online sources and process and visualize them in a simple graphic chart. The prototype is developed as a web application to make it accessible on both desktop and mobile devices.

Keywords: Bitcoin · Visualization · Web · Mobile

1 Introduction

Bitcoin is a cryptocurrency that was introduced in 2008 by an unknown person or group of people under the name Satoshi Nakamoto [1]. Satoshi left the project in late 2010 without revealing much about himself. The community has grown exponentially, with many developers working on Bitcoin. Satoshi's anonymity often raises concerns, many of which are linked to a misunderstanding of the open-source nature of Bitcoin.

The world's first cryptocurrency, Bitcoin, is stored and exchanged securely on the internet through a digital ledger known as a blockchain. Bitcoins are divisible into smaller units known as "satoshis"—each "satoshi" is worth 0.00000001 bitcoin. The main benefit is that nobody owns the Bitcoin network, much like no one owns the technology behind email. Bitcoin is controlled by all Bitcoin users around the world [2].

A blockchain represents a distributed database of records. In other words, it is a public ledger of all transactions or digital events that have been executed and shared among all participants. Each transaction in the public ledger is verified by at least half of the participants in the system. Once recorded, information can never be erased. The blockchain contains a specific and verifiable record of every single transaction ever made [3].

The essential principles of blockchain technology are [4]:

© Springer Nature Switzerland AG 2021
J. Bentahar et al. (Eds.): MobiWIS 2021, LNCS 12814, pp. 74–81, 2021.
https://doi.org/10.1007/978-3-030-83164-6_6

- Distributed database – each party on a blockchain has access to the entire database and complete database history. Nobody can modify the records, and everybody can verify the records.
- Peer-to-Peer transmission – communication occurs directly between peers instead of through a central node.
- Transparency with pseudonymity – every transaction is visible to anyone with access to the system. Each node has a unique alphanumeric address that identifies it.
- Irreversibility of records – once a transaction is entered the system, it cannot be altered because following transactions are linked to this transaction – that is why the term "chain" is used.
- Computational logic – the digital nature of the ledger means that blockchain transactions can be tied to computational logic and programmed.

In the last decade, Bitcoin went from a currency for enthusiasts and experts to a currency used worldwide and daily. Some people are using Bitcoin as everyday currency, although its reach is still somewhat limited. For other people, Bitcoin became an opportunity to invest money and is existing as a means of preserving value. Such a person is either trying to "buy cheap and sell high" or just buying to preserve the value for future years while hoping the value will substantially grow. These people need to monitor the Bitcoin value to sell when profitable or to see if the price is rising.

Visualization is the transformation of data and information into a visual form. Today, data visualization applications became helpful to understand features, properties, dependencies, and behavior of different phenomena and quantities. That is not only a form of graphical presentation but also a method to explore and analyze. A visualization of Bitcoin price in a simple and clear chart can help users make a good decision about strategy purchase or sale.

According to type data taxonomy [5], Bitcoin price, which changes over time, can be classified as 1-dimensional temporal data. It is a data sequence, where every sample is assigned to specific points in time, often in equally spaced time series. This kind of data can be visualized as static or dynamic visual representation [6]. In the case of a static visual representation, the Bitcoin price is shown by a line chart [7]. There are many applications showing charts of prices with a lot of different kinds of information. These can be difficult to read for users who do not understand more detailed indicators or for people who do not have the necessary background. But even for somebody who understands these matters, it is still unnecessary and less clear to present more information if they only care about the price. And even if someone understands them, it might still be more convenient to show something simpler. Our proposed solution aims in this direction because existing applications seemed too complicated to us when we wanted to see just a simple chart with the price. Our other goal is to have an application that is available on both desktop and mobile devices. That would make it possible to use it easily everywhere. The application should also provide the possibility to choose different time ranges and their comparisons.

In the methodological part of the paper, the entire processing pipeline is described. This process consists of data acquisition, processing, and visualization. The results chapter shows possible graphical outputs in the form of graphs generated by the prototype application.

2 Methodology

The main goal is to design a simple web application that enables the visualization of the Bitcoin price in an appropriate form. To show any data, it is necessary to acquire them ideally from an online data source. The principal tasks of our solution are acquiring, processing, and visualizing data. Deployment of the implemented application is the last step.

2.1 Acquire Data

Many servers providing online services of the current price of Bitcoin are available. It is common to access this information through API (Application Programming Interface) that presents data in a machine-readable format. Examples of servers providing these services are CoinDesk [8], CoinGecko [9], or Blockchain [10]. CoinGecko API has a limit of 100 requests per minute. Although our application can hardly reach this limit, we decided not to use this server. Blockchain server provides completely free API but only after registration. In the end, we decided to use CoinDesk because it offers several completely free public APIs [11] that are perfectly suitable for our needs. We use two API calls, one for getting the current price of Bitcoin and the second for obtaining historical prices.

Fetched data are not stored on the device, so the application always requires a connection to the internet. Data retrieval is performed on-demand by the user, who can press various buttons to request historical data. Bitcoin price is fetched on a "one value per one day" basis for different periods – 24 h, 1 week, 1 month, 3 months (a quarter of a year), 6 months (half a year), 1 year, and the whole history since 2010/07/18.

The user can choose a currency in which the price of Bitcoin is downloaded and visualized. The prototype application supports the United States Dollar (USD), Euro (EUR), and Czech Crown (CZK). Information about the selected currency is saved into the device.

Data from the API are returned in a standard JSON format, which is processed in the client application. For examples of queries to CoinDesk API, see the following figures (Fig. 1, 2) to view the result of calling these links. Previous and historical data are not stored in the application, and in case of a change of period or date, the application updates data by a new request to the server.

2.2 Data Processing

Nowadays, websites and mainly the ways of website development are changing. In the past, it was not uncommon that bigger web applications had performance problems. To answer this issue, developers from Facebook implemented a light JavaScript library called ReactJS [12]. This library helps to build declarative, modular, fast, and scalable front-end applications using JavaScript language. ReactJS also works with the Document Object Model (DOM), representing an HTML document with a logical tree structure using a cross-platform and language-independent interface. The library makes it easier to organize data flow and helps thinking about user interface elements as individual components [13].

```
{
  "time": {
    "updated": "Jun 14, 2021 19:20:00 UTC",
    "updatedISO": "2021-06-14T19:20:00+00:00",
    "updateduk": "Jun 14, 2021 at 20:20 BST"
  },
  "disclaimer": "This data was produced from the CoinDesk Bitcoin Price Index (USD). Non-USD currency
    data converted using hourly conversion rate from openexchangerates.org",
  "bpi": {
    "USD": {
      "code": "USD",
      "rate": "39,395.0383",
      "description": "United States Dollar",
      "rate_float": 39395.0383
    }
  }
}
```

Fig. 1. Example of raw data in JSON format. This example shows the current Bitcoin price in USD. Retrieved from https://api.coindesk.com/v1/bpi/currentprice/USD.json on 2021/06/14 at 19:20 UTC.

```
{
  "bpi": {
    "2021-04-01": 58726.6833,
    "2021-04-02": 58981.1117,
    "2021-04-03": 57065.38,
    "2021-04-04": 58221.755,
    "2021-04-05": 59140.685,
    "2021-04-06": 58011.415,
    "2021-04-07": 55950.97,
    "2021-04-08": 58087.18
  },
  "disclaimer": "This data was produced from the CoinDesk Bitcoin Price Index. BPI value data returned as
    USD.",
  "time": {
    "updated": "Apr 9, 2021 00:03:00 UTC",
    "updatedISO": "2021-04-09T00:03:00+00:00"
  }
}
```

Fig. 2. Example of raw data in JSON format. This example shows the Bitcoin price in USD for a 7 days period from 2021/04/01 to 2021/04/08. Retrieved from https://api.coindesk.com/v1/bpi/historical/close.json?currency=USD&start=2021-04-01&end=2021-04-08.

As was already mentioned, creating JavaScript applications can be challenging. Fortunately, there are multiple frameworks and libraries to choose from. For our application, we decided on a framework called NextJS [14]. There is usually a high learning curve before a developer can build a proper application. That is because developers need to learn about client-side routing, page layout, APIs, customization, performance, etc. NextJS framework brings important features for developing the prototype application. Framework Gatsby [15] was considered as a second possible option for the author's research. After testing and prototyping, the authors chose NextJS. The main reasons are [14]:

- an intuitive page-based routing system,
- automatically statically optimizes page(s) when possible,
- server-side renders page(s) with blocking data requirements,
- automatic code splitting for faster page loads,
- client-side routing with optimized page prefetching,
- webpack-based environment which supports Hot Module Replacement (HMR),

- and customization with community plugins and with your own Babel and Webpack configurations.

2.3 Visualization

For visualization purposes, we used library Chart.js [16]. It is an open-source library that enables the creation of several different types of charts using a short JavaScript code. For the prototype application, it is appropriate to use a line chart with linear Cartesian axes and labeling. Plotting data points on one or two lines is often used to show trends or comparisons of two data sets. Chart.js library is available freely, even for commercial uses.

The chart displays the price on the vertical axis and the time on the horizontal axis in the application. Both the price and time axes have a linear scale. Aside from presenting the price for the chosen period, the application also shows historical data for the previous period of the same length. That makes it easy to see the trend of the price change in the selected period. Therefore, the chart contains two lines, one for the actual price of the chosen period and the second for the historical price of the previous period. To make the prototyped application even more explicit and well-arranged, either of these lines can be switched off. That is mainly important for user experience.

The minimal and maximal values on the vertical price axis are adjusted according to the price values that are loaded for the chosen period. This means it does not start from zero. Consequently, it might look like the price is changing a lot in some cases, or the price is approaching to values close zero when not checking the axis closely. So, it is important to keep that in mind while looking at the lines of the presented chart. The exception is the option where complete historical data is displayed. In this situation, the price is rising from zero since Bitcoin started to be traded, and the vertical axis of this chart starts from zero. On the other hand, adjusting the axis makes it possible to see small changes in the price that would otherwise be more difficult to recognize if the axis were including the entire possible price range.

The horizontal axis is simpler to describe. When the user chooses a period, the axis holds one value for each day in that period. The previously described line for the previous period of the same length does not have corresponding values on the axis.

2.4 Deployment

The application runs in the Node.js environment, and the virtual server runs in the cloud. Due to good experiences with the Heroku platform, the authors used this platform for this research [17]. The implemented prototype application is publicly available online at http://www.easy-crypto.online/. It is possible to use the application on both desktop and mobile devices, and it has a responsive design, so it adapts to any mobile device regardless of its screen size.

3 Results

The implemented prototype application is freely available online at the public webserver http://www.easy-crypto.online/. The following three screenshots (Fig. 3, 4 and 5) present the main functionalities of the application. In all cases at the top of the screen, there is an element to change the currency of price. Information about the current exchange rate is also available. The buttons bar enables the user to choose the period for which the price data is fetched and visualized. The chart's horizontal (X) axis contains time, and it has one tick per day. The vertical (Y) axis contains the price, and its tick values are calculated dynamically. The first two screens (Fig. 3, 4) include full charts with all previously described elements. The third figure (Fig. 5) shows detail of one day with a

Fig. 3. Graphical result of the prototype application for the selected period. The figure is presenting a chart for a week (blue line). The red line shows the Bitcoin price from the previous week. The vertical axis range is automatically set according to the price values for the selected time period. Prices are in USD currency. (Color figure online)

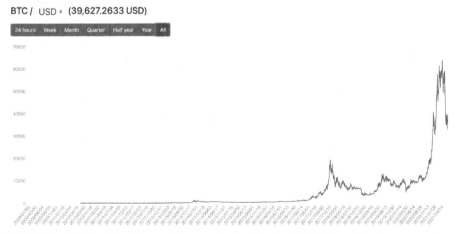

Fig. 4. Graphical result of the prototype application for the whole history The figure presents a chart for the entire period of existence since 2010/07/18. The vertical axis starts at zero. Prices are in USD currency.

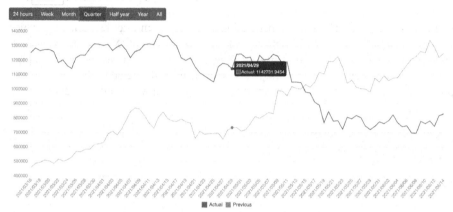

Fig. 5. Graphical result of the prototype application for detailed view. The figure shows the possibility of displaying a popup element with the exact price for the selected day when the cursor is placed on the day on the line. Prices are in CZK currency.

popup element showing the precise price for that day. This feature is available all the time.

4 Discussion

Implementation of the suggested solution proved that simple visualization of the time dependency of Bitcoin price historical data is easy yet powerful and persuasive in its way of providing practical information. Due to the nature of the idea, the proposed application does not show much information. Therefore, it is not suitable for seeking detailed and specific information about other Bitcoin indicators. But as many applications provide this service, this is not considered a disadvantage, and it was not the intention.

Despite the simplistic solution, the prototyped application enables selecting the time interval of the current Bitcoin price. It compares this epoch to historical data in the previous period of the same length by displaying two lines in one chart. The prototype shows the price in a simple chart, and in this sense, the main goal was met. The application also provides a few options, namely currency settings and switcher for both lines. To sum up the results, the application delivers the expected outcome, and all goals have been reached.

5 Conclusions

The implemented solution presents a good result for simple and clear online visualization of Bitcoin price. Comparing current data to historical values for the chosen period enables a quick and brief view of the actual price situation. That is useful for users who deal with Bitcoins as a matter of trade or for people who are only interested in this subject out of curiosity. The goal that we set for ourselves was met.

There is not much space to improve the application by adding more functionalities. Our motivation was to develop it as simple as possible and adding more features would break our main intention. But further research could explore the possibilities of using the same approach for other cryptocurrencies. Visualizing other cryptocurrencies is expected to be easy and possible only by switching to different data API, although we did not try that.

Another course of future research could analyze the possibilities of even more obvious visualization. For example, different chart line colors have not been tested, although they might positively affect the chart's readability.

Acknowledgments. This work and the contribution were supported by a project of Students Grant Agency (SPEV) - FIM, University of Hradec Kralove, Czech Republic.

References

1. Nakamoto, S.: BITCOIN: A peer-to-peer electronic cash system. Bitcoin, **4** (2008). https://bitcoin.org/bitcoin.pdf
2. FAQ - Bitcoin (2021). https://bitcoin.org/en/faq [27 Mar 2021]
3. Crosby, M., et al.: Blockchain technology: beyond bitcoin. Appl. Innov. **2**(6–10), 71 (2016)
4. Lakhani, K.R., Iansiti, M.: The truth about blockchain. Harv. Bus. Rev. **95**(1), 119–127 (2017)
5. Shneiderman, B.: The eyes have it: a task by data type taxonomy for information visualizations. In: The Craft of Information Visualization. Morgan Kaufmann, pp. 364–371 (2003)
6. Müller, W., Schumann, H.: Visualization for modeling and simulation: visualization methods for time-dependent data-an overview. In: Proceedings of the 35th Conference on Winter Simulation: Driving Innovation, pp. 737–745 (2003)
7. Wilkinson, L.: The grammar of graphics. In: Gentle, J., Härdle, W., Mori, Y. (eds.) Handbook of Computational Statistics, pp. 375–414. Springer, Berlin (2012). https://doi.org/10.1007/978-3-642-21551-3_13
8. Coindesk—Leader in blockchain news. CoinDesk (2021). https://www.coindesk.com/ [27 Mar 2021]
9. Reliable & Free Cryptocurrency Data API. CoinGecko (2021). https://www.coingecko.com/en/api [5 Mar 2021]
10. Bitcoin Price API: Bitcoin Ticker & Exchange Rate API - Blockchain (2021). https://www.blockchain.com/en/api/exchange_rates_api [5 Mar 2021]
11. Bitcoin Price Index API. CoinDesk (2021). https://www.coindesk.com/api [27 Mar 2021]
12. React – A JavaScript library for building user interfaces (2021). https://reactjs.org/ [28 Mar 2021]
13. Fedosejev, A.: React. js essentials. Packt Publishing Ltd., Birmingham (2015)
14. Learn | Next.js (2021). https://nextjs.org/learn [28 Mar 2021]
15. GatsbyJS. GatsbyJS (2021). https://www.gatsbyjs.org [28 Mar 2021]
16. Chart.js | Open source HTML5 Charts for your website (2021). https://www.chartjs.org/ [28 Mar 2021]
17. Cloud Application Platform | Heroku (2021). https://www.heroku.com/ [28 Mar 2021]

Networking and Communication

Optimizing 5G VPN+ Transport Networks with Vector Packet Processing and FPGA Cryptographic Offloading

Bruno Dzogovic[1]([✉]), Bernardo Santos[1], Boning Feng[1], Van Thuan Do[1,2], Niels Jacot[2], and Thanh Van Do[1,3]

[1] Oslo Metropolitan Univeristy, Pilestredet 35, 0167 Oslo, Norway
{bruno.dzogovic,bersan,boning.feng}@oslomet.no
[2] Wolffia AS, Haugerudvn. 40, 0673 Oslo, Norway
{vt.do,n.jacot}@wolffia.net
[3] Telenor ASA, Snarøyveien 30, 1331 Fornebu, Norway
thanh-van.do@telenor.com

Abstract. Network slicing is the crucial prerogative that allows end users and industries to thrive from 5G infrastructures, however, such a logical network component can deteriorate from security vulnerabilities that prevail within cloud environments and datacenters. The Quality of Experience in 5G is a metric that takes into consideration sets of factors, which play role in the definition of the end-to-end performance, which is indeed latency, packet processing, utilization of legacy protocols, old hardware, encryption, non-optimized network topologies, routing problems and multitude of other aspects. This research sheds light on the inherent networking stack performance issues that translate into 5G environments, in a use-case where encrypted VPN tunneling is used to secure the backhaul transport network between the 4G/5G cores and the frontend networks.

Keywords: 5G · Enhanced VPN+ · Vector packet processing · FPGA SoC

1 Introduction

5G engrosses various sectors of the modern society, including healthcare, transport, smart infrastructure, industrial and other spheres. One of the most important environs that 5G aims to support is the Massive Internet of Things (MIoT). In healthcare, IoT enables providers to assist patients in various ways by providing wearables, sensors and implants for various medical conditions and monitoring [1] etc. The devices require stringent security measures for preserving the confidentiality and data privacy of patient information. Nevertheless, the healthcare sectors are constantly targeted by cyber criminals and additional considerations from that aspect are desirable to prevent private information leakage and mitigate repercussions [2]. The information retained about healthcare services and patients is of substantially sensitive nature and therein the need for additional protection and threat mitigation. An example of eccentric cyber-attacks during the COVID-19 pandemic from 2020, indicates that the adversaries are utilizing APT

© Springer Nature Switzerland AG 2021
J. Bentahar et al. (Eds.): MobiWIS 2021, LNCS 12814, pp. 85–98, 2021.
https://doi.org/10.1007/978-3-030-83164-6_7

(Advanced Persistent Threat) attacks and is attributed to the possibility that the intention is to compromise and exfiltrate research data regarding COVID-19 vaccines [2]. The increase of cyber threats on healthcare institutions in Central Europe has increased exponentially in November 2020, namely by 145%, which is an astoundingly elevated figure [3]. The enhanced quality of service is what 5G delivers to the smart healthcare and in parallel security threats that it is accompanied with [4]. Most of the research is focused on the stated Quality of Service and performance, but the security remains a highly misjudged domain, therein the upsurge of cyber-attacks on healthcare institutions in the last two years.

Adversaries are continuously developing new practices to enhance their attack vectors and exploit various vulnerabilities for fulfilling their malicious goals. One rather traditional technique to secure a communication is encrypted tunneling, namely employing VPNs to support the communication between endpoints. In this paper, we examine a previous work on a 5G infrastructure for IoT in healthcare and address a performance issue that arises as a result to the encryption in the transport network between the 5G network core (5GC) and the Centralized Unit (CU) in a cloud environment. This is achieved by combining improvements in the Linux kernel for packet processing and introducing an additional FPGA hardware to offload the cryptographic operations from the 5G core compute node. The improvements of performance in 5G VPN+ network slice encrypted with AES-256 are thereby substantial.

1.1 Motivation and Problem Statement

Smart healthcare involves medical devices that are issued to patients and communicate through a 5G network. In simple terms, the transport network that connects the Core Networks of the service providers with contiguous Centralized Units for baseband processing is as secure as the infrastructure itself, which signifies that threats can emerge when adversaries are able to access the network through any means (either from the internet or on-premises). 5G establishes the concept of network slicing that separates the tenants in the network based on their use case. A typical method to resolve the communication and restrict access to the corresponding actors is by using policy-based networking and selective routing of traffic, VLAN segmentation, compute nodes isolation as well as firewalls and traffic filtering. These techniques are incorporated at the orchestration layer of the SDN controller and the same are insufficient to prevent adversaries from commencing various attacks. To strengthen the security of the transport network in 5G between the CU and Core Networks, we have established an infrastructure that allows provisioning of a custom network slice, crafted for healthcare purposes, and utilizes an enhanced VPN+ tunneling to secure the communication. Nevertheless, the symmetric encryption in the tunnel adversely affects the performance of the communication at scale and requires optimizations to provide satisfactory quality of experience for the increasing number of MIoT devices and the end users in healthcare.

This paper begins with an introduction and explaining background work in the related field. Further, a brief explanation of the methodology and implementation follow and correspondingly, the results of the experiments are represented. To finalize, the paper discusses certain limitations and advantages of the proposed approach and concludes on the lessons learned.

2 Background and Related Work

2.1 5G Architecture

The 5G system consists of User Equipment (UE), Access Network (next-generation Node-B, or gNB) and Next-Generation Core Network (5GC). By combining Software-Defined Networking (SDN) and open Application Programming Interfaces (APIs), users can have virtual Network Functions (vNFs) tailored and customized according to a specific scenario. Figure 1 represents an overview of the 5G architecture, which is separated into two main group functions: Control Plane (CP) core of 5GS and User Plane (UP) functions. The control-plane group has different elements defined in terms of Network Functions (NF). It is comprised of a common framework and offers services to other authorized NFs or users. This Service-Based Architecture (SBA) allows modularity, scalability, and reusability [5].

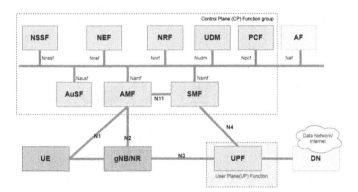

Fig. 1. 5G core architecture

Network Slicing
The concept behind network slicing is based on logical network components, situated on a common physical infrastructure also dissected into virtual networks. The network softwareization concept [6] enables network slicing through software-based solutions. For that purpose, network slicing in 5G utilizes Software-Defined Networking (SDN), Network Function Virtualization (NFV) in clouds and the Edge for the realization of slices over the same physical infrastructure of the service providers. Each slice is controlled independently and can scale according to requirements.

Compared to 4G LTE, 5G replicates the function of physical hardware in form of software. SDNs can thus be easily adapted to serve the needs of backends (such as SD-WAN) as well as local deployments for customizing network slices in 5G. In a previous work at the Secure 5G4IoT lab by the Oslo Metropolitan University, we underlined the details on network slicing using a slicing controller and an SDN controller to provide virtual network functions for connectivity to the corresponding network slice [7, 8]. VNFs can be implemented in different ways. One common method is to separate a physical network interface into manifold virtual functions, assign these virtual networking end-points to a VNF/CNF (Container Network Function) and implement policy and routing via the SDN controller through these terminals for the network slice. Figure 2 represents a working example of virtual network function provisioning for 5G cloud radio access network (C-RAN) with a single Centralized Unit (CU) in OpenStack cloud. Another traditional method for separating vNFs is by using VLAN (Virtual LAN) on Layer-2. According to the working example in the Secure 5G4IoT Lab at the Oslo Metropolitan University, the virtual functions are delivered using SR-IOV (Single Root – Input Output Virtualization) of the network. The 5G core functions are containerized and use the Kuryr plugin to interface the containers with the OpenStack Neutron [9].

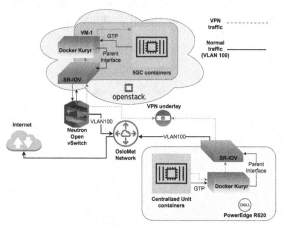

Fig. 2. VLAN segmentation using SR-IOV and VPN instance in the transport network between the centralized unit containers and the 5G cloud core network

High-performance Vector Packet Processing Stack

To handle low-level packet processing issues the VPP (Vector Packet Processing) is used. By enabling a software routing using the VPP driver, we deliver a VPN underlying network for securing the communication between the C-RAN network and the core networks in the cloud. VPP does not process packets on sequential basis as is the case with the scalar model, but instead it processes the entire vector of packets through a graph node before proceeding to the next graph node. There is a support for hardware acceleration through plugins for offloading the packet processing functions to external hardware [10]. VPP uses vector processing as opposed to scalar processing, treats more than one packet at a time. One of the benefits of the vector approach is that it fixes the I-cache thrashing problem. It also mitigates the dependent read latency problem (pre-fetching eliminates latency). This approach fixes the issues related to stack depth/D-cache misses on stack addresses by improving the cycle of capturing all available packets from the device RX ring, forming a vector that consists of packet indices in RX order, running the packets through a directed graph of nodes, and returning to the RX ring. As processing of packets continues, the circuit time reaches a stable equilibrium based on the offered load. As the vector size increases, processing cost per packet decreases because the I-cache misses over a larger N are being amortized [10]. VPP is integrated in OpenStack using the Neutron Modular Layer-2 (ML2-VPP) mechanical driver, as shown in Fig. 3.

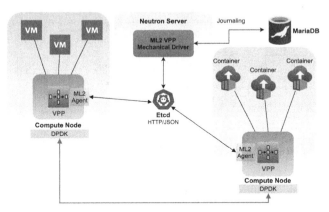

Fig. 3. VPP native integration with the OpenStack Neutron Modular Layer 2 (ML2) driver

For the production-scale cloud, the VPP ML2 agents are deployed via the OpenDaylight SDN controller in OpenStack, which are referred to as *"Honeycomb data-plane agents"* where Kubernetes and Ansible are used for orchestration [11–13]. VPP is shown to massively improve performance in relatively low-power computing environments [14–16].

2.2 Enhanced VPN+ and Cryptographic Functions Offloading to FPGA SoC

One way to enable transport network VPN connection is to bypass application layer VPNs and perform tunneling at transport network layers. In the style of VPN as a Service (VPNaaS) and On-demand network slice provisioning NSaaS (Network Slice as a Service), tenants can request a network slice with VPN tunneling integrated as a custom vNF. The ACTN framework (Abstraction and Control of Traffic-Engineered Networks) is thereby introduced [17] to define the ability for customers to deploy private networks without the understanding of the backend. ACTN defines the Virtual network slicing service function chaining (SFC) model. This same model serves for provisioning 5G transport networks by utilizing the CNC (Customer Network Controller), MDSC (Multi-Domain Service Coordinator) and PNC (Provisioning Network Controller) [18]. CNC is responsible for 5G 3GPP access-network communication with the underlying network of the 5G infrastructure and is also known as Traffic Provisioning Manager (TPM) [19]. The TPM functions as a CNC from ACTN reference point of view and can be deployed in a carrier network as shown in Fig. 4, TPM can be deployed in Mobile Network A - Domain 1 and Domain 2, while the CMIs interfaces are connected to SDN controllers (in this case we refer to the PNC from the ACTN framework reference) [19].

For the current experiments, we employ a hybrid model, in which the SDN controller imports the information of the underlay network through BGP-LS (BGP-Link State) [20]

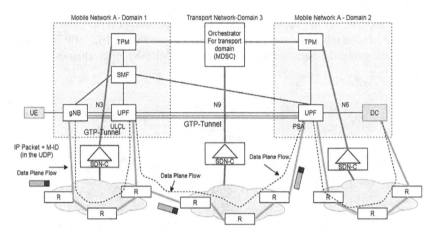

Fig. 4. Enhanced 5G transport network architecture in a multi-region cloud model [19]

via RestCONF APIs, and the traffic engineering (TE) information is collected and shared to external components of the network. Therefore, a Traffic Engineering Database (TED) is formed [21], which stores information about the TE information for dynamic Quality of Service parameters regulation as in the case with MPLS and GMPLS networks [20]. This way, the tenants can decide to instantiate an enhanced VPN+ at the network underlay, while avoiding overlay application-layer overheads at scale.

Field Programmable Gate Arrays are used in clouds for various functions. A SoC (Silicon on a Chip) architecture allows the FPGA to be programmable remotely and without direct access. This combination usually is followed by an ARM architecture device tightly integrated with the FPGA, which allows interfacing to the FPGA fabrics. The FPGA can then be used for various applications that require specific and customized computational properties and are task intensive for the general x86 architecture CPUs [22, 23], which is programmed to perform cryptographic operations for AES-256 in the VPN tunnel. The FPGA is programmed in Verilog to access the memory directly and interact with the VPP kernel module, which opens a potential to scale the FPGA fabrics into cluster of multiple FPGA SoC units. The cluster can then be served as a service to the specific network slicing virtual functions that request it.

3   Methodology and Implementation

The Fig. 5 represents a 4G and 5G infrastructure deployed at the Oslo Metropolitan University with three different slices: a 5G New-Radio, 4G standard LTE access and an IoT network slice with IEEE 802.11 Wi-Fi access. The core networks have their own SR-IOV endpoints and is considered a separate virtual cluster sharing the same cloud. The experimentation methodology is based on network testing performed with the iperf tool to measure traffic performance at scale. Before conducting the evaluation of the throughput in the network, the Maximum Transmitted Unit (MTU) is adjusted to 9000 from the default 1500 value to minimize fragmentation incurred variance in the network flows. This is because the traffic between the Centralized Unit and the 5G Core Network is encapsulated to support the transmission of GTP traffic in an extended IP header. With a MTU value of 1500, the traffic between the UE (User Equipment) and the Internet will experience packet drop, jitter and additive error, therefore it is adjusted accordingly on all interfaces, including the SR-IOV physical functions, virtual functions, as well as the container-plane network.

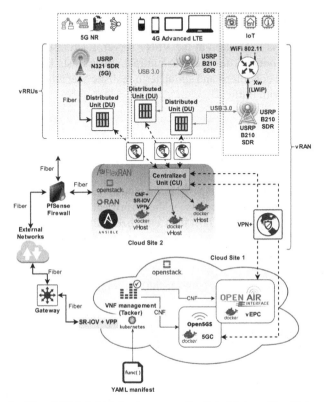

Fig. 5. 4G and 5G hybrid infrastructure at the Oslo Metropolitan University

The compute nodes are Dell R620 servers running Linux Ubuntu server 18.04 operating with low-latency kernel version 14.18.0-25. The Core Network vNFs require a stable environment to operate and thus any fluctuations incurred by the CPU on a hardware level in terms of frequency, voltage, heat-related inconsistences and multitenancy can cause unpredictable result. To minimize experimental error, CPU hyperthreading is disabled as well as power states (C-states, P-states) and the unit overclocked to fixed 3.0 GHz. For testing the connectivity between the Centralized Unit and the Core Networks, network overlays are avoided to eliminate overhead and perform the control experiments directly on the 10 Gbps optical network fabrics between the physical compute nodes. This experimental data is stored and used to compare to the performance impact virtualization can have on the nodes in terms of bandwidth and CPU resources utilization combined. Further, we proceed with tests on the VPN+ tunneling in between the compute nodes, which are followed by tests on the VPN+ endpoints on virtualization layer between the Centralized Unit containers and the Core Network containers. This will shed light on the difference between the impact of hardware networking compared to virtualization with SR-IOV and direct VPN tunneling compared to virtualization-layer VPN+ tunneling.

As a final realignment, we change the generic Linux networking kernel modules with Vector Packet Processing and compare these results to the previously obtained data. That will represent the real status of the performance improvements that can be expected from utilizing vector processing compared to scalar processing. Last but not least, the FPGA SoC is introduced at the VPN+ server. Each test is performed in two stages: single-stream network testing and multiple-stream tests in parallel. The latter exaggerates the traffic conditions and simulates a realistic scenario where the transport network is saturated with traffic.

3.1 Evaluation

The obtained data is classified as follows:

- Scenario A: Hardware-level testing of the compute nodes at the optical network fabrics
- Scenario B: Virtualization-plane tests via the corresponding SR-IOV virtual functions translated in the containers that host the Centralized Unit and the Core Networks
- Scenario A1: VPN+ connectivity between the two compute nodes directly
- Scenario B1: Virtualization-plane tests of the VPN+ connectivity through the same SR-IOV virtual functions
- Scenario A2: VPN+ connectivity between the two compute nodes directly, with Vector Packet Processing Linux kernel module
- Scenario B2: Virtualization-plane tests of the VPN+ connectivity with Vector Packet Processing Linux kernel module
- Scenario A3: VPN+ connectivity between the two compute nodes directly with Vector Packet Processing Linux kernel module and FPGA SoC cryptographic offloading
- Scenario B3: Virtualization-plane tests of the VPN+ connectivity with Vector Packet Processing Linux kernel module and FPGA SoC cryptographic offloading

The A and B scenarios are the experimental control group for comparison with the further test scenarios. This will shed light on the performance detriment that is inflicted on the link. For that purpose, the network flows are measured together with CPU utilization and compared. Correspondingly, the A1 and B2 scenarios test the VPN+ connectivity and the impact it has on the deployment compared to the default state from the A and B scenarios. In the A2 and B2 scenarios, the VPP Linux kernel module is introduced, which will represent the mean performance gain that is otherwise lost due to the packet processing issues from the default scalar approach. Finally, the scenarios A3 and B3 implement an FPGA SoC for offloading the encryption from the CPU of the compute node. These tests are performed only in multiple-stream examinations, in order to assess the performance improvement at scale (in worst-case scenarios).

The traffic of the single-stream and multiple-stream tests is adjusted in such a manner that respects a constant threshold under the total maximum capacity of the node's performance. The experiments do not examine latency-related issues.

4   Results

The results from the experiments are obtained using the iPerf3 network testing tool and the following arguments are passed. The time of execution is 5 min (300 s), with an interval of transmission each 1 s. The TCP buffer size is set as a constant to 32 Megabytes and the test runs as a client-server model with the server being executed at the 10.0.0.1 host, which is the Core Network and the 10.0.0.2 is the Centralized Unit host. Results are summarized in Table 1 and Table 2, denoting CPU resource utilization and maximum bandwidth, correspondingly.

To determine the impact of the VPN on the backhaul network, we establish causal relationships between the hardware-level tests, virtualization layer tests and compare the results with the improvement from utilizing the VPP module. Finally, the results are also compared with the inclusion of the FPGA SoC offloading. For that purpose, the multiple linear regression analysis is used.

The value of the correlation coefficient ("multiple R") is 0.850086999, indicating a good relationship between the CPU utilization, bandwidth, and the number of occurring retransmissions. The significance F-test of the null-hypothesis is less than 0.05 (i.e., S-F = 0.003116316). Figure 6 and Fig. 7 show the overall distribution of CPU utilization compared to the speed per each scenario. During the hardware-level tests, the overall utilization of the CPU in the node was 41.7224%, whereas during the SR-IOV parallel stream tests, the total usage amounts for 27.36%. Nevertheless, there is an unavoidable variation in the system processes at the different times of testing, for which if we calculate the offset, we get 33.4466% during hardware-level tests and 22.9254% during SR-IOV tests, results in $\Delta_{SR-IOV(m)} = 10.5212\%$. This value is subtracted from the overall performance in order to isolate the effects of virtualization during the multiple stream tests, that is 41.7224% during the hardware-level tests and 27.36% during the SR-IOV tests. The difference of 14.3624% subtracts the system resources difference by 10.5212%, obtaining 3.8412% impact on the virtualization plane during the SR-IOV tests with multiple streams. The overhead increases when the traffic scales over the same VNF (Fig. 8 and Fig. 9).

Without provisioning additional VNFs, it is likely that the impact would be more than linear over a threshold of difference between the kernel's scalar packet processing capability and the absolute number of scaled VNF functions for the SR-IOV drivers, accounting for the traffic generated also in the 5G network on top of the diverse network slices. Furthermore, as the number of retransmissions increase, the level of computational resources required for retaining maximal bandwidth will increase, adding on the bottleneck of the operating system's kernel at the physical nodes and is represented through the CPU underutilization. This is further amplified through an encrypted VPN tunnel, accentuating the I-cache thrashing problem with the scalar packet processing. The VPP allows the CPU to have time-series workloads allocated for submitting each encrypted packet to the network interface, thereby increasing the bandwidth of the tunnel and showing 100% CPU utilization. Additional rectification is achieved when the FPGA fabric is introduced, further restoring the traffic performance (~8.87 Gbps).

Table 1. Summary of the CPU utilization at the 5GC core side and the CU side. The values represent total CPU utilization, divided between user resources and system namespace services. Each scenario is characterized with single-stream and multi-stream test results.

Scenario	CPU utilization (%) 5GC_total	CPU utilization (%) 5GC_user	CPU utilization (%) 5GC_system	CPU utilization (%) CU_total	CPU utilization (%) CU_user	CPU utilization (%) CU_system
A/S-S	61.9658	8.23386	53.7319	35.983	5.03469	30.9483
A/M-S	95.9105	18.9873	76.9232	41.7224	8.2758	33.4466

Scenario	CPU utilization (%) 5GC-SRIOV_total	CPU utilization (%) 5GC-SRIOV_user	CPU utilization (%) 5GC-SRIOV_system	CPU utilization (%) CU-SRIOV_total	CPU utilization (%) CU-SRIOV_user	CPU utilization (%) CU-SRIOV_system
B/S-S	63.5708	8.62531	54.9455	21.4606	3.48127	17.9793
B/M-S	96.2447	20.1134	76.1313	27.36	4.43466	22.9254

Scenario	CPU utilization (%) 5GC-VPN_total	CPU utilization (%) 5GC-VPN_user	CPU utilization (%) 5GC-VPN_system	CPU utilization (%) CU-VPN_total	CPU utilization (%) CU-VPN_user	CPU utilization (%) CU-VPN_system
A1/S-S	37.1798	10.0446	27.1352	3.54544	0.36947	3.17597
A1/M-S	44.2623	8.84595	35.4163	4.68069	0.944212	3.73648
B1/S-S	36.9928	10.078	26.9148	1.89289	0.22533	1.66756
B1/M-S	44.0171	8.80109	35.216	3.11648	0.811096	2.30538

Scenario	CPU utilization (%) 5GC-VPN-TN_only	CPU utilization (%) 5GC-VPN-TN_user	CPU utilization (%) 5GC-VPN-TN_system	CPU utilization (%) CU-VPN-TN_only	CPU utilization (%) CU-VPN-TN_user	CPU utilization (%) CU-VPN-TN_system
A2/M-S	100.0	49.257	50.743	7.121	0.782	2.51
B2/M-S	100.0	48.290	51.71	8.234	0.913	2.912
A3/M-S	59.34	2.173	23.439	7.856	0.828	2.87
B3/M-S	63.17	3.012	27.126	9.162	0.711	4.451

Table 2. Summary of the bandwidth tests at the sender and receiver side. The results include the total retransmissions and duration of the tests in seconds. Each scenario is represented with single-stream and multi-stream tests

Scenario	Send duration (s)	Sent data (GB)	Send speed (Gbps)	Retran. (total)	Rec. duration (s)	Rec. data (GB)	Rec. speed (Gbps)
A/S-S	300.036	371.04267	9.89328	0	300.036	371.04249	9.89327
A/M-S	300.015	371.16965	9.89736	1	300.015	371.16546	9.89725
B/S-S	300.039	371.18716	9.89704	0	300.039	371.18684	9.89703
B/M-S	300.021	371.17811	9.89739	22	300.021	371.17443	9.89729
A1/S-S	300.037	19.591886	0.522386	163311	300.037	19.591432	0.522374
A1/M-S	300.021	20.563469	0.54832	347139	300.021	20.559070	0.548203
B1/S-S	300.038	19.921978	0.531218	170510	300.038	19.922784	0.531207
B1/M-S	300.022	21.049824	0.561288	348553	300.022	21.045380	0.56117
A2/M-S	300.021	223.00132	5.347821	3	300.021	223.00412	5.347733
B2/M-S	300.023	219.34128	5.330129	2	300.023	219.34115	5.331604
A3/M-S	300.030	360.21275	8.928763	0	300.030	360.21478	8.972871
B3/M-S	300.021	343.33713	8.873988	0	300.021	343.33711	8.873569

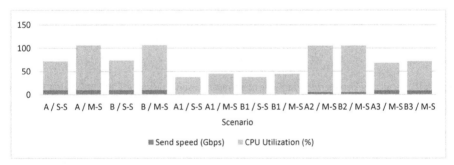

Fig. 6. Distribution of the multiple linear regression analysis of the correlation between relative bandwidth (in Gbps) and CPU utilization in percentage (%) by scenario

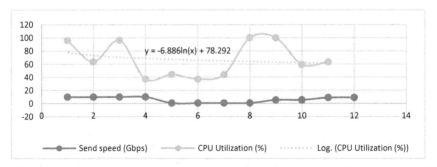

Fig. 7. Multiple linear regression analysis of the relative bandwidth in Gbps and total CPU utilization in percentage (logarithmic distribution)

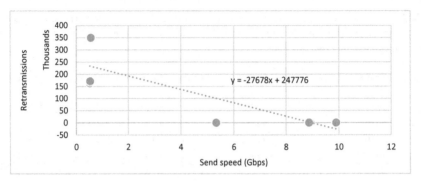

Fig. 8. Correlation between the relative bandwidth and the number of retransmissions

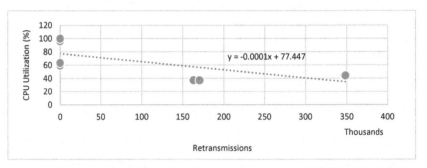

Fig. 9. Dependency between the number of retransmissions and total CPU utilization (system namespace and user running the 5GC core network and VPN)

5 Discussion

One of the main hindrances to performance loss in a software-defined 5G backhaul networking is the utilization of legacy hardware in datacenters. The modern workloads require improved hardware, especially CPU processing units and in general new architectures in order to run with higher efficiency. Datacenters are usually equipped with specialized processing hardware for particular workloads, such as GPUs or FPGAs, which at scale can have detrimental impact on the execution of required tasks. In the case with VPN, the technique that combines Vector Packet Processing and FPGA offloading can be scaled to accommodate bigger infrastructures and negate the requirement of horizontally scaling the same.

Using FPGA SoC requires tedious implementation methodology and incurs latency penalties on the network. Despite that this work is not focused on examining the latency related impacts in the network, an external SoC managed FPGA forwards packets from the SDN controller that directs the network flows through the FPGA and back to the CPU of the compute nodes. A better performing FPGA layer combined with tight integration with the SDN networking stack of the backhaul, can resolve the said issues.

6 Conclusion

Utilizing a vNF passthrough, minimizes the impact of virtualization on the performance of 5G backhaul transport networks at scale. A rather simpler approach that attains flat infrastructure, easier to automate and self-organize, the virtualization layer can be supplemented with vector packet processing to annul some ramifications that arise due to inherent networking kernel limitations in Linux. This implication becomes intensified when the transport network is tunneled via VPN, which can encrypt the communication with various algorithms. The symmetric encryption needs to scramble every packet that traverses the transport network endpoints, which is highly taxing for the CPU and the available resources at the compute nodes in the cloud. The communication becomes severely bottlenecked and the overall potential of the 5G transport network substantially diminished. A prodigious and cost-efficient solution is to integrate FPGA fabrics to handle the encryption of the tunneling and use vector packet processing to increase the flow rates and minimize packet retransmissions, which can drastically improve the performance.

Acknowledgement. This paper is a result of the H2020 Concordia project (https://www.concor dia-h2020.eu) which has received funding from the EU H2020 programme under grant agreement No 830927. The CONCORDIA consortium includes 23 partners from industry and other organizations such as Telenor, Telefonica, Telecom Italia, Ericsson, Siemens, Airbus, etc. and 23 partners from academia such as CODE, university of Twente, OsloMet, etc.

References

1. Zhong, M., Yang, Y., Yao, H., Fu, X., Dobre, O.A., Postolache, O.: 5G and IoT: towards a new era of communications and measurements. IEEE Instrum. Meas. Mag. **22**(6), 18–26 (2019). https://doi.org/10.1109/MIM.2019.8917899
2. Lakshmanan, R.: Healthcare industry witnessed 45% spike in cyber attacks since November 2020. The Hacker News. https://thehackernews.com/2021/01/healthcare-industry-witnessed-45-spike.html. Accessed 26 Mar 2021
3. Muthuppalaniappan, M., Stevenson, K.: Healthcare cyber-attacks and the COVID-19 pandemic- an urgent threat to global health. Int. J. Qual. Healthc. J. Int. Soc. Qual. Health Care 33, 1 (2021). https://doi.org/10.1093/intqhc/mzaa117
4. Ahad, A., Tahir, M., Yau, K.A.: 5G-based smart healthcare network: architecture, taxonomy, challenges and future research directions. IEEE Access **7**, 100747–100762 (2019). https://doi.org/10.1109/ACCESS.2019.2930628
5. Khan, M.Q.: Signaling storm problems in 3GPP mobile broadband networks, causes and possible solutions - a review. In: 2018 International Conference on Computing, Electronics & Communications Engineering (iCCECE), Southend, UK, pp. 183–188. (2018). https://doi.org/10.1109/iCCECOME.2018.8658708
6. Afolabi, I., Taleb, T., Samdanis, K., Ksentini, A., Flinck, H.: Network slicing and softwarization - a survey on principles, enabling technologies, and solutions. IEEE Commun. Surv. Tutorials **20**(3), 2429–2453 (2018). https://doi.org/10.1109/COMST.2018.2815638
7. Dzogovic, B., van Do, T., Santos, B., Van Thuan, D., Feng, B., Jacot, N.: Thunderbolt-3 backbone for augmented 5G network slicing in cloud-radio access networks. In: 2019 IEEE 2nd 5G World Forum (5GWF), Dresden, Germany, pp. 415–420 (2019). https://doi.org/10.1109/5GWF.2019.8911710

8. Yousaf, F.Z., Bredel, M., Schaller, S., Schneider, F.: NFV and SDN—key technology enablers for 5G networks. IEEE J. Sel. Areas Commun. **35**(11), 2468–2478 (2017). https://doi.org/10.1109/JSAC.2017.2760418

9. OpenStack cloud software: Kuryr plugin official documentation. https://docs.openstack.org/kuryr/latest/. Accessed 19 Mar 2021

10. Fd.io: Vector packet processing. https://fd.io/vppproject/vpptech/. Accessed 16 Jan 2021

11. RedHat OpenShift: About Single Root I/O Virtualization (SR-IOV) hardware networks. https://docs.openshift.com/container-platform/4.4/networking/hardware_networks/about-sriov.html. Accessed 16 Jan 2021

12. RedHat: Ansible automation tool. https://docs.ansible.com/ansible/latest/index.html. Accessed 16 Jan 2021

13. Fd.io: Vector Packet Processing – RDMA ibverb Ethernet driver. Version 19.08-27-gf4dcae4. https://docs.fd.io/vpp/19.08/rdma_doc.html. Accessed 16 Jan 2021

14. Pitaev, N., Falkner, M., Leivadeas, A., Lambadaris, I.: Characterizing the performance of concurrent virtualized network functions with OVS-DPDK, FD.IO VPP and SR-IOV. In: Proceedings of the 2018 ACM/SPEC International Conference on Performance Engineering (ICPE 0218), pp. 285–292. Association for Computing Machinery, New York (2018). https://doi.org/10.1145/3184407.3184437

15. Miao, L., Hu, H., Cheng, G.: The design and implementation of a dynamic IP defense system accelerated by vector packet processing. In: Proceedings of the International Conference on Industrial Control Network and System Engineering Research (ICNSER2019), pp. 64–69. Association for Computing Machinery, New York (2019). https://doi.org/10.1145/3333581.3333588

16. Yan, J., Li, T., Wang, S., Lv, G., Sun, Z.: Demonstration of path-based packet batcher for accelerating vectorized packet processing. In: 2018 15th Annual IEEE International Conference on Sensing, Communication, and Networking (SECON), Hong Kong, China, pp. 1–3 (2018). https://doi.org/10.1109/SAHCN.2018.8397154

17. IETF: RFC 8453 – Framework for Abstraction and Control of Traffic Engineered Networks (ACTN). https://datatracker.ietf.org/doc/rfc8453/?include_text=1. Accessed 27 Mar 2021

18. Metro-haul project: What is ACTN framework? https://metro-haul.eu/2018/08/30virtu/what-is-actn/. Accessed 27 Mar 2021

19. Lee, J.K: Applicability of ACTN to Support 5G Transport, TEAS Working Group IETF (2019) . https://tools.ietf.org/pdf/draft-lee-teas-actn-5g-transport-00.pdf

20. V. Roux: Path Computation Element (PCE) Communication Protocol (PCEP). IETF, (2008). https://tools.ietf.org/html/rfc5440. Accessed 27 Mar 2021

21. IETF: Traffic Engineering Database Management Information Base in Support of MPLS-TE/GMPLS. https://tools.ietf.org/html/rfc6825. Accessed 27 Mar 2021

22. Zhang, K., Chang, Y., Chen, M., Bao, Y., Xu, Z.: Engaging heterogeneous FPGAs in the cloud. In: Proceedings of the 2019 ACM/SIGDA International Symposium on Field-Programmable Gate Arrays (FPGA 2019). Association for Computing Machinery, New York (2019). https://doi.org/10.1145/3289602.3294001

23. Xilinx Zynq-7000 SoC: Datasheet – Overview. Version 1.11.1. https://www.xilinx.com/support/documentation/data_sheets/ds190-Zynq-7000-Overview.pdf. Accessed 27 Mar 2021

Quadratic p-Median Formulations with Connectivity Costs Between Facilities

Cesar Sandoval[1] , Pablo Adasme[1(✉)] , and Ali Dehghan Firoozabadi[2]

[1] Department of Electrical Engineering, Universidad de Santiago de Chile,
Avenida Ecuador 3519, Santiago, Chile
{cesar.sandoval.n,pablo.adasme}@usach.cl
[2] Department of Electricity, Universidad Tecnológica Metropolitana,
Av. Jose Pedro Alessandri 1242, 7800002 Santiago, Chile
adehghanfirouzabadi@utem.cl

Abstract. In this paper, we consider the problem of minimizing simultaneously the total connectivity cost of a set of users to a set of facility nodes and between facilities themselves. The problem arises as an extension of the p-Median problem, which is a classical combinatorial optimization problem. We propose two mixed-integer quadratic programming models which allow obtaining optimal solutions. Example application domains where the proposed models can be utilized include modeling and management of smart transportation and wireless networks, to name a few. Our first model is derived as an extension of the classical p-Median formulation. Whereas the second one is an alternative set-covering model. Finally, we linearize these models and strengthen them by imposing additional linearized quadratic cuts. We solve hard instances with up to 60 facility nodes and 350 users with the Gurobi solver. Our preliminary numerical results indicate that the linear set-covering formulation allows solving all tested instances to optimality in significantly less computational effort, which is not possible to achieve with the other proposed models.

Keywords: Mixed-integer quadratic and linear programming ·
p-Median problem · Smart transportation and Wireless networks
applications

1 Introduction

The p-Median problem is a classical combinatorial optimization problem which can be described as follows. First, we are given a set of facility nodes $\mathcal{J}$ and a set of users (customers) $\mathcal{I}$ with cardinalities n and m, respectively. Then, the problem consists of finding an optimal subset of facility nodes $\mathcal{P} \subseteq \mathcal{J}$ with cardinality p that minimizes the total connectivity cost in such a way that each user of $\mathcal{I}$ is assigned to a unique facility node in $\mathcal{P}$. It is a discrete type location problem with many real-life applications including the location of industrial plants, warehouses, public facilities, and network design problems, to name a few

© Springer Nature Switzerland AG 2021
J. Bentahar et al. (Eds.): MobiWIS 2021, LNCS 12814, pp. 99–107, 2021.
https://doi.org/10.1007/978-3-030-83164-6_8

[1,8]. In particular, for network design problems, it provides a useful modeling framework as it allows forming backbone network structures [1,2,8,9].

In this paper, we consider the problem of minimizing simultaneously the total connectivity cost of users to facilities, as in the classical p-Median problem, plus the total connectivity cost between pairs of facilities. Notice that the latter cost is not usually incorporated in the classical p-Median problem. We argue that the motivation for doing so can be justified within many application domains. For example, when moving patients from one hospital to another one under pandemic situations like covid-19. Similarly, in a wireless network, it is highly required that the facilities forming a backbone network structure are installed as close as possible since this would allow more rapid transmission of the data and at lower power consumption. Notice that even though the proposed models provide a generic modeling framework, they can be straightforwardly applied and adapted to many optimization problems related to smart transportation and wireless networks [1]. Also notice that in a graph layout configuration of a network, the connectivity cost between two facilities can be computed as a function of the shortest path distance between them [5]. We propose two mixed-integer quadratic programming models. The first one is derived as an extension of the classical p-Median formulation. Whereas the second one is formulated based on an alternative set-covering formulation related to the p-Median problem [3]. Then, we apply the Fortet linearization method [6] and obtain two additional mixed-integer linear programming (MIP) models. Finally, each linearized model is further strengthened by imposing additional linearized quadratic cuts. In particular, we derive a cardinality cut that allows tightening the linear programming relaxations significantly.

As far as we know, our proposed models are new to the literature. A similar problem was studied in [10] where the author reports a new integer quadratic formulation of a general hub-location problem. The author discusses a variety of alternative solution strategies and proposes two heuristics for the task of siting 2, 3, or 4 hubs to serve interactions between sets of 10, 15, 20, and 25 cities. Other related works, from the domain of wireless networks and urban planning, where our proposed formulations can be applied, are reported in references [7,11]. In particular, in [7], the author proposes a distribution location plan for multi-sink nodes in a wireless sensor network based on the p-median problem. The author also proposes a heuristic algorithm and shows that the proposed strategy can effectively reduce the overall energy consumption, improve the efficiency of the network service and extend the network lifetime. Analogously, in [11], the authors incorporate big data in urban planning for better modeling of urban dynamics and more efficiently allocating limited resources. The authors propose a high-performance computing-based algorithm based on random sampling and spatial voting techniques to solve large-sized p-median problems. Numerical results show that their proposed algorithm provides high-quality solutions and reduces computing time significantly. They also demonstrate the dynamic scalability of their proposed algorithm.

The paper is organized as follows. In Sect. 2, we present and explain the quadratic and linear mathematical formulations. Then, we explain how we derive quadratic cuts, which allow tightening each of the linear programming (LP) relaxations. Subsequently, in Sect. 3, we conduct preliminary numerical experiments in order to compare all the proposed models. Finally, in Sect. 4, we present our main conclusions and provide some insight for future research.

2   Mathematical Formulations and Quadratic Cuts

In this section, we first present and explain the proposed mixed-integer quadratic and linear models. Then, we describe how we obtain the quadratic cuts, which are added to the MIP models.

2.1   Proposed Mathematical Formulations

In order to write a first quadratic model, we define the following binary variables

$$y_j = \begin{cases} 1, & \text{if facility node } j \in \mathcal{J} \text{ belongs to subset } \mathcal{P}. \\ 0, & \text{otherwise.} \end{cases}$$

and

$$x_{ij} = \begin{cases} 1, & \text{if user } i \in \mathcal{I} \text{ is assigned to facility node } j \in \mathcal{J}. \\ 0, & \text{otherwise.} \end{cases}$$

We also define the input matrices $C = (C_{ij})$ for all $i \in \mathcal{I}$ and $j \in \mathcal{J}$, and $D = (D_{ij})$ for all $i, j \in \mathcal{J}$ as the required distance matrices. Notice that each entry in each of these input matrices represents the distance between elements i and j. Consequently, a first model can be written as follows

$$Q_1 : \min_{\{x,y\}} \sum_{i \in \mathcal{I}} \sum_{j \in \mathcal{J}} C_{ij} x_{ij} + \sum_{i \in \mathcal{J}} \sum_{\substack{j \in \mathcal{J} \\ (i \neq j)}} \frac{1}{2} D_{ij} y_i y_j \tag{1}$$

$$\text{s.t.:} \sum_{j \in \mathcal{J}} x_{ij} = 1, \quad \forall i \in \mathcal{I} \tag{2}$$

$$\sum_{j \in \mathcal{J}} y_j = p \tag{3}$$

$$x_{ij} \leq y_j, \quad \forall i \in \mathcal{I}, j \in \mathcal{J} \tag{4}$$

$$x \in \{0,1\}^{mn}, y \in \{0,1\}^n \tag{5}$$

where the first and second terms in the objective function (1) represent the connectivity costs between users and facilities, and between facilities themselves, respectively. The constraints (2) ensure that each user $i \in \mathcal{I}$ is connected to a unique facility node $j \in \mathcal{J}$. Next, the constraint (3) is used to select p out of n facilities from $\mathcal{J}$. Subsequently, the constraints (4) ensure that each user $i \in \mathcal{I}$ is connected to a facility node $j \in \mathcal{J}$ if and only if j is active. Finally, constraints (5) are the domain constraints for the decision variables.

In order to obtain an equivalent MIP formulation for Q_1, we apply the Fortet linearization method [6]. This method consists of replacing each quadratic term in the objective function (1) with a new variable $z_{ij} = y_i y_j$ for all $i, j \in \mathcal{J}, (i < j)$ while simultaneously adding linearization constraints. This leads to the following equivalent MIP model

$$M_1 : \min_{\{x,y,z\}} \sum_{i \in \mathcal{I}} \sum_{j \in \mathcal{J}} C_{ij} x_{ij} + \sum_{i \in \mathcal{J}} \sum_{\substack{j \in \mathcal{J} \\ (i<j)}} D_{ij} z_{ij} \tag{6}$$

$$\text{s.t.:} \ (2) - (4)$$

$$z_{ij} \leq y_i, \quad \forall i, j \in \mathcal{J}, (i < j) \tag{7}$$

$$z_{ij} \leq y_j, \quad \forall i, j \in \mathcal{J}, (i < j) \tag{8}$$

$$z_{ij} \geq y_i + y_j - 1, \quad \forall i, j \in \mathcal{J}, (i < j) \tag{9}$$

$$x \in \{0,1\}^{mn}, y \in \{0,1\}^n, z \in \{0,1\}^{\frac{n(n-1)}{2}}, \tag{10}$$

where the objective function (6) is no longer a quadratic one, but a linear one. The constraints (7)–(9) are the linearization constraints and ensure that variable $z_{ij} = 1$ if and only if both $y_i = y_j = 1$ for all $i, j \in \mathcal{J}, (i < j)$. Otherwise, if either y_i or y_j equals zero, then $z_{ij} = 0$. Notice that we do not use both variables z_{ij} and z_{ji} in M_1 as each connection link is considered only once.

In order to write an equivalent set-covering formulation, we first add an artificial facility node to set $\mathcal{J}$. Denote this new set by $\hat{\mathcal{J}}$. Next, we define an additional input matrix $\hat{C} = (\hat{C}_{ij})$ for each $i \in \mathcal{I}$ and $j \in \hat{\mathcal{J}}$. This new extended matrix is constructed as follows. First, let $\hat{C}$ be an empty matrix. Then, for each $i \in \mathcal{I}$, we sort in ascending order the corresponding row vector of matrix $C = (C_{ij})$, for all $j \in \mathcal{J}$ and add the resulting sorted vector to the i_{th} row of matrix $\hat{C}$. Finally, we add an extra zero column vector to the left of matrix $\hat{C}$. Similarly, we define the input symmetric matrix $\hat{D} = (\hat{D}_{ij})$ for all $i, j \in \hat{\mathcal{J}}$. This matrix $\hat{D}$ is constructed by adding zero column and row vectors to the left and at the top of matrix D, respectively. To terminate, we define the following cumulative variables

$$w_{ij} = \begin{cases} 1, & \text{if the distance cost of user } i \in \mathcal{I} \text{ is at least } \hat{C}_{ij}, \text{ for all } j \in \hat{\mathcal{J}} \\ & \text{no matter which median it is allocated to.} \\ 0, & \text{otherwise.} \end{cases}$$

Thus, a quadratic p-Median formulation can now be written as

$$Q_2 : \min_{\{w,y\}} \sum_{i \in \mathcal{I}} \sum_{j \in \hat{\mathcal{J}} \backslash \{1\}} (\hat{C}_{ij} - \hat{C}_{i,j-1}) w_{ij} + \sum_{i \in \hat{\mathcal{J}} \backslash \{1\}} \sum_{\substack{j \in \hat{\mathcal{J}} \backslash \{1\} \\ (i \neq j)}} \frac{1}{2} \hat{D}_{ij} y_i y_j \tag{11}$$

$$\text{s.t.:} \ \sum_{j \in \hat{\mathcal{J}} \backslash \{1\}} y_j = p \tag{12}$$

$$w_{ik} + \sum_{\substack{j \in \hat{\mathcal{J}} \setminus \{1\} \\ \{C_{ij} < \hat{C}_{ik}\}}} y_j \geq 1, \quad \forall i \in \mathcal{I}, k \in \hat{\mathcal{J}} \setminus \{1\} \tag{13}$$

$$w \in \{0,1\}^{m(n+1)}, y \in \{0,1\}^{n+1} \tag{14}$$

Analogously as for Q_1, we can obtain its linearized version as

$$M_2 : \min_{\{w,y,z\}} \sum_{i \in \mathcal{I}} \sum_{j \in \hat{\mathcal{J}} \setminus \{1\}} (\hat{C}_{ij} - \hat{C}_{i,j-1}) w_{ij} + \sum_{i \in \hat{\mathcal{J}} \setminus \{1\}} \sum_{\substack{j \in \hat{\mathcal{J}} \setminus \{1\} \\ (i<j)}} \hat{D}_{ij} z_{ij} \tag{15}$$

$$\text{s.t.: } (12) - (13)$$

$$z_{ij} \leq y_i, \quad \forall i, j \in \hat{\mathcal{J}} \setminus \{1\}, (i < j) \tag{16}$$

$$z_{ij} \leq y_j, \quad \forall i, j \in \hat{\mathcal{J}} \setminus \{1\}, (i < j) \tag{17}$$

$$z_{ij} \geq y_i + y_j - 1, \quad \forall i, j \in \hat{\mathcal{J}} \setminus \{1\}, (i < j) \tag{18}$$

$$w \in \{0,1\}^{m(n+1)}, y \in \{0,1\}^{n+1}, z \in \{0,1\}^{\frac{(n+1)n}{2}} \tag{19}$$

Notice that the Fortet linearization constraints (16)–(18) are now imposed in M_2 for all $i, j \in \hat{\mathcal{J}} \setminus \{1\}$.

2.2   Quadratic Cuts Used to Strengthen the MIP Models

In this subsection, we explain how we obtain quadratic cuts, which are then linearized to further strengthen the LP relaxations of the MIP models. By doing so, we intend to measure the impact of these cuts on the performance of the branch and cut algorithm of the Gurobi solver [4] when solving M_1 and M_2. We denote by M_1^s and M_2^s the strengthened versions of models M_1 and M_2, respectively. The set of linearized quadratic cuts we add in M_1^s are

$$\sum_{j \in \mathcal{J}} z_{ij} = p y_i, \quad \forall i \in \mathcal{J} \tag{20}$$

$$\sum_{\substack{i,j \in \mathcal{J} \\ (i<j)}} z_{ij} = \frac{p(p-1)}{2} \tag{21}$$

$$y_i + y_j \leq 1 + z_{ij}, \quad \forall i, j \in \mathcal{J}, (i < j) \tag{22}$$

The first cut (20) is obtained by multiplying constraint (3) by each y_i, for all $i \in \mathcal{J}$. Whilst the cardinality cut (21) is obtained by multiplying constraint (3) with each variable y_i for all $i \in \mathcal{J}$. Then, we take the sum over all the resulting constraints and obtain the equality $\sum_{i,j \in \mathcal{J}} y_i y_j = p^2$, which is equivalent to

$$\sum_{i,j \in \mathcal{J}, (i \neq j)} y_i y_j = p(p-1)$$

and

$$\sum_{i,j \in \mathcal{J}, (i<j)} z_{ij} = \frac{p(p-1)}{2}$$

Subsequently, the cuts in (22) are obtained from the quadratic valid inequalities $(1 - y_i)(1 - y_j) \geq 0$ for all $i, j \in \mathcal{J}, (i < j)$. Observe that each term in these inequalities is nonnegative since $y_i \leq 1$ for each $i \in \mathcal{J}$. Finally, notice that the cuts (20)–(22) can be straightforwardly adapted for M_2 while using the set $\hat{\mathcal{J}} \setminus \{1\}$ instead of $\mathcal{J}$.

3   Numerical Experiments

In this section, we present preliminary numerical results for all the proposed models. For this purpose, we implement a Python program using Gurobi solver [4]. In particular, we solve each quadratic model while setting the Gurobi option parameter *Nonconvex* to a value of 2. This option allows one to solve a nonconvex quadratic problem with spatial branch and bound algorithms. We decided to use this option as it proved to be the most effective one in terms of CPU time required to solve the quadratic models. Whilst for the MIP and LP models, we use the Gurobi solver with default options. This implies solving the linear models with state-of-the-art branch and cut-based algorithms. The numerical experiments have been carried out on an Intel(R) 64 bits core (TM) with 3 GHz and 8G of RAM under Windows 10. So far, we generate eight instances with dimensions of $n = \{50; 60\}$ and $m = \{200; 250; 300; 350\}$, and each of them is solved for values of $P = \{10; 20\}$. We mention that this range of parameter values was arbitrarily chosen in order to ensure that hard instances were obtained. In a larger version of this paper, a wider range of parameter values will be considered. The input matrices $C = C_{uj}$ and $D = D_{ij}$ for all $u \in \mathcal{I}$ and $i, j \in \mathcal{J}$ are generated by computing the distances between users and facilities and between facilities themselves. Notice that matrix D is symmetric. The coordinates of each user and facility node are randomly drawn from the interval $(0; 1)$.

In Table 1, we present preliminary numerical results obtained with models Q_1 and M_1. More precisely, in columns 1–4 we present the instance number, and the values of p, m, and n, respectively. Next, in columns 5–8 we report for Q_1, the best objective function value obtained in at most 1h of CPU time, the number of branch and bound nodes, CPU time in seconds required to solve the model, and the *MipGap* parameter value of Gurobi solver, respectively. Gurobi computes this parameter by subtracting from the best incumbent solution the best lower bound obtained. Then, it divides this result by the incumbent solution again. Notice that this value is reported as a percentage. Also notice that if the Gurobi solver terminates with an optimal solution, then the *MipGap* parameter should be equal to zero. Subsequently, in columns 9–15 we report for M_1, the best objective function value obtained in at most 1 h, the number of branch and bound nodes, CPU time in seconds, the optimal objective value of its LP relaxation, and CPU time in seconds required to solve it, and the gap and *MipGap* values, respectively. The gap is computed by $\left[\frac{Best-LP}{Best}\right] * 100$.

Table 1. Numerical results obtained with Q_1 and M_1.

#	P	m	n	Q_1				M_1						
				Best	B&Bn	CPU(s)	MipGap%	Best	B&Bn	CPU(s)	LP	CPU(s)	Gap%	MipGap%
1	10	200	50	45.76	59834	2133.63	0	45.76	10494	1015.92	24.17	0.43	47.18	0
2		250		53.59	45816	2090.6	0	53.59	6398	1156.28	31.15	0.58	41.86	0
3		300		60.54	36938	1964.24	0	60.54	4850	1246.64	37.34	0.61	38.31	0
4		350		66.97	26966	1824.55	0	66.97	2456	703.56	43.96	0.83	34.35	0
5	10	200	60	45.55	50480	3600	0.06	45.55	19046	3229.7	24.03	0.55	47.24	0
6		250		53.35	46754	3600	0.05	53.35	11860	3600	31.04	0.72	41.8	0.03
7		300		60.39	41313	3600	0.05	60.39	11310	3600	37.26	0.81	38.3	0.03
8		350		66.77	33585	3600	0.05	66.77	10374	3600	43.92	0.96	34.21	0.02
1	20	200	50	88.19	2595	962.54	0	88.19	233	120.82	18.4	0.19	79.13	0
2		250		96.21	5095	2129.14	0	96.21	521	375.69	23.47	0.36	75.6	0
3		300		104.17	7559	3600	0.02	104.17	1725	1118.44	28.44	0.5	72.69	0
4		350		110.67	5372	3600	0.04	110.67	1457	1062.42	33.29	0.76	69.91	0
5	20	200	60	84.91	4278	3600	0.06	84.91	1153	858.49	17.81	0.29	79.02	0
6		250		93.24	3566	3600	0.09	93.24	1140	1473.24	22.83	0.55	75.51	0
7		300		101.44	2966	3600	0.12	101.44	1574	3600	27.7	0.67	72.68	0.02
8		350		108.47	2771	3600	0.13	108.36	1513	3600	32.49	0.9	70.01	0.03

Table 2. Numerical results obtained with Q_2 and M_2.

#	P	m	n	Q_2				M_2						
				Best	B&Bn	CPU(s)	MipGap%	Best	B&Bn	CPU(s)	LP	CPU(s)	Gap%	MipGap%
1	10	200	50	45.76	5799	1122.08	0	45.76	188	91.79	24.17	0.77	47.18	0
2		250		53.59	5963	1499.08	0	53.59	124	113.52	31.15	1.29	41.86	0
3		300		60.54	2050	767.52	0	60.54	1	45.86	37.34	1.52	38.31	0
4		350		66.97	2101	872.13	0	66.97	1	37.74	43.96	1.89	34.35	0
5	10	200	60	45.55	9298	3600	0.04	45.55	1196	934.09	24.03	1.24	47.24	0
6		250		53.35	7716	3600	0.05	53.35	791	767.94	31.04	1.79	41.8	0
7		300		60.67	5756	3600	0.04	60.39	312	424.37	37.26	2.44	38.3	0
8		350		66.77	4642	3600	0.02	66.77	1	145.03	43.92	2.81	34.21	0
1	20	200	50	88.19	1383	727.43	0	88.19	17	44.02	18.4	0.43	79.13	0
2		250		96.21	1795	998.88	0	96.21	145	73.65	23.47	0.58	75.6	0
3		300		104.17	3036	1721.66	0	104.17	61	84.32	28.44	0.81	72.69	0
4		350		110.67	4148	2266.1	0	110.67	116	110.93	33.29	1.15	69.91	0
5	20	200	60	84.91	2962	3600	0.04	84.91	43	164.47	17.81	0.62	79.02	0
6		250		93.24	2456	3600	0.06	93.24	325	404.15	22.83	1.07	75.51	0
7		300		101.53	2701	3600	0.07	101.44	635	1118.62	27.7	1.24	72.68	0
8		350		108.42	2229	3600	0.08	108.35	816	1909.16	32.49	1.71	70.01	0

In Table 2, we report numerical results for the models Q_2 and M_2. The column information of Table 2 is analogous to Table 1. Finally, in Table 3 we report preliminary numerical results for the linear models M_1^s and M_2^s. Its legend is analogous as for the linear models reported in Tables 1 and 2 for M_1 and M_2, respectively.

From Table 1, we first observe that both models Q_1 and M_1 allow obtaining the same objective function values except for the instance #8, for which we obtain a slightly smaller value with M_1. Regarding the number of branch and bound nodes, we see that Gurobi reports a significantly less number of nodes

Table 3. Numerical results obtained with M_1^s and M_2^s.

#	P	m	n	M_1^s							M_2^s						
				Best	B&Bn	CPU(s)	LP	CPU(s)	Gap%	MipGap%	Best	B&Bn	CPU(s)	LP	CPU(s)	Gap%	MipGap%
1	10	200	50	45.76	7702	928.61	34.63	0.41	24.32	0	45.76	158	115.51	34.63	1.39	24.32	0
2		250		53.59	5063	1105.62	41.62	0.48	22.33	0	53.59	9	75.24	41.62	1.46	22.33	0
3		300		60.54	3644	1008.27	48.26	0.71	20.27	0	60.54	1	46.72	48.26	1.76	20.27	0
4		350		66.97	4062	1107.03	54.79	0.88	18.18	0	66.97	1	42.38	54.79	1.98	18.18	0
5	10	200	60	45.55	16213	3600	33.48	0.7	26.48	0.01	45.55	1062	869.88	33.48	2.03	26.48	0
6		250		53.35	10270	3600	40.5	0.65	24.08	0.03	53.35	1068	1454.03	40.5	2.09	24.08	0
7		300		60.39	8741	3600	47.2	0.83	21.85	0.04	60.39	257	520.99	47.2	2.6	21.85	0
8		350		66.77	7240	3600	53.77	0.99	19.45	0.02	66.77	1	146.25	53.77	2.98	19.45	0
1	20	200	50	88.19	876	221.09	71.69	0.35	18.7	0	88.19	1	41.15	71.69	1.34	18.7	0
2		250		96.21	1088	368.09	76.93	0.39	20.03	0	96.21	1	52.63	76.93	1.55	20.03	0
3		300		104.17	1327	768.92	82.22	0.46	21.07	0	104.17	1	77.44	82.22	2.0	21.07	0
4		350		110.67	3674	2335.46	87.34	0.55	21.07	0	110.67	55	88.82	87.34	2.33	21.07	0
5	20	200	60	84.91	1156	683.22	66.37	0.46	21.83	0	84.91	1	118.39	66.37	1.76	21.83	0
6		250		93.24	2254	1905.38	71.68	0.59	23.12	0	93.24	1	175.0	71.68	2.4	23.12	0
7		300		101.44	2545	3600	76.92	0.73	24.17	0.02	101.44	223	482.71	76.92	2.9	24.17	0
8		350		108.35	1903	3600	82.08	0.75	24.24	0.03	108.35	488	866.76	82.08	3.31	24.24	0

for M_1. The CPU times show that we can obtain the optimal solution of the problem for a larger number of instances with M_1 in less than 1h. Next, we observe that the *MipGap* values reported for both models are close to zero. The latter indicates that the solutions reported are near-optimal. Notice that from these values, we can obtain tight lower bounds for the problem as well. Finally, we see that the LP relaxation of M_1 is not tight when compared to the best objective function values and that the gaps obtained increase with p.

From Table 2, we observe similar trends for Q_2 and M_2. We notice that M_2 significantly outperforms model Q_2 in terms of the best objective function and CPU time values obtained. Indeed, we obtain the optimal solution to the problem with proven optimality for all tested instances. This cannot be achieved by any of the other proposed models reported in Tables 1 and 2. This achievement can also be observed by looking at the number of branch and bound nodes obtained, which are significantly lower for M_2. Finally, we observe that the LP relaxation of M_2 is not tight either. Similarly, from Table 3 we observe that M_2 outperforms M_1 in terms of all column information reported. In particular, we confirm that M_2 allows obtaining the optimal solution of the problem for all the instances. Perhaps, one of the most interesting observations of Table 3 is that the LP bounds obtained with M_2^s are significantly higher than those reported in Tables 1 and 2, respectively. Ultimately, we observe that the impact of adding linearized quadratic cuts in M_2 is not so strong in terms of CPU time values obtained. However, we see that for most of the instances, the number of branch and bound nodes decreases when these cuts are added to the models.

4   Conclusions

In this paper, we considered the problem of minimizing simultaneously the total connectivity cost of a set of users to a set of facility nodes and among facilities themselves. The problem is motivated by the potential development of future smart transportation and wireless network applications where interacting facilities will be required to be connected and nearly reachable. We proposed two mixed-integer quadratic programming models, which are further linearized. The first one is obtained as an extension of the classical p-Median formulation. Whereas the second one corresponds to an alternative set-covering model. Finally, we strengthen the linear models by imposing additional linearized quadratic cuts. So far, we solved hard instances with up to 60 facility nodes and 350 users. Our preliminary numerical results indicated that the linearized set-covering formulation outperforms all the other proposed models as it allows solving all the instances with proven optimality and in significantly less computational effort.

As future research, new models and algorithms should be investigated in order to tackle this hard combinatorial optimization problem. Complementarily, new cutting plane approaches should be proposed in conjunction with the new models. This would allow a complete validation of the proposal. Ultimately, the study problem in this paper should be adapted to more specific transportation and telecommunication network problems as part of future work.

Acknowledgments. The authors acknowledge the financial support from Projects: FONDECYT No. 11180107 and FONDECYT No. 3190147.

References

1. Adasme, P.: p-Median based formulations with backbone facility locations. Appl. Soft Comput. **67**, 261–275 (2018)
2. Adasme, P., Andrade, R., Lisser, A.: Minimum cost dominating tree sensor networks under probabilistic constraints. Comput. Netw. **112**, 208–222 (2017)
3. García, S., Labbé, M., Marín, A.: Solving large p-median problems with a radius formulation. INFORMS J. Comput. **23**(4), 546–556 (2011)
4. Achterberg, T.: Gurobi solver. https://www.gurobi.com/
5. Cormen, T.H., Leiserson, C.E., Rivest, R.L., Stein, C.: Introduction to Algorithms. MIT Press and McGraw-Hill, Cumberland (2009)
6. Fortet, R.: Applications de lálgebre de boole en recherche operationelle. Rev. Fr. Rech. Oper. **4**, 17–26 (1960)
7. Haicheng, L.: Research on distribution of sink nodes in wireless sensor network. In: 2010 Third International Symposium on Information Science and Engineering, pp. 122–124 (2010). https://doi.org/10.1109/ISISE.2010.56
8. Hakimi, S.L.: Optimum location of switching centers and the absolute centers and medians of a graph. Oper. Res. **12**, 450–459 (1964)
9. Ho-Yin, M., Zuo-Jun, M.S.: Integrated Modeling for Location Analysis. In: Now Foundations and Trends, p. 164 (2016)
10. O'Kelly, M.E.: A quadratic integer program for the location of interacting hub facilities. Eur. J. Oper. Res. **32**, 393–404 (1987)
11. Wangshu, M., Daoqin, T.: On solving large p-median problems. Environ. Planning B Urban Anal. City Sci. **47**(6), 981–996 (2020)

Applying Game Theory Concept to Improve Resource Allocation in Mobile Edge Computing

Dashty Mohammed Khudhur[1], Tara Ali Yahiya[2], and Pinar Kirci[3(✉)]

[1] University of Kurdistan Hewler, Erbil, Iraq
[2] University of Paris Saclay, LRI, Gif-sur-Yvette, France
[3] Bursa Uludag University, Bursa, Turkey
pinarkirci@uludag.edu.tr

Abstract. The implementation of the game theory approach represented by Shapley value is done through a design of network based on WLAN with three types of applications, namely video streaming, file sharing, and Web Access equipped with DB. Python is used to implement the Shapely value while OPNET is used to simulate the proposed architecture. The comparison data shows that using game theory approaches minimize data rate wasting and fair distribution of data rate among each application, this is because game theory approach itself has a coalition between users and allocates resources fairly between users, and the results of simulation focusing on traffic sent and received are compared to verify this fact. The performed comparison shows that the game theory results are performing better than the normal one adopted by the WLAN which is Round Robin with PCF.

Keywords: Game theory · Shapley value · Round robin · PCF

1 Introduction

Cloud computing is a concept that has been developing rapidly and has made enterprises changing the way they used to deal with technology. Cloud computing is delivering computing services over the internet from a remote location on-demand using other computing resources other than owning computing resources. This concept caused many enterprises to change their strategies toward using this technology. Enterprises do not have to spend thousands of dollars on purchasing computing resources but they can access the resources they require from cloud computing providers [1].

Cloud service providers can be classified into three categories: software as a service (SaaS), platform as a service (PaaS), and infrastructure as a service (IaaS). In the SaaS category, the service provider aims to provide application developer services to the client. The client can use applications through web services or by using web browsers. The client doesn't need to know how the infrastructure works. It is the usage of applications over the internet.

In the PaaS model, users can deploy complete applications on the cloud infrastructure, without controlling it. In the model, the cloud service provides tools and libraries for

© Springer Nature Switzerland AG 2021
J. Bentahar et al. (Eds.): MobiWIS 2021, LNCS 12814, pp. 108–118, 2021.
https://doi.org/10.1007/978-3-030-83164-6_9

users and developers to develop and deploy their services without having the required environment on their own computers.

In the third model which is IaaS, computer resources, data storing and networking and all other infrastructure related computing resources are provided as services. The infrastructure is seen as a virtual infrastructure and clients can use the resources whenever and wherever they require them [1].

Edge computing is a new paradigm that brings the service of the cloud provider in the proximity of the users. Edge computing can be considered as an extended cloud which is geographically located close to the users. The idea behind the introduction of edge computing is mainly depending on the actual form of cloud computing. The simplest term of cloud computing is storing and running data on the internet instead of the local hard drive of the computer. Cloud computing uses the internet as a tool to access storage. In other words, cloud computing refers to two main ideas that handle by cloud computing. First one is, distributing workloads on the internet in the provider's datacenter remotely that is called as public cloud, for example: Amazon, Microsoft (Azur). And, if more than one public cloud works remotely for the same purpose it is called as multi-cloud. The second idea explains that how virtualized domain works when a user requests resources through very advance automation, to gain network resources, storage, or any other functionality on the cloud, to balance workload. As mentioned earlier, cloud computing provides resources in different ways of service which is: IaaS, SaaS, and PaaS which makes cloud computing an advance technology. All these services are sometimes located geographically far from the users in case of a public-private deployment. As a consequence, this may violate the Quality of Service of real-time applications that require very low end-to-end latency. For instance, managing, processing, and analyzing huge amounts of data will be one of the challenges of the cloud. Sending huge amounts of data to the cloud provider through the current network architecture i.e., the backhaul, will increase the probability of having congestion and decreasing the performance of the network accordingly [2].

2 Literature Review

Collaborative resource allocation in mobile edge computing with using game theory has challenges in involving different techniques. This is due to increasing requirements of mobile users on MEC, such as, cloud storage, decreasing latency, offloading. Computation-intensive in MEC is worked in [3]. The study focused on resource allocation. Due to resource limitation in mobile terminals, they can not provide a good capacity of computing for data processing which is one of the requirements for the computation-intensive applications. In addition to the demand on cloud that increases each minute, most of the computing tasks will proceed in the cloud in the close future. This will cause an increase in transmission latency and decrease in Quality of service (QoS). To be able to minimize this, MEC offers to address many issues such as latency, with using MEC servers close to the base station, or mobile vehicles, or devices with idle resources.

In the study, it is worked on resource sharing in mobile edge cloud among multiple service providers while each service provider has its own utility provider in [4]. Also, the study defined limitations of resources in edge cloud that might not satisfy the application requests. Because each edge cloud provides service to edge computing where each edge cloud located at the edge of the network which is different from the application. An application runs in each mobile or in internet environment and while communicating between applications an edge cloud forms. Also, application latency is decreased which requires more resources.

Revenue sharing in the edge cloud computing worked in [5]. Computing service providers in both cloud provider and edge provider as a hybrid system examined. Here, edge provider represented IoT, while cloud provider provides computing services to a client, and together they are called as edge-cloud system. The idea is to create a mechanism to distribute tasks. It is compared with the revenue resources from the client and build the revenue sharing to split service providers. And later service providers compete among them to identify utilities to re-share resources fairly to the system.

Mobile edge computing worked in [6]. The bankruptcy game model for computational resource allocation in MEC was considered in the paper.

Data offloading in the multi-MD and multi-MEC-server scenario studied in [7]. Besides, a coalition based structure proposed in the paper. The proposed structure incorporated with MD scheduling, MEC server selection, and offloading encouragement.

3 Game Theory and Shapley Value

Edge computing can take a different form of deployment, although they have the same functionality represented by offloading cloud computing. In the following, the different edge computing technologies are described justifying the motivation of using one of them in the paper.

Mobile users' demands for internet increases on daily basis and mobile hardware in terms of heat, battery life and hardware is quite poor. One of the presented solutions is could computing. However, wireless LAN is quite slow and delays interaction in terms of user application in cloud computing. Also, the main solution for that is an implementation of cloudlet, which adds closest small cloud to mobile users through LAN. Moreover, cloudlet represents a cluster of computers that are connected to the internet. They are located at the edge of the network and connected through LAN or wireless [8].

Fog computing is an extension of cloud computing that creates closer links between ground infrastructure and cloud. Fog comes from fogging which brings services to ground infrastructure and network infrastructure [9].

The European Telecommunications Standards (ETSI) defines Mobile Edge Computing (MEC) as the environment that provides IT services including cloud computing at the very edge of the mobile network with Radio Access Network (RAN) within the range of close nearness to the mobile subscribers [10]. Moreover, MEC provides application builders, cloud computing services, and IT services at the edge of the network. MEC provides capabilities for operators to open their RAN to the approved third parties and allowing operators to deploy their applications rapidly to the enterprises and mobile subscribers.

3.1 Game Theory Concept

Game theory (GT) applied in many domains such as economics, politics and management. Here, the applied mathematics for studying and analyzing different interactions between different players involve punish and reward. Also, GT involves a collection of analytic tools that makes the facility in the decision-making process for a specific case in between economic and social situations that needs to have input from individuals through having different favorites [11].

To improve the decision process in single objectives, the game theory covers different decision strategies. For example, in economics and sociology, the focus is about creating the good design of payment. But structural engineering will focus on design efficiency. In wireless networks, each node represents a player, each player has its own strategy and it should contribute its own value to gain. An example of a coalition game with network components is given in Table 1.

Table 1. Coalition game in network [12]

Network component	Game theory network
Nodes	Act as a player
Available adaptations	Action set
Performance metrics	Utility functions

GT has two main types, cooperative GT and non-cooperative GT. Cooperative GT focuses on how all nodes are working together as a coalition which makes entity not only depends on single nodes but depends on the strategy of other nodes. For this reason, the cooperative GT is more collaborative. It elaborates especially in the case that represents realistic ideas where nodes are attended in several coalitions that makes it more complex. To simplify this complexity a principle should to be applied. In non- cooperative GT, each player tries to achieve its own goal and reduce its own cost. One of the concepts that is used for non-cooperative GT is Nash equilibrium. The main purpose of Nash equilibrium is presenting a strong solution for none of the players. They alternate their own actions or not try to change their own utility, which leads Nash equilibrium to predict the result of the game [12].

3.2 Shapley Value

The game theory provides different models in decision making for any strategic situation which involves mathematical thinking where more than one player participates. For many kinds of problems, it needs different thinking and decision through cooperative and or non-cooperative player's participation to get the mathematical application of game theory.

In general, the cost allocation increases in many different situations. One of them is used when many participants are available to work together. For example, to increase patient care quality with reducing cost allocation, healthcare suppliers who coordinate patient's care, use same principle and methodology of game theory. Also, many different ideas are suggested to manage fair cost allocation. But, some of them become a practical solution [13].

3.3   Wireless Local Area Network (WLAN) and WLAN Medium Access Methods

WLAN is one of the quickest technologies that grows in the industry of telecommunications. It can be involved in many market solutions such as companies, hospitals, public business solutions, airports and even in minimarkets. The technology of WLAN is used to save cost and to avoid a crowd of cables. However, it's the only solution to supply the internet for very high speeds in the industries. In addition to this, there are many technologies and non-technology standards that involve WLAN with throughput, power consumption, coverage range, cost, and price.

802.11a standard: This standard is the first WLAN standard that was presented in July 1997. It is used for wireless communication with the same protocol of Ethernet. And, it supports two models which are 802.11a and 802.11b. Each of them has its own specification and qualification, for instance, 802.11a reaches the speed of 54 Mbps and uses Orthogonal Frequency division multiplexing (OFDM) technology. Moreover, it is supported by the specification of Wired Equivalent Privacy (WEP) as it is implemented by IEEE that provides authentication and encryption.

802.11b standard: This standard is the most common one in 802.11 standards and it was presented in 1999. It depends on Direct Sequence Spread Spectrum (DSSS) 802.11 version. It uses 2.4 GHz. It is used more widely than 802.11a. Also, DSSS is simpler than OFDM. 802.11b standard supports the capacity of 11Mbps and enabled WEP.

Furthermore, 80.2.11 has many other standards such as 802.11g that supports high speed reach in 2.4 GHz. There are other models like 802.11e, 802.11f, 802.11i and 802.11h. Many criteria influence WLAN solutions in making better specifications in terms of speed, power requirement, interference concerns, high-speed timing, capacity requirement, etc. [14].

Distributed Coordination Function (DCF) depends on CSMA/CA (Carrier Sense Multiple Access with Collision Avoidance) and the state of the medium is sensed by the wireless station to send packets. Moreover, packets are transferred when the medium is idle and the time interval is greater than DIFS (Distributed inter-frame space). On the other hand, if packets are not sent then the medium remains idle and it is tracked by the station. Additionally, when the medium is idle, it waits for DIFS and starts to reduce the counter to gather packets from the station.

The Point Coordination Function (PCF) is a polling based scheme in IEEE 802.11. The scheme includes either simplified round-robin technique or priority-based tips. Additionally, this scheme possesses a super frame architecture that comprises both contention-free period and contention period [15].

4   Collaborative Resource Allocation in MEC Using Shapley Value

A scenario is set up for presenting the operation of PCF and DCF. To achieve this methodology, two terms are used with comparing their operations. These are, Constant

Bit Rate (CBR) which uses UDP and File Transfer Protocole (FTP) which uses TCP. Firstly, in the CBR case, the transmitting CBR starts in parallel with the starting of the simulation and finishes with its ending. Additionally, 1 s is used for latency while CBR stations sent 100 packets. And it is anticipated from server stations to receive 100 packets where the size is 256 bytes. The results of this scenario showes that the packet ratio is higher in PCF whereas it is lower in DCF.

On the other hand, the FTP scenario shows that the packet size is specified by the simulator itself. Also, to get the PDR ratio, it is noticed that there should be many packets sent and received by the client and server. Then, results shows that PDR rises in the PCF round-robin scheme while it deducts in DCF because of ACK piggyback on the packet [16, 17].

In the paper, the used method in resource allocation over MEC is detailed. This starts with a description of the system model which is used as the basic scenario for the whole work. Then, the Shapley value is used as a method of allocating data rate to the different applications deployed in the cell. The main reason to use Shapley Value is because Shapley value is one of the common concepts in cooperative game theory. It assigns a unique distribution among all players, in total profit generated by coalition of all players. Moreover, the Shapley value algorithm focuses on the coalition of players. It cooperates and obtains a certain overall gain from the cooperation and depends on the amount of contribution to the coalition. The resource allocation is carried out into two-steps. First, the Shapley value is used. Then, a scheduling algorithm is used to schedule the allocated resources to the different types of traffic to guarantee their QoS parameters through using game theory approach.

The network architecture under consideration for the whole work in the paper is partitioned into two parts, namely as the MEC network and the service requesters. The radio access network is composed of Access Points (AP). They are equipped with a WLAN interface which is based on IEEE 802.11g. The APs are collocated with MEC servers that are connected in their turn via backhaul links to the Internet and then to the network of the cloud provider. Generally, MEC servers work in standalone fashion or they may collaborate with the storage in the network of the cloud provider to send a part of the computation and caching process to the cloud itself (Fig. 1).

The main problem in a wireless network architecture where several MEC servers are deployed and their access is regulated through the Access Points is the resource allocation. Resource allocation is a matter of interest when there are several types of applications offloaded to the MEC servers and each of which has different requirements in terms of QoS parameters. In the paper, real-time and non-real-time applications are used. Hence, they differ in their requirements in terms of delay, response-time throughput, packet loss, etc.

In the paper, a joint resource allocation and scheduling algorithm is proposed in order to efficiently use the network resources. The resource allocation is based on collaborative game theory with using Shapley value.

In order to proceed, each service requesters (players) in the network should form a coalition to cooperate with each other to obtain a gain from this cooperation. The gain is represented by the total data rate offered by the AP. However, since some service requestors are contributing more than others, the data rate should be divided among them

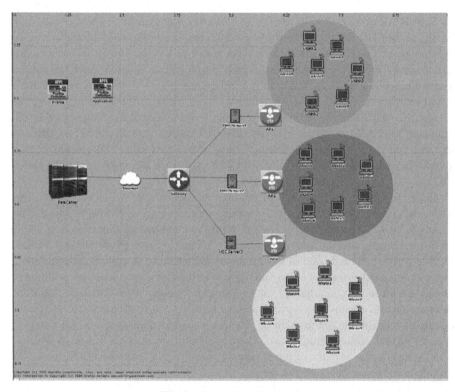

Fig. 1. Network architecture.

in a fair way with taking their contribution into consideration. Each service requestor should obtain the gain or the required data rate to guarantee its QoS by collaboration. Once the resource is distributed fairly among the users, a scheduling algorithm should be carried out in order to allocate the resources. This is the main task that is handled by Shapley value. In the paper, a Round Robin scheduler is implemented in the AP in order to allocate resources among different types of traffic.

In the paper, Shapley value is implemented with python and the results are gained on OPNET simulator in order to determine the data rate distribution in the AP.

5 Simulation Methodology

The model for simulation methodology starts with identifying scenarios based on a realistic case study through defining their nodes and attributes. Then, it continues with deploying connections between nodes, and finding a suitable configuration for each node and finally running the scenario. For proceeding in simulation, the Opnet simulator is identified as a basis for creating all the scenarios.

Simulation is a regeneration of real-world networks through creating models in simulation software. The main steps to create a simulation scenario consist of three-phases; namely the planning phase which identifies the real problem to be simulated and selecting the data rate that is selected for each application to be used in Shapley value. The second phase implements the scenario and node models to be used in the simulation process. And the third phase is testing the defined scenario to validate the simulation model and have numerical results.

Basically, there are two different techniques to evaluate the performance of the network; modelling to provide accurate estimates of performance in large heterogeneous internet works or simulation.

The network architecture used in the paper consists of several WLANs that are collocated with MEC servers through Ethernet cables. Each WLAN device is connected to the Access Point through IEEE 802.11g technology. All of them uses the service of MECs for real-time and non-real-time applications. In their turn, the servers are connected through backhaul link to the Internet then it is connected to the cloud computing service and represented as Infrastructure as a Service. The OPNET network of this network architecture includes node configuration, link setup, and traffic generation.

In the paper, simulation results are presented according to two scenarios; the first one is based on a joint resource allocation using Shapley value with Round Robin and PCF mechanism in WLAN, while the second is based on Round Robin with PCF only.

The first scenario will be based on the combination between Shapley value and the RR scheduling algorithms deployed in the AP before configuring the AP according to Shapley values. It is important to consider the MAC data rate values specified in IEEE802.11g standard.

In the scenario, the 54 Mbps in the AP is used as a total data rate for all MEC applications without any kind of resource allocation.

In this section, simulation results will be obtained for both scenarios explained previously. For each MEC application, some QoS parameters are studied to show the impact of Shapley value on the resource distribution and allocation.

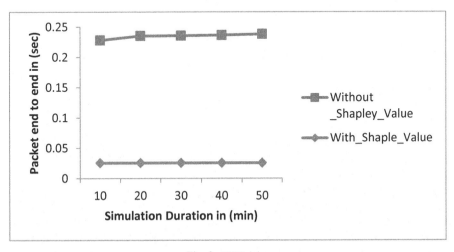

Fig. 2. E2E delay

End to end (E2E) delay for video streaming is represented by the delay from the UE to the MEC server that is depicted in Fig. 2. The legends of the figure is represented by without_Shapley_Value and with_Shapley_Value for both scenarios respectively. Since delay is one of the most important QoS parameters for video application, this is why it is compulsory to study it. It is shown that the packets travelling from UE to the MEC are experienced higher delay in the case where Shapley value is not used. This is due to the fact that, in the Shapley value resources are distributed and reserved for each type of traffic and Round Robin scheduling algorithm is performed with this allocated resource among only UEs which have the same type of application. Unless Shapley values are used, the resources will not be distributed ahead and video traffic is treated as the other application. RR algorithm will operate in the AP and it is well-known that RR is violating the QoS of real-time applications as it has fair and equal treatment of real-time and non-real-time applications.

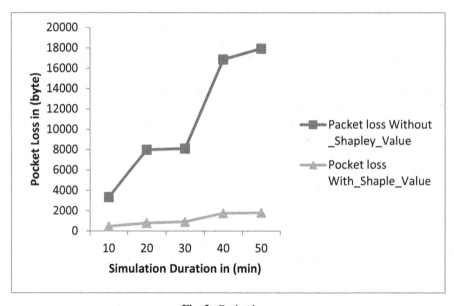

Fig. 3. Packet loss.

The second QoS parameter to be studied for the video streaming application is the packet loss (PL) in Fig. 3. The PL determines the quality of image that is received by the UEs and determines consequently its quality of services. While using the Shapley value, the value of PL is close to zero. As the quality of image is preserved due to the enough data rate allocated to each UE for sending its video. Since, all of the UEs share their data rate with the others in the case of non-use of Shapley value, there will be no priority for them. And as a consequence, PL occurs as the date rate of the cell and it will not be enough to accommodate all of the requests of video traffic of all UEs.

6 Conclusion

Mobile Edge Computing has rapidly developed after cloud computing which provides different services in the network of the operator, like cloud services to the mobile user. MEC is recognized with many characteristics like proximity, real-time access, low latency and offloading. However, due to the fact that MEC servers are located in the access network, because they consume the resources of the access network. Since resources are limited in terms of the data rate, this may lead to a violation of the QoS for MEC applications.

Allocating resources to each type of applications is a challenging issue. And, it depends on how popular is the application and its requirements in terms of QoS. Since MEC servers are collocated with the base stations, it is important to solve this issue by using an appropriate resource allocation in the level of the base station. For providing this, the paper tackled the collaborative game theory approach using Shapley value. The comparisons show that the game theory results perform better than the normal ones adopted by the WLAN which are Round Robin with PCF.

References

1. Wyld, D.C.: Moving to the cloud: an introduction to cloud computing in government. IBM Center for the Business of Government (2009)
2. Clinch, S., Harkes, J., Friday, A., Davies, N., Satyanarayanan, M.: How close is close enough? Understanding the role of cloudlets in supporting display appropriation by mobile users. In: 2012 IEEE International Conference on Pervasive Computing and Communications. pp. 122–127 (2012)
3. Gu, B., Chen, Y., Liao, H., Zhou, Z., Zhang, D.: A distributed and context-aware task assignment mechanism for collaborative mobile edge. Sensors **18**(8), 1424–8220 (2018)
4. Zafari, F., Li, J., Leung, K.K., Towsley, D., Swami, A.: A game-theoretic approach to multi-objective resource sharing and allocation in mobile edge. In: Proceedings of the 2018 on Technologies for the Wireless Edge Workshop, pp. 9–13 (2018)
5. Cao, Z., Zhang, H., Liu, B., Sheng, B.: A game-theoretic framework for revenue sharing in edge-cloud computing system. In: 2018 IEEE 37th International Performance Computing and Communications Conference (IPCCC), pp. 1–8 (2018)
6. Abedin, S.F., Hong, C.S.: Bankruptcy game based computational resource scaling in mobile edge computing. 2018 Korean Netw. Oper. Manage. (2018)
7. Zhang, T.: Data offloading in mobile edge computing: a coalition and pricing based approach. IEEE Access **6**, 2760–2767 (2017)
8. Bahtovski, A., Gusev, M.: Cloudlet challenges. Procedia Eng. **69**, 704–711 (2014)
9. Al-Doghman, F., Chaczko, Z., Ajayan, A.R., Klempous, R.: A review on fog computing technology. In: 2016 IEEE International Conference on Systems, Man, and Cybernetics (SMC), pp. 001525–001530 (2016)
10. www.etsi.org: 2019 Multi-access Edge Computing (MEC). [ONLINE] Available at: https://www.etsi.org/technologies/multi-access-edge-computing. Accessed 17 July 2020
11. Serrano, R.: Cooperative games: Core and Shapley value (No. 2007–11). Working Paper
12. Hadzic, S., Mumtaz, S., Rodriguez, J.: Cooperative game theory and its application in localization algorithms. In: Game Theory Relaunched, p. 173, Intech. (2013)
13. Iturralde, M., Wei, A., Ali-Yahiya, T., Beylot, A.L.: Resource allocation for real time services in LTE networks: resource allocation using cooperative game theory and virtual token mechanism. Wireless Pers. Commun. **72**(2), 1415–1435 (2013)

14. etutorial.org. 2019. Wireless Local Area Networks (WLANs). [ONLINE] Available at: http://etutorials.org/Mobile+devices/mobile+wireless+design/Part+One+Introduction+to+the+Mobile+and+Wireless+Landscape/Chapter+3+Wireless+Networks/Wireless+Local+Area+Networks+WLANs/. Accessed 12 August 2020

15. Published IEEE 802.11 Point Coordination Function (PCF), Intel Services Forum. https://software.intel.com/content/www/us/en/develop/topics/networking.html. Accessed 5 August 2020

16. Software.intel.com.2008. MAC 802.11 Point Coordinator Function. [ONLINE] Available at: https://software.intel.com/content/www/us/en/develop/articles/mac-80211-point-coordinator-function.html. Accessed 5 August 2020

17. Gast, M.: 802.11 wireless networks: the definitive guide. O'Reilly Media, Inc. (2005)

Intelligent Information Systems

Improving Autonomous Vehicles Safety in Snow Weather Using Federated YOLO CNN Learning

Gaith Rjoub[1] , Omar Abdel Wahab[2] , Jamal Bentahar[1]([⊠]) ,
and Ahmed Saleh Bataineh[1]

[1] Concordia Institute for Information Systems Engineering,
Concordia University, Montreal, Canada
{g_rjoub,ah_batai}@encs.concordia.ca, bentahar@ciise.concordia.ca
[2] Department of Computer Science and Engineering,
Université du Québec en Outaouais, Quebec, Canada
omar.abdulwahab@uqo.ca

Abstract. Accurate object detection (e.g., buildings, vehicles, road signs and pedestrians) is essential to the success of the idea of autonomous and self-driving cars. Various object detection techniques have been proposed to enable Autonomous Vehicles (AVs) to achieve reliable safe driving. Most of these techniques are adequate for normal weather conditions, such as sunny or overcast days, but their effectiveness drops when they are exposed to inclement weather conditions, such as days with heavy snowfall or foggy days. In this paper, we propose an object detection system over AVs that capitalizes on the You Only Look Once (YOLO) emerging convolutional neural network (CNN) approach, together with a Federated Learning (FL) framework with the aim of improving the detection accuracy in adverse weather circumstances in real-time. We validate our system on the Canadian Adverse Driving Conditions (CADC) dataset. Experiments show that our solution achieves better performance than traditional solutions (i.e. Gossip decentralized model, and Centralized model).

Keywords: Autonomous Vehicles · Federated Learning · YOLO CNN · Edge Computing · Object Detection

1 Introduction

Increased vehicular activity has triggered considerable traffic congestion, collisions and pollution emissions. The World Health Organization (WHO) has estimated that over a million people were killed on the World's roads in 2016 according to their status report in Global Road Safety Insight of the yearbook

Supported by NSERC and Innovation for Defence Excellence and Security (IDEaS), The Department of National Defence, Canada.

J. Bentahar et al. (Eds.): MobiWIS 2021, LNCS 12814, pp. 121–134, 2021.
https://doi.org/10.1007/978-3-030-83164-6_10

2018 [10]. Thus, in average there are 3700 deaths per day on the World's roads. Over the past decade, significant investments have been put into automated vehicles performance and safety enhancements. Specifically, Information Technology (IT) has been seen as a means to revolutionize vehicle networks. Connecting vehicles via vehicular networks [2, 9, 28] can be used for safety purposes, such as collision alert and crash detection, as well as for supporting other applications, such as vehicle-to-vehicle and vehicle-to-cloud communications.

On the other hand, deploying services at the edge of the network has attracted increasing interest from both academia and industry to address the constraints in terms of onboard computing, connectivity, storage, and energy, while minimizing unnecessary latency in cloud computing scenarios. The next-generation wireless networks are supposed to provide ultra-reliable and ultra-low latency whenever/on-the-move. This will fully meet the current connectivity limitations for the inevitable real-time development demands for automated vehicles. In this respect, integrating machine learning capabilities into vehicles allows for more informed and real-time driving decisions such as pedestrians and cyclists detection.

While most of the current state-of-the-art object detection models are trained and benchmarked on datasets with ideal weather conditions, the aim of this paper is to improve the decision-making process of Autonomous Vehicles (AVs) in snowy conditions. One of the main challenges in object detection in AVs settings is the fact that the amount of labeled data is limited when each vehicle is learning by itself without sharing data with other vehicles. Due to limited resources on each vehicle, any image to be included in the training process requires considerable effort to collect and record. To address this challenge, we employ in this work *Federated Learning (FL)* [22] with the You Only Look Once (YOLO) method, a single Convolutional Neural Network (CNN) that simultaneously predicts multiple bounding boxes and class probabilities for those boxes. The YOLO method has the advantage of being faster than the traditional CNN approaches including faster R-CNN. However, it is less accurate, so by adding the FL to the model, which adds more resource data from the vehicles and the main edge server, we increase the YOLO prediction accuracy. The main advantage of FL is that the vehicles do not share data, but rather train a single shared machine learning model locally on their own data. YOLO has recently been used to handle the object recognition models' difficulties in real-time. It can run up to 155 frames per second and processes its 24 convolutional layers at a very fast speed.

Another challenge of object detection in snowy weather environments is the high communication cost and delay needed to transfer the data (e.g., road conditions, traffic status, etc.) between vehicles, given the high number of data instances that can be collected and the long-distance communications. This challenge is also addressed by the use of the FL paradigm which allows the devices to perform mutually-distributed training of one large machine learning model without having to share the data among the endpoints. FL includes two major phases, namely, small-scaled local training and large-scale global training. At the beginning of the local training, a parameter processor (e.g., an edge server) initiates the machine learning model and provides the initial parameters to the end devices. Then, the edge server combines all the obtained updates in the local computation process to build a global machine learning model. This method is repeated until a certain degree of accuracy is achieved.

1.1 Contributions

The main contributions of the paper can be summarized as follows:

- We propose a FL-based object detection model that capitalizes on the edge computing technology to enable AVs to meet the rapid-growing demands of self-driving and object detection.
- We employ the YOLO CNN that simultaneously predicts multiple bounding boxes and class probabilities for those boxes. This allows the vehicles to make accurate predictions in real-time.
- We study the performance of the proposed solution experimentally on the Canadian Adverse Driving Conditions Dataset (CADC)[1]. The experimental results suggest that our solution achieves a better performance compared to the traditional predicting approaches that could be used to execute FL for objects detection.

1.2 Organization

The rest of the paper is organized as follows. In Sect. 2, we conduct a literature review on the existing FL approaches in cloud and edge computing settings. We also survey the main deep and convolutional neural network learning-based image recognition approaches. In Sect. 3, we describe the details of the proposed solution. In Sect. 4, we explain the experimental environment, evaluate the performance of our solution, and present empirical analysis of our results compared to other benchmarks. Section 5 concludes the paper.

2 Related Work

In this section, we first survey the main approaches that employ FL over edge computing. Then, we study the approaches that study FL over autonomous vehicles. Finally, we give an overview of the deep learning approaches that are used for object detection over autonomous vehicles.

2.1 Federated Learning over Edge Computing

In [26], the authors propose an edge FL (EdgeFed) in which the outputs of the mobile nodes are combined at the edge server to increase the learning performance and decrease the global level of contact and communication frequency.

---

[1] https://cadcd.uwaterloo.ca.

In [29], the authors suggest a FL architecture, called *FedMEC*, that simultaneously combines partition techniques and differential privacy. By breaking a DNN model into two sections, *FedMEC* suggests to offload the complicated computations to the edge servers. In addition, the authors use a differential private data perturbation approach to avoid the leakage of privacy from the local model parameters where Laplace noise interferes with the updates from the local devices to the edge server.

In [23], the authors propose a Mobile Edge Computing (MEC) architecture that embeds a multi-layer, FL protocol named *HybridFL*. *HybridFL* seeks to enhance the performance and alleviate the unreliability of end-users by modulating client choice regionally, leading to an appropriate amount of local cloud updates. In [19], the authors use a Double Deep Q Learning (DDQN) to develop a trust-based and energy-aware FL scheduling method for IoT environments. The trust mechanism aims to detect the IoT devices that over-use or under-use their resources during the local training. Then, the authors develop a DDQN scheduling algorithm to take suitable scheduling decisions that take into consideration the trust values and energy levels of the IoT devices. In [8], the authors suggest a modern federated reinforcement learning architecture wherein each agent independently uses a different device to exchange knowledge, and merges individual models as well as learning parameters with the other agents to form a more mature model. The authors employ the Actor-Critic Proximal Policy Optimization algorithm for exchanging the gradients.

2.2   Federated Learning over Autonomous Vehicles

A selective model aggregation method is proposed in [25], where "fine" local DNN models are chosen and submitted by local image quality assessment and computer capabilities to their central server. The authors use two-Dimensional contract theory as a distributed paradigm for overcoming knowledge asymmetry to promote the connections between central servers and vehicle clients. In [15], the authors examine a new form of vehicular network model, i.e., a Federated Vehicle Network (FVN). This model can be regarded as a robust distributed vehicular network for supporting high-database applications such as computer distribution and FL. In order to enable the transfers and prevent the malicious behaviour, authors capitalize on auxiliary Blockchain-dependent systems.

In [7], the authors suggest an aggregation model for a FL navigation framework called *FedLoc* in the vehicular fog. They argued that their scheme effectively defends model changes trained locally and facilitates participants' fluency in a flexible way. With regards to the idea of connected automobiles that use WiFi Access Points (AP), the authors of [14] use a FL method to investigate the viability of the automobiles. Via an in-depth mathematical study, the authors were able to see how a network control FL algorithm can be better implemented with respect to the existing WiFi specifications and TCP protocol.

In order to increase cache efficiency and preserve vehicle privacy, the authors of [27] propose a modern mobility-aware proactive edge cache model for FL, known as *MPCF*. *MPCF* employs a context-conscious Auto Encoder model to approximate the popularity of content and then positions common content expected at the edge of vehicle networks to minimize latency. In addition, *MPCF* incorporates a cache replacement mobility-aware policy that allows network edges, in reaction to mobility patterns and vehicles' preferences, to add and evict contents.

2.3 Deep Learning for Object Detection over Autonomous Vehicles

In [16], the authors provide a new obstacle detection method that uses a new deep learning approach. A newly developed completely convolutional network model is presented to achieve a semantic pixel-wise marking i the following scenarios: free-space, on-road unexpected barriers, and background. The geometric cues are used with an advanced detection method that uses predictive model-based experiments to determine whether or not there are any hazards in the stereo input pictures. A real-time and lightweight traffic light detector for autonomous vehicle platforms is proposed in [11]. This system identifies all potential traffic lights in a heuristic manner and builds the training model on the GPU server and feeds it with numerous public datasets. It then classifies the outcomes using a lightweight CNN model.

In [6], the authors propose a solution that uses a multi-directional closed-loop steering controller with CNN-based feedback to increase vehicles' handling capabilities and performance in comparison to previous techniques that used pure CNN. This study shows that DAVE-2SKY, a neural network that learns how to steer vehicle lateral control using supervised pre-training and reinforcement learning using images from a camera placed on the vehicle, can perform inference steering wheel angles for self-driving vehicle. In order to achieve a better trajectory prediction, the authors introduce a sequential model in [24], that employs a neural network consisting of a CNN and a long short-term memory network. To obtain valid trajectory data, they use a box-plot to identify and exclude data from the vehicle's trajectories that seem anomalous. Moreover, the trajectories of nearby cars are predicted using CNN space expansion and LSTM time expansion.

3 Our Method

We propose to leverage FL for object detection in AVs environments. FL is an efficient technique to enable distributed training of the YOLO CNN model by involving AVs with edge cloud servers in a practical communication network. This form of collaborative learning helps the vehicles achieve fast and high accurate decisions in real-time.

3.1 FL Mechanism

Let $V = \{v_1, v_2, \ldots, v_x\}$ be a set of x AVs responsible for object detection. Let $D = \{D_1, D_2, \ldots, D_x\}$ be the set of datasets stored in the vehicles where each

D_i is the dataset stored in the vehicle v_i. As shown in Fig. 3, edge cloud adopts a FL structure comprised of the following core components:

- **Edge Server**: The edge server first trains a global YOLO CNN model on a publicly available dataset and then sends the initial parameters to the set of AVs. AVs use these parameters to perform local training on their own data. The edge server then collects the wight of the local models w_{r+1}^v for each vehicle v at the next FL communication round $r + 1$ from the different AVs and aggregates them using the *FedSGD* method [1] as follows:

$$w_{r+1} = \sum_{v=1}^{V} \frac{d_v}{d} w_{r+1}^v \qquad (1)$$

where d_v is the volume of local data available at the v-th vehicle, i.e., $d_v = |D_v|.d$, and d is the size of the whole data across the selected vehicles. The edge server also notifies the AVs about the recent YOLO model updates, resulting from global model aggregation. The objective of the learning model is to minimize the global loss function, i.e.:

$$\min_{w \in \mathbb{R}} L(w) = \frac{1}{|V|} \sum_{v=1}^{V} \frac{d_v}{d} L_v(w) \qquad (2)$$

where $L_v(\cdot)$ is the loss function of each AV v on its own data. L_v can be further written as:

$$L_v(w) = \frac{1}{d_v} \sum_{i=1}^{d_v} \ell_i(w) \qquad (3)$$

where $\ell_i(w)$ is the loss function on each single data sample.
- **Autonomous Vehicles**: As illustrated in Fig. 2, AVs include embedded sensors, such as cameras, tachographs, GPS, lateral acceleration sensors, and are often prepared to host computational and connectivity tools such as CPU, memory, and data communication [27]. Data communication is the process of using computing and communication technologies to transfer data from one place to another, or between participating parties. Images captured using built-in sensors are used to train the local models to predict objects. AVs connect to the edge server to obtain the initial and aggregate model parameters, and each one trains its own YOLO CNN model using its own collected image data and hence derives an updated set of the parameters. AVs upload new local versions to the edge server (using Eq. 4) where they are compiled by the edge server into a new one.

$$w_{r+1}^v = w_r^v - \gamma \nabla L_v(w) \qquad (4)$$

where γ is the fixed learning rate, and $\nabla(\cdot)$ denotes the gradient operation.

Fig. 1. Communication process of AVs federated learning in edge cloud

3.2 YOLO CNN

The latest state-of-the-art CNNs object detections have been trained and benchmarked in ideal weather datasets, suchas the KITTI dataset [5]. However, those datasets do not show how effectively these CNNs function in real-world driving scenarios in which the weather conditions are complicated and changing over time. To address this shortcoming, we use in our work the CADC dataset, which contains annotated Light Detection and Ranging (LiDAR) and camera data in adverse weather conditions, including snow [12]. The CADC dataset can expand the CNN models to more adverse and critical weather conditions (Fig. 1).

A single CNN simultaneously predicts multiple bounding boxes and class probabilities for those boxes. YOLO is one of the most promising state-of- the-art, real time object detection systems [17]. YOLO utilizes features from the whole picture in order to identify and classify each bounding box as well as the classes to which they belong. Like humans, YOLO is capable of quickly recognizing both what items are inside a picture as well as where within the picture those items are located. Our model will first use an input picture, which is divided into a $N \times N$ grid. Each grid cell predicts B bounding boxes and a confidence score β for each box, where our model used $N = 13$ and $B = 5$. This confidence score estimates the probability that the item belongs to a given class, which is successfully detected. This is formally defined as per Eq. 5:

$$\beta = Pr(Object) \times IOU_{pred}^{truth} \tag{5}$$

where IOU_{pred}^{truth} is intersection over the union between the predicted box and the ground truth.

The following five predictions are included in each bounding box: cx, cy, m, h, and β. The box's centroid in reference to the grid cell's bounds is represented by the (cx, cy) coordinates, while m and h are the relative width and height. Each grid cell predicts ζ conditional class probabilities, which are expressed mathematically as follows:

$$\zeta = Pr(Class_i | Object) \tag{6}$$

Finally, we compute the bounding boxes weight by their actual probabilities of containing that object. We compute these weights by multiplying the conditional class probabilities and the individual box confidence predictions [30] as follows:

$$Pr(Class_i | Object) \times Pr(Object) \times IOU_{pred}^{truth} = Pr(Class_i) \times IOU_{pred}^{truth} \tag{7}$$

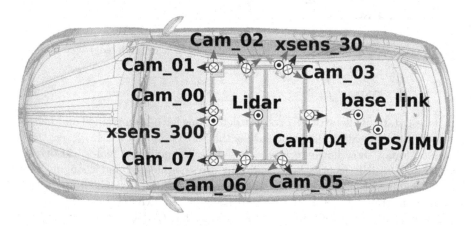

Fig. 2. Overhead view of the vehicle for sensors and cameras (from [13])

4   Implementation and Experiments

4.1   Experimental Setup

We carry out our experiments using the CADC dataset [13], which was produced using the Lincoln MKZ, modified with the Autonomoose AV platform. This autonomous driving dataset, compiled throughout the winter in the region of Waterloo, Canada, is the first dataset to examine and address several types of bad driving circumstances such as low visibility, fog, excessive precipitation snow, etc. It contains 7,000 frames of annotated data from 8 cameras (Ximea MQ013CG-E2), LiDAR (VLP-32C), and a GNSS + INS system (Novatel OEM638), collected through a variety of winter weather conditions. We train a YOLO CNN model on the dataset to determine our algorithm's efficiency and effectiveness. The YOLO model is made up of 24 convolutional layers one after the other and 2 fully connected layers at the end. For pre-training, we use the first 20 convolutional layers followed by an average-pooling layer and a fully connected layer. Keras and TensorFlow (TF) are used to implement the model. Keras is a Python-based neural network API that supports TF. TF, an open-source software framework for dataflow programming created by the Google Brain team, is widely used for a variety of purposes. The FL model is trained on AVs using the Stochastic Gradient Descent (SGD) algorithm, and the training dataset was distributed over 1000 AVs as a Non-IID setting where each AV sampled images randomly but from different subsets of the training data, standing for a more challenging but realistic setting. We varied the number of the selected AVs from 25 to 500 randomly (if its available within the coverage of the edge server) to train the local model. We evaluate the performance of the proposed solution against 1) The decentralized gossip model which does not require an aggregation server or any central component; and 2) The centralized model, the most prevalent strategy, in which a huge quantity of training data is acquired centrally and used to train models across a set of AVs.

4.2   Experimental Results

In Fig. 3, we provide experimental comparisons in terms of training and test accuracy. We run the experiments over 1000 iterations. We observe from this figure that our proposed solution achieves the highest training and test accuracy level compared to the traditional CNN approach and exhibits a better scalability and a faster convergence. This can be justified by the fact that our solution uses YOLO that is designed to be fast and includes a FL component to compensate the lack of data from which some edge servers might suffer and recover this lack by training the model on each AV's local data.

Different from Fig. 3, where we compare the training and test accuracy of our solution against the traditional CNN model, we compare in Fig. 4 the test accuracy of our solution against the centralized and gossip machine learning approaches. We provide experimental comparisons in terms of average test accuracy. The test accuracy quantifies the accuracy obtained by each AV after using the global model trained in a federated fashion to make predictions on its own data. We ran the experiments over 1000 iterations. We observe from this figure that the test accuracy obtained by our model is much higher than those obtained by the gossip and centralized approaches. In particular, the average test accuracy obtained by our model, gossip, and centralized approaches are $90.4\% - 95.2\%$, $82.4\% - 88.1\%$, and $71.4\% - 76.16\%$, respectively. This mean that our model approach enables the AVs to better learn and predict objects in bad weather conditions.

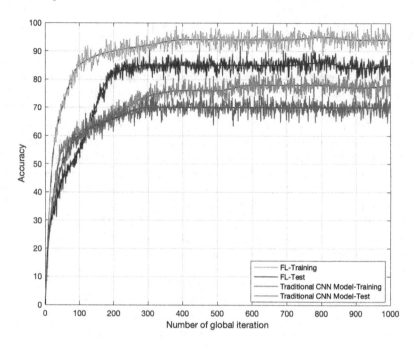

Fig. 3. Comparison of accuracy of final global model

In Fig. 5, we measure the learning time of the different studied approaches, while varying the number of AVs from 25 to 500. The main observation that can be drawn from this figure is that increasing the number of AVs leads to a modest increase in the learning time in the different studied solutions. The figure also reveals that our proposed model achieves the lowest learning time. This is justified by the fact that it distributes the training over the different AVs and aggregates the global model on the edge server, while the gossip model directly exchanges and aggregates models locally at the level of the AVs, which only have a limited resource capabilities. On the other hand, the centralized model needs to gather the training data and train the model on one of the AVs before distributing it across a set of AVs.

In Fig. 6, we measure the accuracy of the different studied approaches, while varying the number of AVs from 10 to 100 and varying also the size of the data available on each AV from 50 to 400. We notice from this figure that increasing the number of AVs leads to a modest increase in the accuracy in the different studied solutions. In fact, the less the data are on AVs, the less the features that can be capitalized on to improve the prediction accuracy would be.

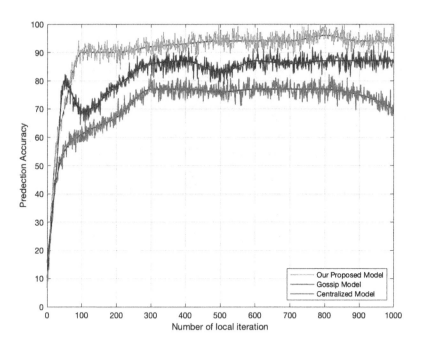

Fig. 4. Comparison of prediction accuracy of local model

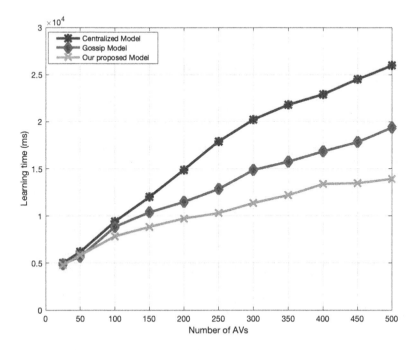

Fig. 5. Learning time versus the number of AVs

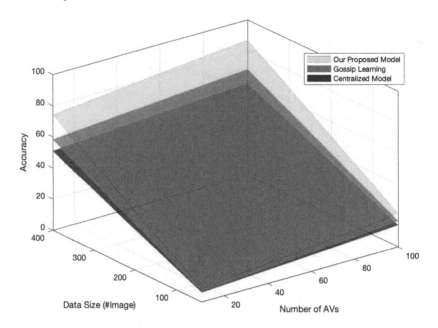

Fig. 6. Accuracy: we study in this figure the impact of varying both the number of AVs and size of data on the accuracy

5   Conclusion

In this work, we proposed a FL-powered YOLO-based approach to improve the real-time object detection predictions over AVs in bad weather conditions. Experiments conducted on the Canadian Adverse Driving Conditions (CADC) dataset reveal that our solution assures the best trade-off between speed and detection accuracy compared to three existing approaches. In the future, we plan to extend this work by investigating a scheduling approach that capitalizes on Deep reinforcement learning [20,21] and trust modeling [3,4,18] to further reduce the training time by avoiding unnecessary computations on untrusted AVs.

References

1. Amiri, M.M., Gündüz, D.: Machine learning at the wireless edge: distributed stochastic gradient descent over-the-air. IEEE Trans. Sig. Process. **68**, 2155–2169 (2020)
2. Cui, J., Wen, J., Han, S., Zhong, H.: Efficient privacy-preserving scheme for real-time location data in vehicular ad-hoc network. IEEE Internet Things J. **5**(5), 3491–3498 (2018)
3. Drawel, N., Bentahar, J., Laarej, A., Rjoub, G.: Formalizing group and propagated trust in multi-agent systems. In: Bessiere, C. (ed.) Proceedings of the Twenty-Ninth International Joint Conference on Artificial Intelligence, IJCAI, pp. 60–66 (2020)

4. Drawel, N., Bentahar, J., Qu, H.: Computationally grounded quantitative trust with time. In: Seghrouchni, A.E.F., Sukthankar, G., An, B., Yorke-Smith, N. (eds.) Proceedings of the 19th International Conference on Autonomous Agents and Multiagent Systems, AAMAS, Auckland, New Zealand, May 9–13, pp. 1837–1839. International Foundation for Autonomous Agents and Multiagent Systems (2020)
5. Geiger, A., Lenz, P., Urtasun, R.: Are we ready for autonomous driving? the kitti vision benchmark suite. In: Conference on Computer Vision and Pattern Recognition (CVPR) (2012)
6. Jhung, J., Bae, I., Moon, J., Kim, T., Kim, J., Kim, S.: End-to-end steering controller with CNN-based closed-loop feedback for autonomous vehicles. In: 2018 IEEE Intelligent Vehicles Symposium (IV), pp. 617–622. IEEE (2018)
7. Kong, Q., Yin, F., Lu, R., Li, B., Wang, X., Cui, S., Zhang, P.: Privacy-preserving aggregation for federated learning-based navigation in vehicular fog. IEEE Transactions on Industrial Informatics (2021)
8. Lim, H.K., Kim, J.B., Kim, C.M., Hwang, G.Y., Choi, H.b., Han, Y.H.: Federated reinforcement learning for controlling multiple rotary inverted pendulums in edge computing environments. In: 2020 International Conference on Artificial Intelligence in Information and Communication (ICAIIC), pp. 463–464. IEEE (2020)
9. Obaidat, M., Khodjaeva, M., Holst, J., Ben Zid, M.: Security and privacy challenges in vehicular ad hoc networks. In: Mahmood, Z. (ed.) Connected Vehicles in the Internet of Things, pp. 223–251. Springer, Cham (2020). https://doi.org/10.1007/978-3-030-36167-9_9
10. World Health Organization et al.: Global status report on road safety 2018: Summary. World Health Organization. Technical Report (2018)
11. Ouyang, Z., Niu, J., Liu, Y., Guizani, M.: Deep CNN-based real-time traffic light detector for self-driving vehicles. IEEE Trans. Mob. Comput. **19**(2), 300–313 (2019)
12. Pitropov, M., Garcia, D., Rebello, J., Smart, M., Wang, C., Czarnecki, K., Waslander, S.: Canadian adverse driving conditions dataset (2020)
13. Pitropov, M., et al.: Canadian adverse driving conditions dataset. Int. J. Robot. Res. **40**(4–5), 681–690 (2021)
14. Pokhrel, S.R., Choi, J.: Improving TCP performance over wiFi for internet of vehicles: a federated learning approach. IEEE Trans. Veh. Technol. **69**(6), 6798–6802 (2020)
15. Posner, J., Tseng, L., Aloqaily, M., Jararweh, Y.: Federated learning in vehicular networks: opportunities and solutions. IEEE Network **35**(2), 152–159 (2021)
16. Ramos, S., Gehrig, S., Pinggera, P., Franke, U., Rother, C.: Detecting unexpected obstacles for self-driving cars: fusing deep learning and geometric modeling. In: 2017 IEEE Intelligent Vehicles Symposium (IV), pp. 1025–1032. IEEE (2017)
17. Redmon, J., Divvala, S., Girshick, R., Farhadi, A.: You only look once: unified, real-time object detection. In: Proceedings of the IEEE Conference on Computer Vision and Pattern Recognition, pp. 779–788 (2016)
18. Rjoub, G., Bentahar, J., Wahab, O.A.: BigTrustScheduling: Trust-aware big data task scheduling approach in cloud computing environments. Future Gener. Comput. Syst. **110**, 1079–1097 (2020)
19. Rjoub, G., Abdel Wahab, O., Bentahar, J., Bataineh, A.: A trust and energy-aware double deep reinforcement learning scheduling strategy for federated learning on IoT devices. In: Kafeza, E., Benatallah, B., Martinelli, F., Hacid, H., Bouguettaya, A., Motahari, H. (eds.) ICSOC 2020. LNCS, vol. 12571, pp. 319–333. Springer, Cham (2020). https://doi.org/10.1007/978-3-030-65310-1_23

20. Sami, H., Mourad, A., Otrok, H., Bentahar, J.: Demand-driven deep reinforcement learning for scalable fog and service placement. IEEE Transactions on Services Computing. In Press (2021). https://doi.org/10.1109/TSC.2021.3075988
21. Sami, H., Otrok, H., Bentahar, J., Mourad, A.: AI-based resource provisioning of IoE services in 6G: a deep reinforcement learning approach. IEEE Transactions on Network and Service Management. In Press (2021). https://doi.org/10.1109/TNSM.2021.3066625
22. Wahab, O.A., Mourad, A., Otrok, H., Taleb, T.: Federated machine learning: Survey, multi-level classification, desirable criteria and future directions in communication and networking systems. IEEE Commun. Surv. Tutorials **23**(2), 1342–1397 (2021)
23. Wu, W., He, L., Lin, W., Mao, R.: Accelerating federated learning over reliability-agnostic clients in mobile edge computing systems. IEEE Trans. Parallel Distrib. Syst. **32**(7), 1539–1551 (2020)
24. Xie, G., Shangguan, A., Fei, R., Ji, W., Ma, W., Hei, X.: Motion trajectory prediction based on a CNN-LSTM sequential model. Sci. China Inf. Sci. **63**(11), 1–21 (2020). https://doi.org/10.1007/s11432-019-2761-y
25. Ye, D., Yu, R., Pan, M., Han, Z.: Federated learning in vehicular edge computing: a selective model aggregation approach. IEEE Access **8**, 23920–23935 (2020)
26. Ye, Y., Li, S., Liu, F., Tang, Y., Hu, W.: EdgeFed: optimized federated learning based on edge computing. IEEE Access **8**, 209191–209198 (2020)
27. Yu, Z., Hu, J., Min, G., Zhao, Z., Miao, W., Hossain, M.S.: Mobility-aware proactive edge caching for connected vehicles using federated learning. IEEE Transactions on Intelligent Transportation Systems (2020)
28. Zhang, D., Ge, H., Zhang, T., Cui, Y.Y., Liu, X., Mao, G.: New multi-hop clustering algorithm for vehicular ad hoc networks. IEEE Trans. Intell. Trans. Syst. **20**(4), 1517–1530 (2018)
29. Zhang, J., Zhao, Y., Wang, J., Chen, B.: FedMEC: improving efficiency of differentially private federated learning via mobile edge computing. Mob. Netw. Appl. **25**(6), 2421–2433 (2020)
30. Zhao, Z.Q., Zheng, P., Xu, S.T., Wu, X.: Object detection with deep learning: a review. IEEE Trans. Neural Netw. Learn. Syst. **30**(11), 3212–3232 (2019)

WhatsApp, an Educational Computer System?

Bangisisi Zamuxolo Mathews Nyembe and Grant Royd Howard(⊠)

University of South Africa (Unisa), Florida, South Africa
54830222@mylife.unisa.ac.za, howargr@unisa.ac.za

Abstract. Can WhatsApp be used as an educational computer system? This question had not been answered conclusively by current research and was a global imperative for the computers and education research and practice communities given that over a quarter of the entire world's population used WhatsApp. To advance the field, educational theory and practice and to give meaning to WhatsApp in education, empirical quantitative evidence was gathered with a questionnaire to measure mobile collaborative learning on WhatsApp. The results indicated that increased collaboration on WhatsApp improved academic achievement and improving other key aspects such as active learning, trust, support, formality, interaction and interdependence enhanced collaboration and, in turn, improved academic achievement. The study advanced educational computer theory and mobile collaborative learning theory and provided evidence-based learning design guidelines for incorporating WhatsApp into learning programs for improved academic achievement.

Keywords: Cooperative/collaborative learning · Mobile learning · Post-secondary education · Social Media · 21st century abilities

1 Introduction

The study asked the question, can WhatsApp be used as an educational computer system? This question was significant and relevant to educators and domain researchers globally, since there were about two billion active WhatsApp users globally as at October 2020, which made WhatsApp most widespread social media application behind Facebook and YouTube [1] and accounted for over a quarter of the entire world's population. This included students throughout the global tertiary education community and offered educators worldwide a free-to-use computer system with a large student user base that was already familiar with the application.

To this end, theory development by the research community is necessary to inform educational practice about the design, not specifically WhatsApp software design but educational program and activity design on WhatsApp, and use decisions required for realizing an effective WhatsApp educational computer system.

Recent research has begun to develop such theory, but to date it remains ambivalent, as is evident in contrasting research reporting that WhatsApp may improve learning [2–4] and WhatsApp may not [5–7]. Thus, conducting scientific research on and developing theory relating to WhatsApp and academic achievement was essential for advancing

© Springer Nature Switzerland AG 2021
J. Bentahar et al. (Eds.): MobiWIS 2021, LNCS 12814, pp. 135–148, 2021.
https://doi.org/10.1007/978-3-030-83164-6_11

the field of computers and education and its sub-fields of social media and academic achievement, mobile collaborative learning (MCL) and mobile learning (m-learning). Furthermore, the study builds requisite meaning among the international research and education communities, where evidence-based knowledge is produced on the relationships between technological progress and educational goals. Following a positivistic epistemology, the study develops original knowledge to answer the research question by gathering quantitative data using a questionnaire from relevant students.

The study advances current research. It addresses questions about the role of social media in supporting academic goals and responds to the requests for new research on the use of social media applications and their impact on academic achievement [8], it explores situated social media practices contextualized within a specific social media platform [9], it sets out to test whether generalized findings about social media and academic performance hold for WhatsApp [10] and it investigates MCL using WhatsApp [11, 12].

This section stated the study's problem, question and objective and explained its significance and contribution to the research field, educational practice and theory advancement. Following is the rigorous instrument development process and initial structural model. Section Three details the rigorous empirical method for answering the research question and provides guidance for replication studies. Section Four presents the study's results and explores their implications. Section Five clarifies the study's contribution to theory progression, exposes the study's limitations and offers opportunities for further advancement of the field.

2 Theoretical Framework

Without there being any prior research on the specific constructs and their interrelationships, theoretical framework, involved in MCL on WhatsApp and academic achievement, the study proceeded to review and evaluate instruments in the literature that measured collaboration from various fields and perspectives. Those that had high reliability, applicability and construct validity were retained and input into the instrument development process, which was guided by the MacKenzie et al. [13] scale development framework. The process resulted in a theoretical framework of ten constructs applicable to the research problem with six measurement items per construct and an initial structural model (see Fig. 1) [14]. The ten constructs were Active Learning (AL), Support (S), Interdependence (ID), Interaction (IA), Formality (F), Sense of Community (SC), Trust (T), Information Exchange (IE), Collaboration (C) and self-reported Academic Achievement (AA).

The study defined each of the constructs as follows. Support (S) is the level of learning-related assistance and help that is provided to a student by other students on WhatsApp. Interaction (IA) is the level of learning-related engagement and reciprocal action, such as sharing, discussing, meeting and chatting, between two or more students on WhatsApp. Sense of Community (SC) is the level of belonging to a WhatsApp learning-related group having common goals, needs and interests. Information Exchange (IE) is the level of learning-related information exchanged during learning on WhatsApp. Interdependence (ID) is the level of condition or contingency on other students for learning on WhatsApp. Active Learning (AL) is the level of WhatsApp learning activities involving meaningful and applied learning activities and is contrasted with passive learning. Formality (F) is the level of serious and academically correct learning-related engagement on WhatsApp between students by virtue of their language in contrast to relaxed and casual engagement. Trust (T) is the level of confidence that a student has in other students when learning on WhatsApp. Collaboration (C) is the level of contributing and working jointly on WhatsApp to attain shared learning goals. Academic Achievement (AA) is typically measured by actual student grades obtained from writing a test or examination [15]. However, the study could not obtain access to actual grade information for each of the respondents and therefore defined Academic Achievement (AA) as the level of a student's self-reported academic achievement.

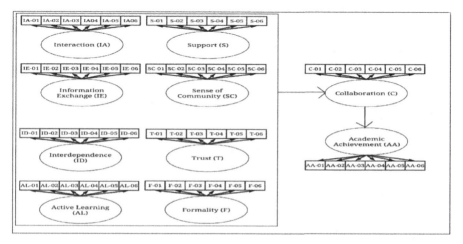

Fig. 1. Initial measurement and structural model.

Since there was no knowledge or theoretical framework available in the literature that specified how these constructs interrelated and it was clear from the literature evaluation that these were key constructs involved in collaboration and collaboration on WhatsApp, the study, at this point, hypothesized that Collaboration (C) influences self-reported Academic Achievement (AA) and the other eight constructs influence Collaboration (C). These hypotheses are described in the study's initial structural model (see Fig. 1).

3   Method

3.1   Strategy and Sampling

The study followed a rigorous positivistic research pattern where primary empirical quantitative data was collected using a questionnaire [16]. The data was gathered from students in two English medium tertiary education institutions located in the Free State province in South Africa. Judgement/purposive sampling was used to select respondents that matched the profile required to address the research problem [17]. The respondents included undergraduate (first- to third-year level) and honours (fourth-year level) students. The sampled students provided relevant data from both academic and vocational qualifications and many different qualification types for breadth of student characteristics and representativeness.

Before any data was collected, written permission was obtained from each of the institutions, ethical clearance was obtained from the researchers' university and each respondent was required to acknowledge informed consent before submitting their questionnaire responses.

Data collection for the main study began in late April 2020 and ended in mid-October 2020 with 393 completed and usable responses from the anonymous Google Forms online questionnaire. 393 responses were considered adequate to address the research problem using structural equation modelling (SEM) since at least two-hundred responses is generally considered enough for effective SEM analysis [18].

4   Results and Discussion

4.1   Reliability

To test the questionnaire's reliability, a pilot study was conducted in early April 2020 with data from sixteen representative students. The data was analyzed with JASP's single-test reliability analysis. JASP was a free multi-platform open-source statistics package implemented in R and a series of R packages and developed and continually updated by researchers at the University of Amsterdam [19]. Subsequently, questionnaire items were amended and/or dropped, which resulted in improved Cronbach's alpha values and acceptable reliability of the final set of questionnaire items [20]. Thereafter, the main study was conducted and the Cronbach's alpha values for each construct based on the main study data are provided in Table 1.

Table 1. Cronbach's alpha reliability analysis – main study.

Construct	Cronbach alpha
(AA) Academic Achievement	0.946
(S) Support	0.927
(IE) Information Exchange	0.925
(SC) Sense of Community	0.923
(C) Collaboration	0.914
(AL) Active Learning	0.899
(T) Trust	0.888
(IA) Interaction	0.884
(F) Formality	0.862
(ID) Interdependence	0.821

4.2 Data Handling

Once the main study data had been collected, data cleaning was performed to identify and address any errors or inconsistencies due to corrupted data or inaccurate data entry. The only changes that were made to the data were in the respondent characteristics section of the questionnaire. These changes included correcting misspelled home languages, modifying the spelling and descriptions of qualifications, and similar. All changes maintained the original meaning of the data. Once cleaned, the data was imported into JASP for all subsequent statistical analyses.

4.3 Respondent Characteristics

Almost two-thirds of the students were female, most students were between the ages of 19 and 24 years old, most of the respondents spoke Sesotho and isiZulu, over eighty percent were registered for bachelor's degrees with a comparatively even distribution across first to fourth year course levels and over a third spent from one to five hours per week on WhatsApp learning with other students. In addition, most students used smartphones at home to learn on WhatsApp and the most frequent barriers to learning on WhatsApp were the cost of data, places with no signal for internet connectivity, places without electrical plug points for charging their devices and places without freely available Wi-Fi hotspots.

4.4 Exploratory Factor Analysis (EFA)

Exploratory factor analysis (EFA) is a statistical technique for exploring the underlying factor structure in a data set and was used to demonstrate whether the items in the questionnaire loaded onto the research model constructs [21] and to assess construct, convergent, discriminant and face validity [22].

Prior to conducting the EFA, a Kaiser-Meyer-Olkin (KMO) test was performed to assess the data set's suitability for EFA. The overall KMO value calculated was 0.95, which demonstrated strong correlation among the items and justified proceeding with the EFA.

Initially, Principal Component Analysis (PCA) was run with varimax rotation, since it is a widely used variable-reduction technique that results in a concise number of principal components with eigenvalues above one [23] and that represent the majority of the variance within the data set [21]. The outcome was nine principal components (see Table 2).

The PCA indicated that only nine principal components accounted for most of the variance in the data, instead of the expected ten per the initial measurement and structural model. In addition, the PCA calculated the loadings of each questionnaire item onto the nine principal components. A factor loading of above 0.4 is generally regarded as a good loading [24], so loadings less than or equal to 0.4 were excluded from the analysis. Based on the PCA, it was decided to drop the construct Sense of Community (SC) as it was evident that all four items relating to SC loaded onto both components PC1 and PC4. However, PC1 also had all four items relating to the construct Support (S) loaded onto it, but with higher loadings than any of the SC items and PC4 also had all four items relating

Table 2. Principal component characteristics.

No.	Eigenvalue	Proportion var.	Cumulative
PC1	18.037	0.451	0.451
PC2	2.619	0.065	0.516
PC3	2.107	0.053	0.569
PC4	1.772	0.044	0.613
PC5	1.538	0.038	0.652
PC6	1.351	0.034	0.686
PC7	1.270	0.032	0.717
PC8	1.064	0.027	0.744
PC9	1.016	0.025	0.769

to the construct Active Learning (AL) loaded onto it, but with higher loadings than any of the SC items. This indicated that the SC items and SC construct could be removed since they did not load uniquely and had weaker loadings than the other construct items that loaded onto PC1 and PC4. The construct Sense of Community (SC) was removed from the initial measurement and structural model and all data relating to the four Sense of Community (SC) items were excluded from further analyses [24].

Thereafter, the often preferred EFA method called Principal Axis Factoring (PAF) [21] with varimax rotation and loadings above 0.4 was conducted based on nine factors indicated during PCA. The PAF demonstrated that each construct's set of four questionnaire items loaded onto a separate factor, which provided support for using the nine-construct model for the subsequent analyses.

4.5   Analysis of Variance (ANOVA)

4.5.1   Objectives and Requirements

To determine if there were any significant systematic variances present in any of the respondent characteristics, such as age or course level, ANOVA was run [25]. Significant systematic variances can provide valuable insights and potentially inform educators about how to structure their teaching with WhatsApp.

Homogeneity of variance is an important assumption of ANOVA, which was determined with Levene's tests. If the p-value for this test was greater than or equal to 0.05 ($p \geq 0.05$), there was no violation of the homogeneity of variance assumption. However, where $p < 0.05$, there was a violation, and ANOVA was not conducted because any interpretation could be misleading.

In addition, ANOVA is an omnibus test that simultaneously tests all possible comparisons to assess whether a statistically significant difference exists amongst any groups, but it cannot specify which groups differ. Specifying the groups that are significantly different required the Tukey's post hoc test, which necessitates a greater difference to establish significance since it controls for Type I errors or a true null hypothesis being rejected.

4.5.2   Gender, Age Range, Home Language, Qualification, Course Level and Hours on WhatsApp every week Learning

Focusing on the gender of the respondents, the Levene's test indicated that ANOVA could proceed for constructs IA, S, ID, T, AL, IE, C and AA ($p \geq 0.05$). However, the ANOVA produced no significant differences on any construct for gender ($p \geq 0.05$). Notably, since the respondents entered either male or female only for gender, an independent samples t-test could have been conducted for each construct to determine any significant differences. This was done for completeness, and the t-tests confirmed no significant differences for gender ($p \geq 0.05$).

Regarding the age range of the respondents, the Levene's test indicated that ANOVA could proceed for constructs IA, S, ID, T, AL, F, IE C and AA ($p \geq 0.05$) and the ANOVA indicated that there were significant differences ($p < 0.05$) on the constructs IA, T, AL, IE and C only.

For construct IA, T and AL, Tukey's test showed that there were significant differences ($p < 0.05$) between the groups 19 to 24 years old and 35 to 39 years old and between the groups 25 to 29 years old and 35 to 39 years old, which suggests that the 35 to 39 years old age group interacted, trusted and actively learned less on WhatsApp than the younger groups as was evident by their lower mean score for these constructs.

For construct IE, Tukey's test showed a significant difference ($p < 0.05$) between the groups 25 to 29 years old and 35 to 39 years old, which suggests that the 35 to 39 years old age group exchanged less information on WhatsApp than the younger group as was evident by their lower mean score for the IE construct.

However, for construct C, Tukey's test showed no significant differences between any of the groups ($p \geq 0.05$). Overall, the ANOVA suggests that the 35 to 39 years old age group, who represented less than 1% of the respondents, may have trusted less on WhatsApp and interacted, actively learnt and exchanged less information than some of the younger groups. Notably, this age group could be at any course level, from first year to fourth year, so these results are independent of the course level findings.

For the home language of the respondents, the Levene's test indicated that ANOVA could proceed for constructs IA, S, T, AL, F, IE, C and AA ($p \geq 0.05$). Subsequently, the ANOVA indicated that there was a significant difference ($p < 0.05$) on the construct AA only and Tukey's test showed a significant difference between the language groups Sesotho sa Leboa and Setswana only for this construct ($p < 0.05$). While it was not clear why there was a significant difference on academic achievement specifically between these two languages and none of the other languages, the descriptive statistics showed that Sesotho sa Leboa had a mean of 10.82 and a standard deviation of 4.81 and Setswana had a mean of 18.10 and a standard deviation of 2.38. Nevertheless, these two languages accounted for only 5.3% of the respondents and further studies with much larger samples of these specific language speakers would be required to investigate whether this finding was valid across their broad populations.

In terms of the qualifications, the Levene's test indicated that ANOVA could proceed for constructs IE, C and AA ($p \geq 0.05$). However, the ANOVA indicated that there were significant differences (p < 0.05) on the constructs IE and AA only and Tukey's test showed significant differences for the construct IE only (p < 0.05).

Tukey's test showed significant differences for the construct IE between each of the qualifications Bachelor of Science (BSc), Bachelor of Education (BEd), Bachelor of Social Sciences (BSocSci), Bachelor of Arts (BA), Postgraduate Certificate in Education (FET) (PGCE) and the group Various other bachelor's and honours degrees, diplomas and certificates (VoDDC). This may be suggestive of information volume differences between the more traditional bachelor's degrees and the various other bachelor's and honours degrees, diplomas and certificates, since the VoDDC group had a lower mean score on information exchange.

With reference to course level, the Levene's test indicated that ANOVA could proceed for constructs IA, S, ID, AL, IE and C (p ≥ 0.05). The ANOVA indicated that there were significant differences (p < 0.05) on the constructs IA, S, IE and C only and Tukey's test agreed on those four constructs (p < 0.05).

For the IA and IE constructs, Tukey's test showed a significant difference between first-year level and third-year level, with third-year level having a higher mean construct score. For the S construct Tukey's test showed significant differences first-year level and third-year level and between third-year level and fourth-year level, with third-year level having the highest mean construct score.

For the C construct Tukey's test showed significant differences between first-year level and third-year level, between first-year level and fourth-year level and between second-year level and third-year level, with third-year level having the highest mean construct score followed by the second-year level then the fourth-year level and finally the first-year level. These results suggest that the more advanced third-year students, who represented almost a third of the respondents, made more use of WhatsApp to interact, support, exchange information and collaborate.

In relation to the hours spent on WhatsApp every week learning, the Levene's test indicated that ANOVA could proceed for constructs IA, ID, F, IE, C and AA (p ≥ 0.05). ANOVA indicated that there were significant differences (p < 0.05) on the constructs IA, ID, F, IE and C only and Tukey's test agreed (p < 0.05).

Tukey's test showed significant differences for the constructs IA and ID between group 0 – <1 h and group 10 – <20 h and between group 0 – <1 h and group 40+ hours, with the group 0 – <1 h having the highest mean construct score.

For the construct F, Tukey's test showed significant differences between group 0 – <1 h and group 20 – <40 h and between group 0 – <1 h and group 40+ hours, with the group 0 – <1 h having the highest mean construct score.

For the construct IE, Tukey's test showed significant differences between group 0 – <1 h and each of groups 1 – <5 h, 5 – <10 h, 10 – <20 h, 20 – <40 h and 40+ hours, with the group 0 – <1 h having the highest mean construct score.

In addition, for the construct C, Tukey's test showed significant differences between group 0 – <1 h and each of groups 5 – <10 h, 10 – <20 h, 20 – <40 h and 40+ hours, with the group 0 – <1 h having the highest mean construct score.

These results suggest that the students who spend between 0 – <1 h on What-sApp every week learning, experience the most interaction, information exchange, collaboration, formality and interdependence.

4.6   Structural Equation Modeling (SEM)

4.6.1   Objectives and Software

To test and evaluate the research model hypotheses, measure the relationships amongst the constructs and answer the research question, SEM was conducted. The SEM was processed in JASP, whose SEM module was based on the lavaan package in R [26, 27], which was a free open-source commercial-quality statistical package for latent variable modeling.

4.6.2   Initial SEM Structural Model Specification

The initial SEM structural model was specified using the following hypothesized inter-relationships and processed using the maximum likelihood (ML) method: Trust (T), Interaction (IA), Interdependence (ID), Support (S), Information Exchange (IE), Formality (F) and Active Learning (AL) influences Collaboration (C) and Collaboration (C) influences Academic Achievement (AA).

However, the χ^2 (absolute/predictive fit Chi-square), RMSEA (root mean square error of approximation) and TLI (Tucker-Lewis index) or NNFI (non-normed fit index) model fit indices (MFIs) were not at acceptable levels and MFIs are necessary to support claims that the theoretical and structural relations adequately agree with the observed data [28]. Thus, the SEM structural model required re-specification.

4.6.3   Re-specified SEM Structural Model

Re-specification of the SEM structural model was done to achieve acceptable MFIs and to ensure that the interrelationships between Active Learning (AL), Formality (F), Interaction (IA), Support (S), Information Exchange (IE), Trust (T) and Interdependence (ID) were measured.

The re-specification was guided by the modification indices calculated in JASP. Modification indices indicate whether changes such as adding paths to the SEM structural model would result in improvements and is the Chi-square (χ^2) value by which the model fit would improve if the changes were made [29]. Table 3 provides the model fit indices for the re-specified SEM structural model.

Given the many significant relationships in the re-specified SEM structural model, it is split into two diagrams also for visual ease, namely Diagram One and Diagram Two. Diagram One is presented in Fig. 2 and shows how the other constructs influence Collaboration (C) and how Collaboration (C) influences Academic Achievement (AA). Figure 2 excludes the interrelationships among the constructs Active Learning (AL), Formality (F), Interaction (IA), Support (S), Information Exchange (IE), Trust (T) and Interdependence (ID). Diagram One suggests that Collaboration (C) had a strong positive influence on Academic Achievement (AA), Active Learning (AL) had a moderate positive influence on Collaboration (C) and the other constructs with solid lines had weak positive influences on Collaboration (C).

Diagram Two is presented in Fig. 3 and shows the influences amongst the constructs Active Learning (AL), Formality (F), Interaction (IA), Support (S), Information Exchange (IE), Trust (T) and Interdependence (ID). Diagram Two highlights that Formality (F) and especially Trust (T) were antecedent constructs that positively influenced

Table 3. Re-specified SEM structural model - MFIs.

MFI	Recommended limit	Calculated value	Acceptable fit?
χ^2 (absolute/predictive fit Chi-square)	≤ 3.0	2.905	Yes
SRMR (standardized root mean square residual)	≤ 0.8	0.045	Yes
RMSEA (root mean square error of approximation)	<0.06 to 0.08 with confidence interval	0.070 (90% confidence interval $= 0.045$–0.095)	Yes
CFI (comparative fit index)	≥ 0.95	0.984	Yes
TLI (Tucker-Lewis index) or NNFI (non-normed fit index)	≥ 0.95 can be $0 >$ TLI $>$ 1 for acceptance	0.961	Yes

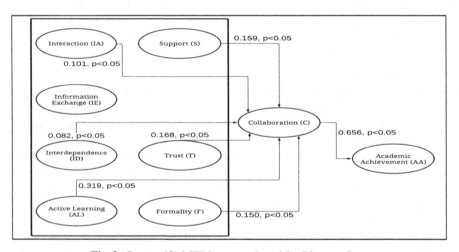

Fig. 2. Re-specified SEM structural model – Diagram One.

the other constructs, while not influencing each other. This could be due to Trust (T) and Formality (F) being constructs relating to necessary mental dispositions, in contrast to Active Learning (AL), Interaction (IA), Support (S) and Information Exchange (IE) that relate to subsequent actions. Diagram Two suggests that Trust (T) had a moderate to strong positive influence on Active Learning (AL), Interaction (IA), Support (S), Information Exchange (IE) and Interdependence (ID) while Formality (F) had a weak positive influence on Active Learning (AL) and Interdependence (ID). Thus, Trust (T) appeared to be an important requirement for all the constructs, while increased Formality (F) may be required for Active Learning (AL) and Interdependence (ID).

Support (S) did not influence any other constructs but was moderately positively influenced by Trust (T), Information Exchange (IE) and Interaction (IA), and weakly positively influenced by Active Learning (AL).

Active Learning (AL) had weak relationships with all the other constructs, except Trust (T), and was either influenced by or influencing them. Interaction (IA) had weak positive influences on Active Learning (AL), Support (S) and Information Exchange (IE), Information Exchange (IE) had a weak positive influence on Support (S) and Interdependence (ID) had a weak positive influence on Active Learning (AL).

Diagram Two supports the study's literature analysis and synthesis which indicated that these constructs were associated with collaboration. While the interrelationships exposed by the re-specified SEM structural model appear complex, they were theoretically justifiable both at face value and in terms of the literature and construct definitions. The SEM provided evidence of the important constructs and their interrelationships when learning with WhatsApp.

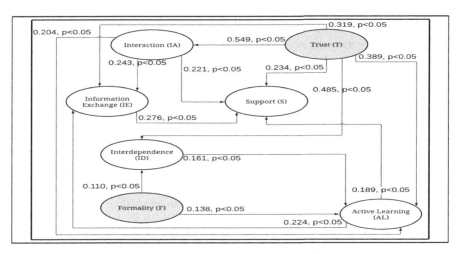

Fig. 3. Re-specified SEM structural model – Diagram Two.

SEM provided an efficient method for specifying and analyzing the interrelationships among the constructs and tested the hypothesized relationships. In particular, it was evident that collaboration had a strong positive influence on self-reported academic achievement, active learning a moderate positive influence on collaboration and trust a moderate to strong influence on all associated aspects including active learning.

5 Conclusion

The study provided empirical evidence that WhatsApp can be used as an educational computer system, which answers an important global question and advances theory and educational practice, especially given the size of the WhatsApp user base and its availability worldwide in educational institutions.

The evidence that collaboration on WhatsApp improves academic achievement progresses and corroborates recent studies reporting that WhatsApp may improve learning [2–4]. Furthermore, in light of contrasting studies that WhatsApp may not improve learning [5–7], the study exposes a replicable, measurable and quantifiable epistemology for knowing key constructs and their interrelationships, the theory, involved in learning on WhatsApp. In addition, the study furthers understanding about how to design learning with WhatsApp for improved learning.

The study moves forward current research, theory and practice by responding to the request for new research on the use of social media applications and their impact on academic achievement [8], explored situated social media practices contextualized within a specific social media platform, namely WhatsApp [9], tested whether generalized findings about social media and academic performance hold for WhatsApp [10] and investigated MCL using WhatsApp [11, 12].

For teaching practice, the findings extend our comprehension of the key elements involved in learning on WhatsApp and provide insights into how these elements should be designed to produce an educational computer system and improve academic achievement. It would be important to design learning activities for a high level of collaboration on WhatsApp since there is a positive relationship between collaboration and academic achievement. Then, the design should consider the development and maintenance of trust and formality during learning activities on WhatsApp as these aspects are indicated as essential for improving active learning, support, interaction and interdependence, all of which influence collaboration. In addition, learning design should include specific activities that require students to actively learn, support one another, interact and foster interdependence as these would enhance collaboration and, in turn, improve academic achievement. Furthermore, educators should design learning activities differently for different course levels so that first- and second-year level students are encouraged more to interact, support, exchange information and collaborate during their learning activities, as third year students appear to require less encouragement. Also, it may be necessary to provide additional support to older students in the 35 to 39 years old age group, who may not trust learning activities on WhatsApp and interact, actively learn and exchanged less information than the younger groups. Interestingly, learning programs making use of WhatsApp should design for short periods on WhatsApp only, such as an hour per week, as these time periods appear to be the most constructive with high levels of interaction, information exchange, formality, interdependence and collaboration.

The study did have limitations, which expose new research opportunities. A limitation relates to the study's sampling method which, while rigorous, relevant and efficient, may constrain generalizability. Future studies could test and advance the theory developed in the study in and across different country, cultural, language and urban contexts. In addition, the study's data was gathered from respondents at one point in time, a cross-sectional study, and studying these phenomena on a longitudinal basis could expose new knowledge about the interactions amongst the research constructs and discover new patterns of student learning behavior.

References

1. Statista.com: Most popular social networks worldwide as of October 2020, ranked by number of active users. https://www.statista.com/statistics/272014/global-social-networks-ranked-by-number-of-users/#professional. Accessed 17 Jan 2021
2. Pimmer, C., Brühlmann, F., Odetola, T.D., Oluwasola, D.O., Dipeolu, O., Ajuwon, A.J.: Facilitating professional mobile learning communities with instant messaging. Comput. Educ. **128**, 102–112 (2019). https://doi.org/10.1016/j.compedu.2018.09.005
3. Eid, M.I.M., Al-Jabri, I.M.: Social networking, knowledge sharing, and student learning: the case of university students. Comput. Educ. **99**, 14–27 (2016). https://doi.org/10.1016/j.compedu.2016.04.007
4. Rasheed, M.I., Malik, M.J., Pitafi, A.H., Iqbal, J., Anser, M.K., Abbas, M.: Usage of social media, student engagement, and creativity: the role of knowledge sharing behavior and cyberbullying. Comput. Educ. **159**, 1–12 (2020). https://doi.org/10.1016/j.compedu.2020.104002
5. Alkhalaf, A.M., Tekian, A., Park, Y.S.: The impact of WhatsApp use on academic achievement among Saudi medical students. Med. Teach. **40**, S10–S14 (2018). https://doi.org/10.1080/0142159X.2018.1464652
6. Whelan, E., Islam, A.K.M.N., Brooks, S.: Applying the SOBC paradigm to explain how social media overload affects academic performance. Comput. Educ. **143**, 1–12 (2020). https://doi.org/10.1016/j.compedu.2019.103692
7. Liebherr, M., Schubert, P., Antons, S., Montag, C., Brand, M.: Smartphones and attention, curse or blessing? - A review on the effects of smartphone usage on attention, inhibition, and working memory. Comput. Hum. Behav. Rep. **1**, 1–8 (2020). https://doi.org/10.1016/j.chbr.2020.100005
8. Lacka, E., Wong, T.C., Haddoud, M.Y.: Can digital technologies improve students' efficiency? Exploring the role of virtual learning environment and social media use in higher education. Comput. Educ. **163**, 1–11 (2021). https://doi.org/10.1016/j.compedu.2020.104099
9. Manca, S., Bocconi, S., Gleason, B.: "Think globally, act locally": a glocal approach to the development of social media literacy. Comput. Educ. **160**, 1–17 (2021). https://doi.org/10.1016/j.compedu.2020.104025
10. Giunchiglia, F., Zeni, M., Gobbi, E., Bignotti, E., Bison, I.: Mobile social media usage and academic performance. Comput. Human Behav. **82**, 177–185 (2018). https://doi.org/10.1016/j.chb.2017.12.041
11. Fu, Q.-K., Hwang, G.-J.: Trends in mobile technology-supported collaborative learning: a systematic review of journal publications from 2007 to 2016. Comput. Educ. **119**, 129–143 (2018). https://doi.org/10.1016/j.compedu.2018.01.004
12. Kirschner, P.A., Sweller, J., Kirschner, F., Zambrano, J.: From cognitive load theory to collaborative cognitive load theory. Int. J. Comput.-Supp. Collab. Learn. **13**(2), 213–233 (2018). https://doi.org/10.1007/s11412-018-9277-y
13. MacKenzie, S.B., Podsakoff, P.M., Podsakoff, N.P.: Construct measurement and validation procedures in MIS and behavioral research: integrating new and existing techniques. MIS Q. **35**, 293–334 (2011). https://doi.org/10.2307/23044045
14. Nyembe, B.Z.M., Howard, G.R.: Development of a Quantitative Instrument to Measure Mobile Collaborative Learning (MCL) Using WhatsApp: The Conceptual Steps. Lecture Notes in Computer Science **12066**, 507–519 (2020). https://doi.org/10.1007/978-3-030-44999-5_42
15. Allen, J.D.: Grades as valid measures of academic achievement of classroom learning. Clear. House A J. Educ. Strateg. Issues Ideas. **78**, 218–223 (2005). https://doi.org/10.3200/TCHS.78.5.218-223

16. Sekaran, U., Bougie, R.: Research Methods for Business: A Skill Building Approach. John Wiley and Sons, Chichester, United Kingdom (2013)
17. Tongco, M.D.C.: Purposive sampling as a tool for informant selection. Ethnobot. Res. Appl. **5**, 147–158 (2007). https://doi.org/10.17348/era.5.0.147-158
18. Hoe, S.L.: Issues and procedures in adopting structural equation modelling technique technique. J. Appl. Quant. Meth. **3**, 76–83 (2008). https://ink.library.smu.edu.sg/sis_research/5168
19. Love, J., et al.: JASP: Graphical statistical software for common statistical designs. J. Stat. Softw. **88**, 1–17 (2019). https://doi.org/10.18637/jss.v088.i02
20. Nunnally, J.C.: Psychometric Theory. McGraw-Hill, New York (1976)
21. Costello, A.B., Osborne, J.: Best practices in exploratory factor analysis: Four recommendations for getting the most from your analysis. Pract. Assessment, Res. Eval. **10**, 1–9 (2005). https://doi.org/10.7275/jyj1-4868
22. Worthington, R.L., Whittaker, T.A.: Scale development research: a content analysis and recommendations for best practices. Couns. Pyschol. **34**, 806–838 (2006). https://doi.org/10.1177/0011000006288127
23. Reinard, J.C.: Communication Research Statistics. Sage, Thousand Oaks, California (2006)
24. Howard, M.C.: A review of exploratory factor analysis decisions and overview of current practices: what we are doing and how can we improve? Int. J. Hum. Comput. Interact. **32**, 51–62 (2016). https://doi.org/10.1080/10447318.2015.1087664
25. Tredoux, C., Durrheim, K. (eds.): Numbers, Hypotheses & Conclusions: A Course in Statistics for the Social Sciences. UCT Press, Cape Town (2005)
26. Rosseel, Y.: lavaan: an R package for structural equation modeling. J. Stat. Softw. **48**, 1–36 (2012). https://doi.org/10.18637/jss.v048.i02
27. Rosseel, Y.: The lavaan tutorial. https://lavaan.ugent.be/tutorial/index.html. Accessed 25 May 2021
28. Schreiber, J.B., Nora, A., Stage, F.K., Barlow, E.A., King, J.: Reporting structural equation modeling and confirmatory factor analysis results: a review. J. Educ. Res. **99**, 323–338 (2006). https://doi.org/10.3200/JOER.99.6.323-338
29. Whittaker, T.A.: Using the modification index and standardized expected parameter change for model modification. J. Exp. Educ. **80**, 26–44 (2012). https://doi.org/10.1080/00220973.2010.531299

Transfer Learning on Inception ResNet V2 for Expiry Reminder: A Mobile Application Development

Wi-Yi Ong, Chian-Wen Too$^{(\boxtimes)}$, and Kok-Chin Khor

Lee Kong Chian Faculty of Engineering Science, Universiti Tunku Abdul Rahman,
Bandar Sg. Long, 43000 Kajang, Malaysia
ongwiyi@1utar.my, {toocw,kckhor}@utar.edu.my

Abstract. Expiry dates are general information that every product has. It represents the recommended period to use a product. However, it is hard to keep track of the expiry date when there are many products to keep. In this work, we aim to solve the problem using the transfer learning technique in deep learning. We trained a Convolutional Neural Network (CNN) - Inception ResNet V2 with a synthetic data set that contains images of near-reality expiry dates. The Inception ResNet V2 has achieved an accuracy of 0.9964 using synthetic images and an accuracy of 0.9612 using real noisy images. Training and deploying the Inception ResNet v2 into the mobile application we built help users record and track expiry dates fast and efficiently. The usability test we conducted gave a score of 85.7 based on the System Usability Scale (SUS). The score shows that users had a good experience using the mobile application.

Keywords: Expiry date · Transfer learning · Inception ResNet V2 · Mobile application

1 Introduction

Food, beverage, medicine, and many other products must have a durable life date – the expiry date. Unfortunately, people nowadays are too busy to care about the expiry date of every product in their home. From the statistics shown by Malaysian Food Waste [1], food waste took up 44.5% of Malaysia's waste composition, followed by plastics waste which is 13.2%. Most of the food waste comes from households, from the expired food and groceries thrown away. A recent news report showed that a substantial amount of food waste could be avoided [2].

Consumers may not remember the expiry date of each product. It is also inconvenient for consumers to record down every product's expiry date manually for reminding purpose. Even if the consumers are willing to do so, they may easily lose track of the expiry dates.

The proposed Expiry Reminder application in this project aims to provide consumers with a way of managing the expiry dates of the products they purchased. The mobile

© Springer Nature Switzerland AG 2021
J. Bentahar et al. (Eds.): MobiWIS 2021, LNCS 12814, pp. 149–160, 2021.
https://doi.org/10.1007/978-3-030-83164-6_12

application makes managing expiry dates easy and helps to reduce household waste. The mobile application uses a deep learning model - Inception ResNet V2, to recognise expiry dates with a camera.

The remaining of the paper is as organised as follows. Section 2 provides a review of the existing mobile applications, mobile application development frameworks and various deep learning models. Section 3 describes the system architecture for the mobile application and the methodology for building the deep learning model. The results of training and testing the model shall be discussed in Sect. 4. Finally, we conclude this project in Sect. 5.

2 Technologies Review

2.1 Overview of Existing Mobile Applications

Five existing Expiry Reminder mobile application are studied: Expiry Wiz [3], Aladdinpro-expiry reminders [4], Expired – Grocery Reminder & Alerts App [5], Before Expiry [6] and Expiry Reminder [7]. Three of them are on the Android platform, while the rest are on the iOS platform. These products have product management features and push notifications to notify users that a product is about to expire. Most applications provide a product categorise feature for customers to monitor their products and a reminder feature to remind users of the product's expiry date. Furthermore, the applications include search by barcode features, enabling users to find a product by simply scanning a barcode.

However, as a product expires, most applications do not handle it properly. The product will either appear in the product list as expired or chosen to be deleted by the consumers. The application can be improved by adding the expired product to an in-app shopping list so that consumers can be reminded to restock the product again.

Apart from that, existing applications only allow users to enter a product detail manually. As a result, the key-in operation becomes very tedious and inefficient, and consumers may lose interest in the application. Expiry date recognition can be implemented to speed up adding expiry dates, which sometimes are tiny and unreadable.

2.2 Mobile Application Development Frameworks

There are several different frameworks available in the industry to allow developers to create a hybrid app effortlessly. Xamarin [8], Flutter [9], and React Native [10] are the famous frameworks used by many developers.

Xamarin

Xamarin is a commercial cross-platform development tool owned by Microsoft. It is built based on the.Net framework and uses C# to create hybrid or cross-platform mobile applications. Xamarin [8] is known for creating applications that have almost native-like performance levels. Plus, Xamarin allows developers to use Xamarin, iOS [11], and Android [12] to customise the applications if needed manually.

Flutter

Flutter is an open-source, cross-platform mobile app development framework created by Google. Dart [13] is the programming language used by Flutter and is a modern language developed by Google in 2011, stated by Thomas [14]. Flutter framework is supported by Android Studio and Visual Studio Code, and it includes a Software Development Kit (SDK) that assists developers in compiling code into native machine code, as well as a platform that contains a collection of reusable UI elements such as buttons, text inputs, sliders, and many more that enable developers to build visually appealing applications. Flutter also enables developers to configure the UI feature and enhance the application's UI.

React Native

React Native is an open-source programming tool for Facebook's cross-platform smartphone software. Its programming language is JavaScript, which is well-known by professional web application developers. React Native includes many native UI elements for both the iOS and Android platforms, giving the application a native feel. The React Native framework can also access native functions such as a camera. Besides, React Native has a hot reload feature, which enables users to make changes to the app in real-time.

2.3 Convolutional Neural Network (CNN)

CNN is a type of feed-forward neural networks based on Artificial Neural Network (ANN) [15–17]. CNN differs from ANN in its hidden layers. Yu et al. [18] stated that CNN's hidden layer comprises three layers: convolutional layer, sub-sampling layer or pooling layer, and fully connected layer.

The convolutional layer uses filters to perform feature extraction. Each filter contains a bias and the activation function, i.e., Rectified Linear Unit (ReLU). A pooling layer is used to down-sampling and reduce the dimension of the feature map. A max-pooling layer can take the highest value and assist in extracting low-level features such as edges, while an average pooling layer is good in extracting smooth features by taking the average value. After performing several rounds of features extracting and down-sampling, a fully connected layer is used to flatten the features into a one-dimensional layer. Lastly, the features are classified at the output layer by using Softmax as the activation function.

Each CNN layer (Convolutional layers+Pooling layers) learns different concepts in each layer. Basic feature detection filters, such as edges, are learned in the first few layers. In the middle layers, feature detection filters such as object parts are learned. The feature detection filters in the final layers learn and identify the entire object in various shapes and positions.

Many pre-trained models, including ResNet [19], GoogleNet [20], EfficientNet [21], uses CNN as their architecture, and these pre-trained networks are performing well in classifying images. According to Kranthi Kumar et al. [22], CNN is used in image classification, feature extraction and recognition. Its simple architecture allows us to create an efficient neural network with high recognition accuracy. It can also be combined with other neural networks to become a modular type for conducting more complex recognition tasks.

3 Methodology

3.1 System Architecture

The development framework for the mobile application is Flutter. Flutter has many libraries and packages that make it easy to integrate with Firebase Backend Services and the tflite deep learning model. Furthermore, Flutter has a collection of UI widgets that can rapidly and easily build an appealing and interactive UI.

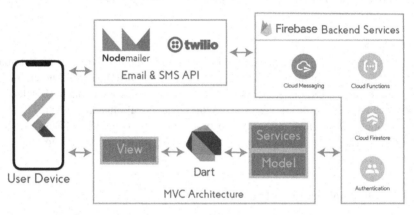

Fig. 1. The system architecture for the mobile application.

The system architecture design used for the mobile application is Model View Controller (MVC) architecture and microservices. The model contains the application's data structure from the database and directly manages the data. The view is any representation of information that accepts user input and display output. The Controller shall process the user input before passing back to the model or manipulate data before passing it to view. On the other hand, cloud microservices are also used to automate backend services. Both architectures are used together to provide a good user experience and, at the same time, ensure easy modification of the code in the future. The overall system architecture design is as shown in Fig. 1. Figure 2 shows the sample screenshots of the mobile application.

3.2 Features of the Mobile Application

The Expiry Reminder application includes:

1. Managing products
2. Managing category of the product
3. Manage the in-app shopping list
4. Automated added product into the in-app shopping list when the product is expired or out-of-stock
5. Use Inception ResNet V2 to recognise expiry date

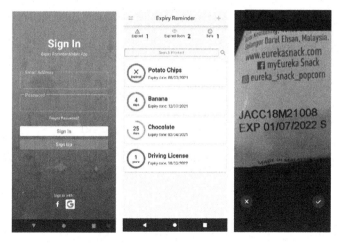

Fig. 2. Sample screenshots of the mobile application.

6. Use a barcode to search a product and retrieve product details
7. Provide multiple Push Notification Alerts, SMS Notification Alerts, and Email Notification Alerts to remind users about the expiry date of the product

Although the mobile application contains the functionalities mentioned above, this paper focuses mainly on the fifth feature – to use Inception ResNet V2 to recognise expiry date. A description shall be given starting from data set creation to model evaluation.

3.3 Transfer Learning Inception ResNet V2

We trained the pre-trained model - Inception ResNet V2 and used it in this mobile application to recognise a product packaging's expiry dates.

Dataset Generation
We generated a close to reality image data set to train the deep learning model. A python script was written to generate the data set automatically with various customisations. The script started by generating dates starting from the defined start date to the end date. Then, date strings with different formats were generated for each date. The dates were stored in a text file and used by the TRDG [23] library to generate images. A folder was created according to the class index, and the TRDG library generates the images into the folder. There were three classes generated for each date and one special class generated for each month. Table 1 shows the date format generated for each date, and Fig. 3 shows the samples of the synthetic dates.

Hyperparameter Tuning
Hyperparameter tuning is critical to train a deep learning model for performance. There are two methods for tuning hyperparameters. The first is to tune the hyperparameter manually, and the second is to computerise the tuning process to find the best hyperparameter. At the start of the experiment, hyperparameters were manually tuned to see

Table 1. Various date formats for training the deep learning model.

Date format	Format included	Example
ddMMyy	ddMMyy	011221
	dd MM yy	01 12 21
	dd MM yy	01 12 21
	dd-MM-yy	01-12-21
	dd - MM – yy	01 - 12 - 21
	dd/MM/yy	01/12/21
	dd/MM/yy	01/12/21
	dd.MM.yy	01.12.21
	dd. MM. yy	01. 12. 21
ddMMyyyy	ddMMyyyy	01122021
	dd MM yyyy	01 12 2021
	dd MM yyyy	01 12 2021
	dd-MM-yyyy	01-12-2021
	dd - MM - yyyy	01 - 12 - 2021
	dd/MM/yyyy	01/12/2021
	dd/MM/yyyy	01/12/2021
	dd.MM.yyyy	01.12.2021
	dd. MM. yyyy	01. 12. 2021
yyyyMMdd	yyyyMMdd	20211201
	yyyy MM dd	2021 12 01
	yyyy MM dd	2021 12 01
	yyyy-MM-dd	2021-12-01
	yyyy - MM - dd	2021 - 12 - 01
	yyyy/MM/dd	2021/12/01
	yyyy/MM/dd	2021/12/01
	yyyy.MM.dd	2021.12.01
	yyyy. MM. dd	2021. 12. 01
MMyyyy	MMyyyy	Dec2021

Fig. 3. Samples of synthetic data generated.

how each parameter interacts with the model. A set of suitable hyperparameters were then generated for later tuning with Grid Search.

The hyperparameters to tune are the batch size, the learning rate and the dropout rate. Batch size is the number of training example fed to the model in an iteration. The larger the batch size, the more data fed in one iteration. Thus, more computing resources shall be needed. On the other hand, the learning rate determines how much a model can adjust to the expected error each time its weights are changed. The model learns more as its learning rate increases and vice versa. However, a high learning rate may result in overfitting, while a low learning rate may prolong the training process or cause the model to stuck at the same accuracy. Dropout is the method used to regularise the model for minimising overfitting and enhancing model generalisation by dropping nodes. The dropout rate represents the probability of nodes being dropped. A dropout rate of 1.0 indicates that no dropout occurred between the layers, while a dropout rate of 0.0 indicates that no output is transmitted to the next layers.

The deep learning models were trained on a laptop equipped with Intel Core i5-9300H@2.40 GHz CPU, 20 GB RAM, and NVIDIA GeForce GTX 1650 (4 GB) GPU. Due to computational constraints, manual hyperparameter tuning was used to figure out each parameter's common range. Testing parameters one by one using solely grid search took much time, and it is computationally infeasible. Based on the manual hyperparameter tuning finding, the common range for learning rate, batch size, and dropout rate were 0.01 to 0.0001, 64 to 128, and 0.2 to 0.4, respectively. After getting the common range of each hyperparameter, the best combination of hyperparameters was obtained using Grid Search.

Data Augmentation

Data augmentation is a commonly used approach for training deep learning models in image recognition. Data augmentation aims to extend the original data set's diversity by generating synthetic data from a training set. Many data augmentation strategies are available, such as random rotation, random contrast, random translation, random zoom, and random brightness. The expiry date of a product may be taken at various angles and contrast levels in real life. Hence, random rotation and random contrast were used for augmenting the data in this project.

Regularisation

Regularisation is the process of preventing overfitting in deep learning. Inception ResNet V2 is a complex deep neural network with hidden layers to capture features. The model is easily overfitted when training data is not large enough. A large number of images for each class is needed to prevent overfitting. The training data has many features, and a complex model is needed to identify the image correctly.

Further, the dropout strategy is used to avoid overfitting. The model complexity can be minimised by randomly removing nodes at each iteration. The strategy ensures that the network is not over trained to pick up noises rather than features from the images and causes a high variance of the deep learning model.

Apart from the above strategies, early stopping is also used to avoid overfitting. When the deep learning algorithm learns all of the features of each image class, it will begin to overfit by capturing unwanted noise as features. Early stopping is used to track the validation loss at each epoch and stop the model training if the validation loss begins to rise, indicating overfitting.

Training, Validation and Testing

The data set contains 5359 image classes, and each class has 130 images. In total, there are 696,670 images in the data set. We divided the data set into three parts: the training set, the validation set, and the testing set. They are in the following proportions: 70:15:15. The training set contains 487,669 training instances, while the validation and testing set each contains 104,500 instances. We used the training set to train the deep learning model by learning the features of each image class and the validation data to evaluate the model performance at each epoch. After the training, the model was evaluated on the testing set (unknown new data) using validation accuracy. The formula we used to calculate the accuracy is as shown in Eq. 1.

$$\text{Accuracy} = \frac{\text{Number of correct prediction}}{\text{Total number of prediction}} \tag{1}$$

Since the project was a multi-class classifier problem, Sparse Categorical Cross Entropy was used to calculate the validation loss, as shown in Eq. 2, where w, N, y_i and $\hat{y}_i$ denote to the model's weight, number of instances, true classes, and predicted classes, respectively.

$$J(w) = -\frac{1}{N} \sum_{i=1}^{N} y_i \log(\hat{y}_i) \tag{2}$$

4 Results and Discussion

4.1 Recognition of Expiry Dates

We performed a grid search to obtain the optimal hyperparameters when training the model for better accuracy. A smaller subset from the training set is taken to perform the grid search hyperparameter tuning. The same training loop was run repetitively with different combinations of hyperparameters. Due to the constraint of computing resources, each hyperparameter combination ran only 1 epoch. The validation loss and validation accuracy were used to determine which hyperparameter performs the best.

The tuning result is shown in Table 2. The result shows that training the deep learning model with 64 batch size, 0.0001 learning rate, and 0.4 dropout gave the best validation accuracy and validation loss.

We plotted the model's learning curve to see how it fits through epochs. Figure 4 shows the learning curve for the model. We then evaluated the model using the testing set taken from the synthetic date images data set generated earlier. Besides, the model was also evaluated using 102 real-world images. Using the mobile application, we developed and installed in smartphones, we captured real-world images on different household products under normal household lighting. Then, the captured images were cropped to show only the expiry dates. The instructions for capturing the images are stated in the mobile application when users first use the function. The performance of the Inception ResNet V2 is as shown in Table 3.

There are 104,500 images in the test set, and the model gave 99.64% accuracy recognising them. The model has a loss of 0.0157, which is close to zero. On the other hand, the model achieved 96.12% accuracy and 0.1440 loss recognising the real-world images. Even though the results are not as good as recognising the synthetic test set, the model can still predict most of the date images correctly.

Table 2. The results of grid search hyperparameter tuning

Epoch	Batch size	Learning rate	Dropout	Validation accuracy	Validation loss
1	64	0.01	0.2	0.000000	76.891197
			0.3	0.000150	59.240292
			0.4	0.000000	45.036331
		0.001	0.2	0.002604	11.707423
			0.3	0.000000	10.809799
			0.4	0.002604	10.709365
		0.0001	0.2	0.000000	9.620681
			0.3	0.000000	9.950025
			0.4	**0.002604**	**9.582140**
	128	0.01	0.2	0.000000	78.836098
			0.3	0.000000	67.211235
			0.4	0.000000	49.153797
		0.001	0.2	0.000000	11.416241
			0.3	0.000000	11.015180
			0.4	0.000000	10.570828
		0.0001	0.2	0.000000	9.700305
			0.3	0.000000	9.664173
			0.4	0.000000	9.551310

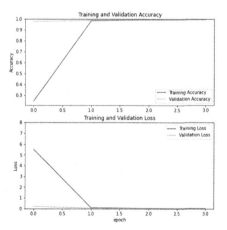

Fig. 4. The learning curve of the inception ResNet V2 model

Table 3. The performance of inception ResNet V2 in both testing set and real-world images

	Accuracy	Loss
Synthetic test set	0.9964	0.0157
Real-world images	0.9612	0.1440

4.2 Usability Test

A System Usability Scale (SUS) developed by Brooke [24] was used to evaluate the application's usability. The respondents gave a scale from 1 (strongly disagree) to 5 (strongly agree) for 10 SUS questions. The table below shows the usability test scores from seven respondents [25]. The average SUS score is 85.71, indicating that the respondents had a good experience of using the application (Table 4).

Table 4. The SUS scores of the mobile application

Respondent	Usability score for each question										Total	Total (100%)
	1	2	3	4	5	6	7	8	9	10		
Respondent 1	3	3	4	2	3	3	3	3	3	3	30	75
Respondent 2	3	3	3	3	4	3	2	3	3	3	30	75
Respondent 3	3	3	3	1	3	3	3	4	2	2	27	67.5
Respondent 4	4	4	4	4	4	4	4	4	4	4	40	100
Respondent 5	4	4	4	4	4	4	3	4	4	3	38	95
Respondent 6	4	4	4	4	4	4	4	4	4	4	40	100
Respondent 7	4	3	4	3	3	4	3	4	4	3	35	87.5
Average SUS score												85.71

5   Conclusion

In this work, a mobile application for expiry reminder has been developed. Besides incorporating the standard features any expiry reminder application has, our mobile application can recognise expiry date using a deep learning model - Inception ResNet V2. Such a feature is not found on other existing mobile applications in the market.

We generated a synthetic data set and collected real-world images to train and evaluate the Inception ResNet V2 in recognising various expiry date formats. The search of optimal hyperparameters was conducted to determine the optimal parameters for the model. The optimal hyperparameters obtained were 64 batch size, 0.0001 learning rate, and 0.4 dropout rate. The model was then trained using the fine-tuned parameters and evaluated using both synthetic testing set and real-world images. The mobile application is outstanding in recognising the expiry dates. On the synthetic data, the deep learning model achieved an accuracy of 0.9964 and a loss of 0.0157. On the real-world images, the model achieved an accuracy of 0.9612 and a loss of 0.1440. The mobile application also performed well in the usability testing, receiving a SUS score of 85.71 from the respondents.

However, there is a limitation in our mobile application. Due to the computational resources' constraint, the number of expiry date formats learnt by the deep learning model is still limited (refer to Table 1). In the future, we shall extend our work by incorporating more formats into the deep learning model.

References

1. Malaysian Food Waste: Poverty Pollution Persecution, 2019. The Star Online: Daily food waste staggering. https://www.thestar.com.my/news/nation/2021/05/20/daily-food-waste-sta ggering. Accessed 10 June 2021

2. The Star Online: Daily food waste staggering. https://www.thestar.com.my/news/nation/ 2021/05/20/daily-food-waste-staggering. Accessed 10 June 2021

3. TerrificMobile: Expiry Wiz. https://play.google.com/store/apps/details?id=com.terrificm obile.expirywiz&hl=en

4. Aladdinpro: Aladdinpro-expiry reminders. https://play.google.com/store/apps/details?id= com.aladdin.pro&hl=en

5. Mobile Farm: Expired – Grocery Reminder & Alerts App. https://play.google.com/store/apps/ details?id=com.mobilefarm.expired

6. Gie Joo, L.: Before expiry. https://apps.apple.com/us/app/id1384262435.

7. AppNextDoor Labs: Expiry reminder. https://apps.apple.com/us/app/expiry-reminder/id1231 732904

8. Microsoft: Xamarin. https://dotnet.microsoft.com/apps/xamarin

9. Google: Flutter. https://flutter.dev/

10. Facebook: React native. https://reactnative.dev/

11. Apple: iOS. https://www.apple.com/my/ios/ios-14/

12. Android. https://www.android.com/

13. Google: Dart. https://dart.dev/

14. Thomas, G.: What is flutter and why you should learn it in 2020. FreeCodeCamp (2019). https://www.freecodecamp.org/news/what-is-flutter-and-why-you-should-learn-it-in-2020/. Accessed 20 Aug 2020

15. Yamashita, R., Nishio, M., Do, R.K.G., Togashi, K.: Convolutional neural networks: an overview and application in radiology. Insights Imaging **9**(4), 611–629 (2018). https://doi. org/10.1007/s13244-018-0639-9

16. O'Shea, K., Nash, R.: An Introduction to Convolutional Neural Networks, pp. 1–11, (2015). http://arxiv.org/abs/1511.08458

17. Kim, P.: Convolutional Neural Network BT - MATLAB Deep Learning: with Machine Learning, Neural Networks and Artificial Intelligence, pp. 121–147. Apress, Berkeley (2017)

18. Yu, H., Yang, L.T., Zhang, Q., Armstrong, D., Deen, M.J.: Convolutional neural networks for medical image analysis: state-of-the-art, comparisons improvement and perspectives. Neurocomputing (2021). https://doi.org/10.1016/j.neucom.2020.04.157

19. He, K., Zhang, X., Ren, S., Sun, J.: Deep residual learning for image recognition. In: Proceedings of the IEEE Conference on Computer Vision and Pattern Recognition, vol. 2016, pp. 770–778 (2016). https://doi.org/10.1109/CVPR.2016.90

20. Szegedy, C., et al.: Going deeper with convolutions. In: Proceedings of the IEEE Conference on Computer Vision and Pattern Recognition, vol. 7–12, pp. 1–9 (2015). https://doi.org/10. 1109/CVPR.2015.7298594

21. Tan, M., Le, Q.: EfficientNet: rethinking model scaling for convolutional neural networks. In: 36th International Conference on Machine Learning, ICML 2019, vol. 2019-June, pp. 10691–10700 (2019)
22. Kranthi, K.K., Dileep, K.M., Samsonu, C., Vamshi, K.K.: Role of convolutional neural networks for any real time image classification, recognition and analysis. Mater. Today Proc. (2021). https://doi.org/10.1016/j.matpr.2021.02.186
23. Belval, E.: Text recognition data generator (2019). https://github.com/Belval/TextRecognit ionDataGenerator
24. Brooke, J.: System usability scale (1986)
25. Nielsen, J.: Why you only need to test with 5 users (2000). https://www.nngroup.com/articles/ why-you-only-need-to-test-with-5-users/

IoT and Ubiquitous Computing

A Game of Fog and Mirrors: Privacy in the World of Internet of Things

Alice F. Parker[1], Tor-Morten Grønli[1(✉)], and Muhammad Younas[2]

[1] Mobile Technology Lab, Department of Information Technology,
Kristiania University College, Oslo, Norway
`Tor-Morten.Gronli@kristiania.no`
[2] School of Engineering, Computing and Mathematics, Oxford Brookes University, Oxford, UK

Abstract. Privacy challenges are a growing point of research in both political science and computer science as the pervasive nature of IoT devices turns Orwell's dystopic state into a potential reality. This research maps out potential scenarios for IoT privacy challenges in the interdisciplinary effort to understand what it means to have privacy in world of internet-enabled sensors.

Keywords: Internet of Things · Information security · Privacy

1 Introduction

One of the greatest challenges facing both technology and politics in the 21st Century is coming together in spearhead, and that spearhead is IoT and ubiquitous computing. Privacy is not a new challenge to either paradigm. This is a research area that started centuries ago. Neither is it a research area that is likely to be solved anytime soon. Yet the pervasive nature of IoT is demanding that the 'balance of privacy' craves an interdisciplinary effort as the two paradigms collide. This research will map out the road leading up to this intersection, as well as visualise the challenges of IoT privacy in both technological and political disciplines.

IoT's boom in recent years has seen it commonplace for internet-enabled devices in homes, transports, and streets around the world. Already, are there almost as many sensors as humans, and soon sensors will be numbered in trillions [1]. As Weiser predicted, these sensors are "so ubiquitous that no one will notice their presence" [2]. Each and every heartbeat and breath taken can be recorded and the data sent into the cloud and out of the control of the individual. Their footsteps, geolocation, smile, and speech are amongst the various things that can be tracked through these ubiquitous sensors placed in our watches, mobiles, fridges and even our ski boots [3]. Whilst the technology is still in its infancy, it is not ridiculous to perceive that one day a sensor in human brains will be able to send bio signal data to into the hands of others. Literally reading our thoughts. Regardless of the current unfeasibility of brain-computer interaction, advancements in AI means that with the data presently available we can already create models to predict what humans may do next. Before they have thought of it themselves.

© Springer Nature Switzerland AG 2021
J. Bentahar et al. (Eds.): MobiWIS 2021, LNCS 12814, pp. 163–174, 2021.
https://doi.org/10.1007/978-3-030-83164-6_13

1.1 Privacy Versus Confidentiality

As a newcomer to privacy in data protect and IoT, it seems as if the researchers from political paradigms like cybersecurity policy and international politics, and the researchers from human-computer interaction and technology, are sitting in the same room with their backs to each other and demand that they talk face to face, yet neither turns. A common way to start a dialogue is to begin with the same language. For that, definitions on key terms need to be established. Privacy is the first definition to agree upon. For a system to protect user privacy, one needs to know what privacy is. The OED definition of privacy is:

"The state or condition of being alone, undisturbed, or free from public attention, as a matter of choice or right; seclusion; freedom from interference or intrusion" [4]. The European Union's legal interpretation is in the form of General Data Protection Regulation (GDPR) which came into force in 2018. The law, whilst only European, applies to all European citizens wherever they are in the world. GDPR "asks you to make a good faith effort to give people the means to control how their data is used and who has access to it" [5]. It is important to note that this is already a break from the common definition of privacy, as it does not necessarily imply one is free from interference or intrusion. An IoT device is GDPR compliant when ensuring that it is transparent with the user about their data and the purpose for keeping it, as well as facilitating a simple way for the user to control where their data is, the IoT device is GDPR compliant. This does not necessarily corelate to privacy. It may be closer to the interpretation of confidentiality. Nor does GDPR protect users for unfaithful actors or define how to implement the law in a technological sense. Neither, does it calm qualms for users with inherent distrust of the law and state.

1.2 Privacy in Philosophy Mirrored in IoT

A debate on the morality of the state will not dominate this research, but it is important to acknowledge the ambiguity and subjective nature of the IoT privacy actors. The discussion on privacy can be traced back to the 18th Century, if not further. Jeremy Bentham, a British political philosopher, devised the Panopticon as a way in for prison guards to easily see all prisoners from one spot, without moving [6]. His argument was that a prisoner, never quite knowing if the guard was watching, would behave and this was to their own benefit. We can draw strong lines between this prison architecture and IoT's ubiquity. The user is never easily aware of when sensors are present [7]. In this sense, individuals are prisoners, captive to the IoT device prison guards.

A century later the French philosopher, Michel Foucault, highlighted the cruel societal ramifications of the Panopticon state. Whilst the thought that an omniscient government might have benefits of both deterring and catching those who act outside the law, regardless of whether the omniscience is presumed or genuine, this leads to dynamic normalization [8]. IoT devices have already appeared in the media as heroes in criminal cases, such as home assistant devices keeping evidence of premeditated murder [9]. In a tyranny this directly facilitates the eradication of freewill, for example the persecutions of minorities or other groups seen as a threat to the survival of the tyrannic state. Even in a democracy, Foucault argues, can also have fundamental consequences on independent thinking and creativity. Thus, leading to the erosion of democracy [8].

If one needs any more elaboration on the dystopic nature that could be entailed with IoT, one only needs to draw upon George Orwell's 1984 [10]. The difference between his fictious writing and present day is that the technology is far more ubiquitous than Orwell's imagination allowed. IoT is the technology that turns his fiction into theoretical possibility. It is very important to note that at no point is the morality of privacy invasion assessed. This research give an objective overview of privacy invasion regardless of the justifications.

1.3 Privacy Versus Security

Cybersecurity is a large research area. It can often take priority over privacy research. It is necessary to distinguish the difference between security and privacy. Alwarafy et al. cover the security and privacy threats to Edge IoT but do not distinguish between the two, nor do they look at what these threats to mean outside boundaries of IoT [11]. The dystopian trajectories illuded about above do not make an obvious case for a threat to security. A scenario where society ends up like Orwell's 1984 is often not considered in cybersecurity. Privacy violations are precursory to security violations and their security implications may not be directly obvious. The privacy violation of the US citizens' Facebook data by Cambridge Analytica was not a threat to security on an individual scale, nor was it a threat to national security until it allowed a small elite to effectively control the outcome of a supposedly democratic election. Cybersecurity research will cover data theft, but research into privacy needs to consider when this data is given either lawfully or with consent. There is an intrinsic link between security and privacy, yet the consequences of IoT privacy breaches warrant their own research in a setting where they are considered a precursor to security threats at both national and personal levels.

2 Methodology

The brief overview of the political and philosophical discussion on privacy makes it evident that Orwellian invasions of privacy can be mirrored and played out through IoT research. This paper follows design science methodology by presenting a map of scenario variables in IoT privacy threats and placing existing research on IoT privacy solutions within this map. The interdisciplinary nature of the subject means research from both political science and technology will be applied. It is important to note that in political science paradigms, the theories of realism, liberalism and critical theory are continuing to throw differing results and predictions. The political science paradigms are used to back up the privacy implications but the theories will not be used to assess the technological nature of the article.

What follows is a literature review of an assortment of different research articles that tackle the challenges in IoT privacy from different perspectives. The backgrounds of the researchers in these articles span across nations (from the US, UK and to China) and research area (legal, political, and computer science).

Following this, we will present the map of IoT privacy scenario variables and ensue in a discussion on the prior literature in relation to produced artefact.

3 Literature Review

3.1 Who's Afraid of the Big Bad Smart Fridge?

Tanczer et al. [12] amply set the scene to a world in which IoT security and privacy threats are left unchecked. Their "future and foresight methodologies allow for the exploration of plausible futures and their desirability." They were able to categorise these areas in 4 common themes: (1) Physical safety, (2) Crime and exploitation, (3) Loss of control, (4) Social norms and structures [12]. By identifying and discussing potential dystopian scenarios, the hope is for IoT researchers to better strategize and tackle issues of IoT privacy and security. An example provided is "The seamless tracking of car users through companies that build and operate such smart cars may also lead to further erosions of privacy and individual's autonomy and sense of autonomy" [12]. Their work very much highlights the trajectory of IoT left unchecked. In a world in which "we give up freedom for convenience", they conclude on two opposing possible outcomes. The first is that mass hysteria and public outcry will force the individuals to shun IoT technology regardless of whether the benefits of their use outweigh the perceived privacy threats. The second is a scenario in which society is complacent, passive and apathetic to privacy invasions. Tanczer et al.'s [12] research also shows that IoT researchers are currently pessimistic that proposed frameworks to govern IoT privacy and security will result in compliance and enforcement measures from the manufacturers of IoT devices. Neither is "keeping out an unauthorised actor through access controls and erecting barriers such as firewalls, is unlikely to remain effective" [12]. Finally, Tanczer et al. [12] articulate that privacy issues in societal discussion are continuously ongoing, IoT entering this debate will only complicate the issues further. Their article presents a depressing trajectory for IoT which allows researchers to focus on important points to address in future research. Left out is the discussion of 'good' and 'bad' privacy invasion, and the mapping of actors causing the privacy invasion.

3.2 The Cloud, the Private Sector and the State

Pre-GDPR, Macropoulos et al.'s [13] IEEE opinion article explores the dangers to an individual's privacy where the state is the main threat. "The private sector has a pivotal role to play in balancing the privacy needs of the individual and the security demands of the state" [13]. Their article illustrates the role that the private sector places in an individual's right to privacy. Not only for the benefit of the individual, but in a scenario where "customers believe their privacy is under threat, their choice of provide will be heavily biased by trust considerations" [13], and the company itself is in jeopardy. Whilst not focusing directly on IoT, but instead at general cloud computing prior to the widespread adoption of edge comping and the implementation of GDPR, the article raises contributions about the location and control of data. A combination of "political, legal and technological approaches" is needed to address the issue. Macropoulos et al., echoing Tanczer et al., state that "information technology is merely the newest arena within which societies are seeking to balance the needs of the state with the expectations individuals" [13]. The contribution this article plays is the perspective of there being more than one actor portrayed as the victim of privacy invasion and more than one actor portrayed as the perpetrator.

3.3 GDPR Compliant User-Centric Privacy Frameworks

GDPR is considered the most far reaching and powerful laws made on data protection in world history. "GDPR aims to give control of personal data back to the user" [14]. Kounoudes et al. propose GDPR-compliant framework for IoT devices. Rather than looking at privacy as a challenge to overcome, they look at providing privacy protocols in a user-centric way "without blocking the evolution of IoT" [14]. They map existing frameworks to GDPR characteristics and look at solutions. Their three main contributions to IoT privacy mechanisms are as follows:

- Machine Learning techniques have been thoroughly used to provide user privacy protection.
- Using policy languages to specify user privacy preferences and to express complicated policies. - Optimising the trade-off between privacy and utility [14].

3.4 Privacy by Design

"Privacy must be addressed not just in terms of static regulatory requirements but also in terms of developing best practices for IoT industry" [15]. As a neglected aspect in the design of IoT, "an understanding of data movement is focal to ensure accurate and complete threat location, system analysis and compliance assessment" [15]. Thorburn et al. look at the methodologies and guidelines needed to ensure IoT privacy compliance. These they categorise into six points:

- Data flow
- IoT Privacy Taxonomy
- Privacy-by-Design Focus
- Audit
- Implementation
- Compliance and risk driven [15]

The significance of the privacy-by-design frameworks are covered in the discussion below.

3.5 Conceptual Privacy Frameworks

Chow creates a conceptual privacy stack framework for a IoT user-centric privacy protectionism [7]. This privacy stack builds on ensuring the control of data is in the hands of the user and enabling the user to customise data flow based on their own preferences. The unique and ubiquitous nature of IoT calls for a more attentive approach to data protection. Visualised in Fig. 1, IoT designs should consider the awareness, inference, preferences and notification that users have when it comes to their data. "A basic privacy principle is that personal data collection should happen only with appropriate notice and choice" [7]. The aim is to build a channel of communication between the IoT provider and the user for preserving the individual's privacy.

3.6 Privacy Mediators

To fulfil demands for user data control, Davies et al. [16] present cloudlets. Cloudlets, a privacy mediator, act as a secure and independent gateway between the IoT device – be it a chip or a system of IoT devices, and the cloud provider or company. The user is in complete control over what information is sent. This is "a scalable and secure solution on the edge of the cloud" [16]. Data is kept local and close to the device rather than being streamed through a vast distributed system. Not only does this protect the user from the technology provider, but also from outside cyber-attacks as the data's surface area is now reduced.

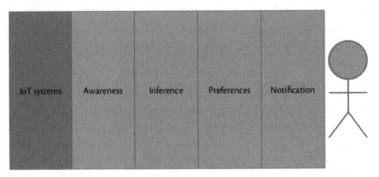

Fig. 1. The privacy stack framework bridges from today's Internet of Things (IoT) systems to users [7].

This architectural framework provides the user with a "rich set of privacy controls" [16]. Mediators can be placed at varying degree of granular.ity and provided by 3rd party providers, much like anti-virus software today, and can be controlled in context-aware setting. Davies et al. also play close attention to detail on video data processing, memory storage location and privacy control settings. The data would be "logically within the trust domain of the end user" [16], state, situating the cloudlets at the edge of the cloud.

3.7 Local Differential Privacy in Edge Computing

Unlike the previous articles shared that have explored giving the control to user's about where their data ends up, Bi et al. [17] propose a more cautious solution that takes into consideration the dishonest and the 'honest-but-curious' third parties that may deliberately or inadvertently leak private data. The authors of the paper focus purely on location data. Bi et al. [17] remark on the similarities between blockchain and edge computing decentralised technology as beneficiary to protecting user's privacy. However, blockchain is still too burdening for processing at the edge to be widely used in IoT. Bi et al. [17] use local differential privacy as method for prevent data collection centres from ever getting users' accurate location data. Local Differential Policy "transfer the privacy process of data to each user, enabling users to individually process and protect personal sensitive information" [17].

3.8 Federated Learning

A similar model for ensuring as little data as possible strays far from the user is proposed by McMahan et al. at Google [18]. Their model also promotes lower latency and energy consumption. Using a miniature version of TensorFlow, machine learning algorithms can process data and create outputs without the input data being sent to the central cloud. Only the aggregated data is ever sent back to the cloud. This technology is just one example of how designers are pushing more and more of the architecture to the edge of the cloud, and closer to the user [18].

4 Discussion

To understand the challenges for IoT in terms of privacy threats, we need to map out all the surface area. Figure 2 shows the variables that can be in play without depicting the relationship between each group. This is not necessarily a comprehensive summary of the different variable elements, but the point is to demonstrate that in order to discuss privacy in IoT, we cannot have a one size-fits-all solution. It is often assumed that the victim of IoT privacy invasion is an individual that either has access to the IoT device itself or access to privacy settings through their mobile device. But there is little consideration that the victim might be an individual that has no knowledge or access to the IoT device or privacy settings. The victim may also be a group of people or a state, which would involve the use of aggregated data rather than specific raw data.

The aggressor, the one inflicting the invasion of privacy, can also be categorised into different groups. The finger is often pointed towards "honest-but-curious third parties" [17] as the violators of privacy. However, a more nuanced approach into the flow of data and why the data is needed. There is also no value in looking at one of the end nodes of the map in Fig. 2 in isolation, we must build a scenario in which the end nodes are used in combination. Figure 3 shows all the possible ways in which Bob can have his privacy violated: either an indirect threat (the violation of his privacy through aggregated data) or a direct threat (where the violation of Bob's privacy can be traced directly back to him). It is important to illustrate the different relationships between the victim and the aggressor as these will indicate at what point the privacy is invaded.

The scenarios illustrated above are not imagined, we can find examples of these expressed in the media. Recent concerns were raised about employee privacy when Amazon vans installed video cameras to make their drivers take rest breaks if the technology determines the driver is tired [19].

Affective computing means emotions are no longer private from Orwellian surveillance. Scenario 2 and 3 demonstrate this in Fig. 3. Carlo, highlights that the "constant monitoring of employees creates an oppressive, distrustful and disempowering work environment that completely undermines workers' rights" [19].

By mapping the threats to Bob's privacy, we can begin to look at where the gaps are in research to address privacy issues in IoT. Tanczer et al. [12] take a similar approach, by calling upon leading IoT experts to express their trajectories of IoT left unchecked. Many of the violations to Bob's privacy at an aggregated level are mentioned in Tanczer et al.'s research [12]. Scenarios marked in green in Fig. 3 show scenarios where privacy could be violated from aggregated data. "We give up freedom for convenience" [12].

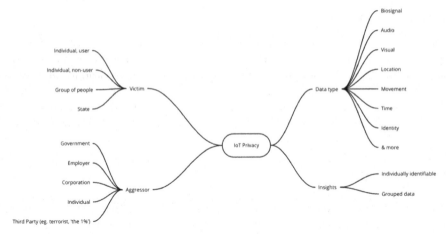

Fig. 2. IoT privacy scenario variables.

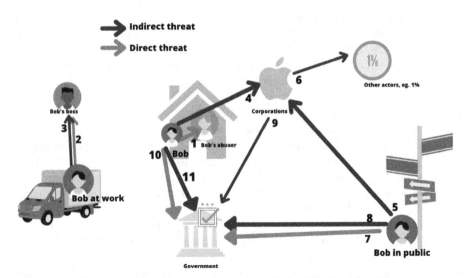

Fig. 3. Privacy scenario map with the individual (Bob) as a victim

Frameworks allow a breakdown of concepts and making it easier to think through concepts when designing and assessing risk. The research for GDPR compliant frameworks in Kounoudes et al. maps their identified challenges to GDPR characteristics, as shown in Fig. 4. Similar to the research from Chow, (private by design) and Davies et al. [16], the privacy preserving mechanisms are reliant on the user being able to make informed decisions about the usage of their data. They both make effort to ensure that services "explicitly provide basic inferences" [7]. There is a considerable amount of privacy preferences research not mentioned in this research that look into enabling users to make empowered privacy preference choices. Tanczer et al.'s research lay challenge to this as one trajectory for IoT privacy challenges is apathy. "Individuals would consequently lack suitable alternatives that provide them with the opportunity to freely give consent and remain in control over how their data is being collected and processed" [12]. No number of choices or power over their own data is sufficient when the user does not care what happens with their data.

Mapping of GDPR characteristics to challenges

	Characteristic	CH1	CH2	CH3	CH4
CR1	Prevent inference	✓			
CR2	Provide data transformation	✓		✓	
CR3	Provide user awareness on data collection				✓
CR4	Provide control of personal data to users		✓	✓	
CR5	Provide monitoring and control of devices that collect data			✓	
CR6	Provide tools for data management to users		✓	✓	✓
CR7	Provide ability for data erasure		✓		
CR8	Provide transparency		✓		✓
CR9	Provide balance of privacy between users and third parties		✓		
CR10	Provide enforcement of user privacy preferences		✓		
CR11	Provide privacy by design or privacy by default		✓		
CR12	Provide ability to users to make informed consent choices		✓		
CR13	Estimate privacy risks of data collection/inference to users		✓		
CR14	Communicate risks of data collection/inference to users		✓		
CR15	Provide ability to users to specify their privacy preferences		✓		
CR16	Prevent excessive data collection		✓		

√= subject addressed; (blank) = not addressed

Fig. 4. Mapping of GDPR characteristics to challenges [16]

Bi et al. [17] take the more cautious route by assuming all data centers are untrustworthy. Whilst not explicitly referred to, McMahan et al. [18] also provides the same solution. Data leaving the edge nodes is aggregated and the user's individual privacy is left undisturbed. Figure 5 from Bi et al. [17] shows how the raw location data never leaves the client's devices. These solutions also allow for the value of the data being sent back to the central cloud not to be weakened. Federated Learning sends the trained dataset back to the shared model [18].

Edge computing has become a popular architectural structure for IoT devices due to its lower latency and keeping the user's data closer to the edge of the network. Additionally, research often uses self-built and self-controlled IoT hubs to sync and manage the interoperability of numerous devices. Consumers opt for commercial IoT hubs such as Google Nest or Amazon Echo which ultimately allow the devices manufacture access to all data flowing through these devices. Understanding that the lawful passing of data as illustrated in scenarios marked in green are central to the concerns raised by Tanczer et al. [12].

Finally, neither current privacy control preferences nor privacy preserving mechanisms within IoT gateways and even GDPR compliant frameworks can protect Bob's privacy from an abusive individual with legal access to IoT devices that monitor his movements. Figure 3 shows this in scenario 1. This is a scenario that Tanczer and Parkin et al. [20] research. The surface area for privacy threat from a domestic abuser is all encompassing as visualised in Fig. 6. Their research is still in the infancy to be able to provide contributable solutions, but they indicate fair usability is an essential part of the design stage in IoT devices. This is something that the research in the literature reviews that create privacy-by-design frameworks for IoT devices does not cover.

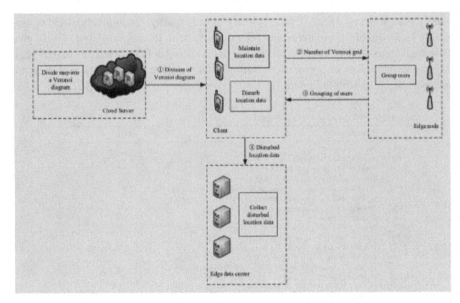

Fig. 5. Bi et al. Voronoi privacy preserving method

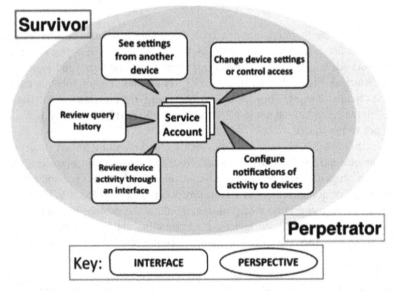

Fig. 6. Perspectives and interfaces onto a service account in a climate of tech-abuse [20].

5 Limitations

There are several limitations in the contributed map and table to lay out the challenges that face IoT privacy. Firstly, and most significantly, the mapping ought to be applied to all major IoT privacy research. There is also a need for stronger research into the privacy violations using aggregated data. This is mentioned in Tanczer et al. [12]'s research on the trajectories of IoT privacy challenges but there is a need to look at it from a purely technical perspective. Whilst this research distinguishes the privacy violation scenario differences from corporation, third party and government aggressors, there requires more attention to the differences of these actors. This is would be similar to the work of [13] yet calls for research specific to IoT devices in a GDPR world. The scenarios listed also only focus on individuals as a victim and it would be useful to look at the scenarios where businesses and states are the victim. Finally, there this is a need for more refined policy on privacy challenges when the data is obtained with informed consent, permission and on an aggregated level.

6 Conclusion

In order for IoT privacy challenge research to thoroughly address weaknesses and understand the potential threats to individual and grouped privacy, we need to begin with a map of the scenarios possible. This calls for an interdisciplinary effort from both political science and computer science researchers. Tanczer et al.'s [12] research shows a promising start to the collaborative work required.

As laid out in the introduction, privacy has been researched for centuries. IoT merely moves this into a new paradigm and complicates the matter further [13]. By acknowledging the unfinished and contentious nature of privacy in philosophical spheres, it prevents naivety of IoT technology researchers to preclude that a simple privacy mediator or mechanism may suffice.

To reiterate, this research does not attempt to label any scenario of privacy violation as justified or not. The first step is to recognise where the privacy is invaded, and then leave it to philosophers and policy makers to decide on the rational. Following this, technology researchers can then implement the desired frameworks for enabling Private-by-design IoT devices. Frameworks covered in the literature review do make a start on privacy-by-design, but the map produced in Fig. 4 shows that not all the scenarios have been designed for. Edge Computing has facilitated more privacy for the end user, but it still leaves many scenarios unchecked.

If not anything, the mapping of the multitude of threats, victims and scenarios in IoT privacy challenges shows that this is truly a game of Fog and mirrors.

References

1. Sharma, C.: Iot data privacy framework. http://www.chetansharma.com/publications/iot-data-privacy-framework/. Accessed 9 Feb 2021
2. Weiser, M.: Ubiquitous computing. Computer **26**(10), 71–72 (1993) https://doi.org/10.1109/2.237456
3. Carv, C.: https://getcarv.com/. Accessed 2 July 2021
4. Oxford University Press: privacy, n. https://www.oed.com/view/Entry/151596?redirectedFrom=privacy. Accessed 11 Feb 2021
5. European Union: Gdpr data privacy. https://gdpr.eu/data-privacy/. Accessed 11 Feb 2021
6. Bentham, J., Bozovic, M.: The Panopticon Writings. Verso, New York (1995)

7. Chow, R.: The last mile for IoT privacy. IEEE Sec. Priv. **15**(6), 73–76 (2017)
8. Foucault, M.: Discipline and Punish: The Birth of the Prison. Pantheon Books, New York (1977)
9. Privacy International. Timeline IoT in court: https://privacyinternational.org/timelineiotincourt. Accessed 12 Feb 2021
10. Orwell, G.: Centennial ed. Tandem Library, 1950 (1984)
11. Alwarafy, A., Al-Thelaya, K.A., Abdallah, M., Schneider, J., Hamdi, M.: A survey on security and privacy issues in edge computing-assisted internet of things. IEEE Internet Things J. **8**(6), 1 (2020)
12. Tanczer, L.M., Steenmans, I., Elsden, M., Blackstock, J., Carr, M.: Emerging risks in the IoT ecosystem: who's afraid of the big bad smart fridge? Living Internet Things: Cybersec. IoT **2018**, 1–9 (2018)
13. Macropoulos, C., Martin, K.M.: Balancing privacy and surveillance in the cloud. IEEE Cloud Comput. **2**(4), 14–21 (2015)
14. Kounoudes, A.D., Kapitsaki, G.M.: A mapping of IoT user-centric privacy preserving approaches to the GDPR. Internet Things **11**, 100179 (2020)
15. Thorburn, R., Margheri, A., Paci, F.: Towards an integrated privacy protection framework for IoT: contextualising regulatory requirements with industry best practices. In: Living in the Internet of Things (IoT 2019), pp. 1–6 (2019)
16. Davies, N., Taft, N., Satyanarayanan, M., Clinch, S., Amos, B.: Privacy mediators: helping IoT cross the chasm. In: Proceedings of the 17th International Workshop on Mobile Computing Systems and Applications, Series HotMobile 2016. Association for Computing Machinery, New York, pp. 39–44 (2016). https://doi.org/10.1145/2873587.2873600
17. Bi, M., Wang, Y., Cai, Z., Tong, X.: A privacy-preserving mechanism based on local differential privacy in edge computing. China Commun. **17**(9), 50–65 (2020)
18. Brendan, M., Daniel, R.: Federated learning. https://ai.googleblog.com/2017/04/federated-learning-collaborative.html. Accessed 9 Feb 2021
19. Jane, W.: BBC|Amazon faces spying claims over AI cameras in vans. https://www.bbc.com/news/technology-55938494. Accessed 4 Feb 2021
20. Parkin, S., Patel, T., Lopez-Neira, I., Tanczer, L.: Usability analysis of shared device ecosystem security: informing support for survivors of IoT-facilitated tech-abuse. In: Proceedings of the New Security Paradigms Workshop, Series NSPW 2019. Association for Computing Machinery, New York, pp. 1–15 (2019). https://doi.org/10.1145/3368860.3368861

A Step Towards More Eco-responsible Computing

Fontaine Richard$^{(\boxtimes)}$ ⓘ, Courdier Rémy, and Payet Denis

Laboratoire d'Informatique et de Mathématiques (LIM),
University of Reunion Island, Saint Denis, France
`richard.fontaine@univ-reunion.fr`

Abstract. On a global scale, the environmental footprint of digital technology represents a continent two to three times the size of France and five times the size of the French car fleet. In order to limit the negative impact of this overabundance and to optimize the emerging computing potential of our environment, we propose an architecture model and its implementation in order to allow the mutualization of the components embedded in our connected devices.

Keywords: Agent · Ubiquitous computing · Eco-computing

1 Introduction

We are at the beginning of a new computing era which is manifested by a trend to integrate computing into the physical objects of everyday life [2,21,24]. While providing a lot of benefits, this technological advance brings with it a set of environmental issues [3,4].

According to the European Union [6], in 2020, there were 30 critical raw materials (against 14 in 2011) and among them, many elements are directly linked to new technologies: Cobalt (lithium-ion batteries); Germanium (optical fibers); Hafnium (processor); Indium (touch screen); Tantalum (liquid crystal displays, dynamic random access memory (DRAM) chips), or Lithium (battery). These elements were generally related to the manufacture of computers, printers and other common digital objects. But since 2015, we notice that a shift has taken place [3]:

- Televisions represented 5 to 15% of the impacts in 2010 against 9% to 26% by 2025;
- Smartphones represented 2 to 6% of the impacts in 2010 against 4 to 16% by 2025;
- Connected objects represented 1% of the impacts in 2010 against 18% to 23% by 2025.

Based on these statistics, we can see that the depletion of our global reserves is fast approaching. We therefore need a new vision of eco-design that focuses not only on the energy impact, but on a direct safeguard of our raw materials.

© Springer Nature Switzerland AG 2021
J. Bentahar et al. (Eds.): MobiWIS 2021, LNCS 12814, pp. 175–184, 2021.
https://doi.org/10.1007/978-3-030-83164-6_14

To do this, we believe it is necessary to see in our connected objects more than their initial functionalities. These hidden and currently unexploited functionalities, which we will call dispositions, represent the core of our approach. We propose, through an architecture model, to reveal them and to mutualize them virtually in order to allow the emergence of new services without systematically adding new physical connected objects. This model has been implemented within an Android framework named Agent Framework For Omnipresent Real Device (AFFORD).

Before highlighting the technical solutions that are used to make this mutualization of dispositions, we will illustrate our concept in order to demonstrate its advantages.

1.1   Example of a Mutualisation of Components: A Monitoring Agent

In this example; we will consider a monitoring agent A which has the objective Ω of alerting in case of a fall. This objective can be divided into three required objectives ω which are:

- ω_1: to detect a fall
- ω_2: to alert the user by a sound
- ω_3: alert the user with a flashing light

In our case, the agent has access to a set of connected devices including: a light bulb, a computer, and an accelerometer. So, we can describe the Obj objects of the environment through the n dispositions they present:

- Obj^1: The accelerometer
  - n_1 detect a fall
- Obj^2: The computer
  - n_2 produce sound
  - n_3 display a picture
- Obj^3: The connected light bulb
  - n_4 make light

In a usual context, the service would be managed by a single entity, whereas in our case, it is possible to dissociate the monitoring service, the capture of information and the response of the system. When the system is started, agent A seeks to accomplish the Ω objective. Because of the presence of the accelerometer Obj^1 in its environment and its disposition n_1 to detect a fall, the objective ω_1 is made permanently active. If a fall is detected, the agent reacts and its ω_2 and ω_3 objectives become active. In an optimal case, where the light bulb Obj^3 and the computer Obj_2 are accessible, the agent has the possibility to activate the behaviours ω_2 and ω_3. In this way, attention is focused on the problem of falling. In the same way, it is interesting to note that this same light bulb Obj^3 and this same computer Obj_2 can be used as an alert source for other types of monitoring (such as intrusion, temperature, or hydrometry monitoring). This vision of our environment thus allows us to reduce redundancies within a system by privileging a more intelligent and reasoned use of the objects that surround us.

2 An Ecological Challenge, but Also a Technical Challenge

To make this vision real and to start this change of habit, three points must be taken into account:

From a conceptual point of view, we believe that it is necessary to propose a high-level solution, which would allow a quick deployment on a maximum of existing devices.

From a technological point of view, considering the ubiquitous aspect, the solution must be light enough to allow its deployment on devices with low computing capacity.

From a human point of view, its use must be as natural as possible. To achieve this, we will emphasize the presence of autonomous entities that can decide individually on the provisions they wish to share.

2.1 Current Technological Possibilities

Before presenting our solution, we will examine the existing technical possibilities that can be used to try to solve our problem. In order to do this, we will look at three different levels of abstraction: middleware, agents, and artifact concept.

Middleware. In ubiquitous systems, the middleware is generally considered as a generic layer which provides basic functions [1,12]. This approach is commonly used [11,16], however a limit to the use of middleware comes with the fact that, usually, a system has as many middlewares as there are communication problems [14,18]. Consequently, the more heterogeneous entities are involved in a system, the more it may contain a large number of middleware in order to hide the communication problems.

Even if some authors propose the implementation of a "middleware of middlewares" in order to provide a unique interface to the applications [23], the system will be unable to adapt as new technologies appear.

Agents. In an ambient intelligence context, an option to overcome the heterogeneity of the environment is the use of agents ([9,13,22,25]). However, if we want to scale up, it is inconceivable to put the responsibility of describing all the connected objects and their possibilities on the level of the agents in charge of the services. Based on this observation, some proposals try to overcome the problems of making connected objects available by linking them to specialized "agent-objects" [15,17,20]. Unfortunately, this option is confronted with a conceptual problem. Indeed, it is not advisable to model an object using the agent concept, because it does not have its characteristics [5,7,13,25].

Artifacts. The A&A (Agent & Artifact) meta-model is characterized by three main abstractions [19]:

- Agents: proactive components of systems, encapsulating the execution of activities in a given environment;
- Artifacts: passive components of systems, such as resources and media, intended to be used by agents to support their behaviour;
- Workspaces: conceptual containers of agents and artefacts, useful for defining the topologies of the environment and notions of the locality.

The concept of artefact, due to its abstract nature and not being conceived for a specific purpose, unfortunately does not directly solve the problem of the mutualisation of the dispositions of objects present in our environment. However, its coherence in terms of agent/object modelling and its polymorphic nature make it an interesting theoretical tool for our model proposal.

3   Concept Description

From the constraints and elements raised above, we can deduce that the current solutions do not meet the requirements of our proposal. From this observation, we propose to modify our vision of the environment by proposing a virtual decomposition of our objects [10] in the form of a dispositional artifact that we will define as follows:

Definition 1 (Decomposition into dispositional artifacts.). *Each object Obj, can be represented by a set of artifacts Art according to the usage such as:*

$$Obj-> \{Art_n\}$$

with Obj a connected object, Art a virtual artifact, n the disposition of the object encapsulated by the artifact.

From this decomposition, it is then possible for the agent to perceive new possibilities within its environment that we will call dispositional opportunities.

Definition 2 (Emergence of dispositional opportunities.). *Let W (an agent-object system) $= (A, Obj)$ and W_p (an agent-artifact system) $= (A, Art_p)$ composed of an artifact Art with a disposition p. A dispositional opportunity exists if and only if there exists an opportunity τ, such that :*

1. $W = (A, Obj)$ does not possess τ

2. $W_p = (A, Art_p)$ possess τ

and $Art_p \in Obj$

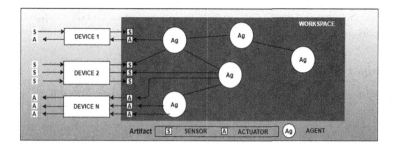

Fig. 1. Mutualisation of components within a workspace

Based on these definitions, we propose an architecture model that involves three types of entities based on the A&A concept: agent, workspace and artifact.

Within this model, the layouts are encapsulated in artifacts that will be used as virtual media to make the dispositions of connected objects accessible to an agent (Fig. 1).

Because the roles of the agent and the workspace are globally unchanged, we will directly focus on the conceptual additions related to the decomposition of the objects into a dispositional artifact tree.

3.1 Architecture Model

We will therefore focus on the seven main artifact classes: Artifact, Composite Artifact, Main Artifact, Final Artifact, Sensor Artifact, Actuator Artifact, Service Artifact.

- Artifact
  This class is the primary component of the layout decomposition. Globally, it defines all the primitives useful for programming the observable behaviours of artefacts in accordance with the frameworks or implementation environments. This first class allows the establishment of the dependency link between artefacts, as well as its observable state within workspaces.
- Composite Artifact
  The CompositeArtifact class is mainly an artifact container. Its role is to keep a trace of the structure of the original connected object. It is also possible that it is itself under the management of an artifact if it is also a component element.
- Main Artifact
  The Main Artifact class virtually represents the object and contains information about it (nature, state, mac address, etc.). It is also responsible for accessing the artifacts and only this class is directly linked to the workspaces.
- Final Artifact
  The elements of this class represent the artifacts that are directly accessible in the workspace. All classes that inherit from it (Sensor Artifact, Actuator

Artifact, Service Artifact) can be seen as the leaves of the decomposition tree of the original object and therefore cannot have artifacts that compose them.

3.2 Properties

Thanks to the artifact classes seen previously, it becomes possible to virtually describe the dispositions of an object in the form of a tree. Within this description, the leaves represent the object's dispositions and the internal nodes, the structure of its decomposition.

The Fig. 2 illustrates a virtual decomposition of a smartphone into a tree where the root represents the original object (Main Artifact), the intermediate nodes the structure of the decomposition (Composite Artifact) and the leaves the dispositions that can be made accessible (Final Artifact).

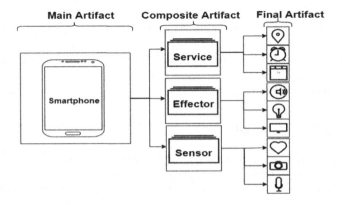

Fig. 2. Example of decomposition

As a result, the object is no more represented in a monolithic way, but is decomposed into a set of dispositional artifacts. It then becomes possible to mutualize them within workspaces in order to propose services that fully use the possibilities of our connected environment. From a conceptual point of view, unlike the use of agents, mutualization is based on a coherent paradigm, and their uniformity and high level of abstraction avoid the overabundance of middleware. The use of artifacts also has the advantage of solving two key problems related to the Publish/Subscribe concept, which is generally used to define the modalities of transmission of sensor information. First, the problem of efficiently linking an event with many subscribers on one type of event can be solved by "relocating" the associated Sensor object to another device. The connected object will only have to manage one Subscriber per sensor. Broadcasting to interested entities will be done through the Sensor artifacts. Second, the problem of efficient multicasting of events within a network of event providers is solved by having the agent connected directly to the desired sensor. Thus, interested entities will only have access to information that is relevant to them.

4   Android Implementation

Fig. 3. An application on the Android platform

An implementation of this model, named Agent Framework For Omnipresent Real Device (AFFORD), has been developed on Android through a framework in order to show the feasibility of the model. AFFORD is based on the "Software Kit for Ubiquitous Agent Development" (SKUAD) platform, which is a platform for creating ambient agents, being able to manage sensors and effectors, whose performances and design allow an embedded use [8]. The application we made, in APK format (9.13 MB), can detect all sensors embedded in an Android device and currently offers seven effectors and two services (Fig. 3).

At runtime, if a component is available and the authorizations allow it, the system proceeds to the creation of artifacts as an instance of the associated class. The user can then choose, via the user interface, which artifacts to make available and which agents to activate within the workspace.

During the test phases, AFFORD was tested on different Android devices (smartphone and tablet) in order to highlight the presence of provisions. This first step confirmed that many possibilities were hidden in our smartphones. In addition to the effectors and services that can be implemented (e.g. ringtone, voice recognition, buzzer.), we can see in the table (Fig. 4) that natively they were able to propose at least twenty artifacts.

Brands	Samsung	Motorola	Samsung	Samsung	Xiaomi
Model	Galaxy s8	One zoom	SM-T870	SM-N960F	Redmi Note 8T
RAM (Go)	4	4	8	6	4
SensorArtifact	26	44	20	27	22

Fig. 4. Some examples of tested smartphones

4.1 Example in Real Environment

A real-world example of this implementation has been proposed through a falling detector. The devices used in this test are: a Samsung Galaxy S8 smartphone, a Samsung Tab A (2016) tablet and an Acer TravelMate P257 laptop. At the end of the layout analysis step, the smartphone offers twenty-six Sensors and the tablet offers five.

To perform this test, we used the artifact encapsulating the accelerometer, present in any smartphone and usually used to determine the orientation of the screen or to stabilize photographs, as a shock sensor. It should be known that a smartphone accelerometer can generally detect movement in the micrometer range. Moreover, in order to show that the possibilities are not limited to the components of the device, we have created an artifact encapsulating synthesis and voice recognition to perform a simple dialogue with a user.

Thus, the intelligent entity, in this implementation a SKUAD agent, becomes able, by adjusting the sensitivity parameters, to discriminate different types of shocks (fall, heights, direction, presence of a final shock). In case of shock, the agent will try to attract the user's attention via the flash or the vibrator of Android devices or by making the computer screen blink. If the agent does not get a response, he can then use voice synthesis and voice recognition to talk to a user. In this case, the agent asks a series of closed questions giving the choice to the user to answer among a set of predefined answers. Each answer pronounced by the user will be transformed into text and then analyzed by the agent in order to make a report of the situation.

4.2 Encouraging Results

Through the previous example, however simple, we find ourselves virtually and schematically in a system with 3 processors, 3 batteries, 12 GB of Ram and 580 GB of storage. This power is much higher than the one required in a current use. This particularity shows us that the sensing and broadcasting entities can be externalized without the necessity of adding components with a processing capacity. We have also shown that the current dynamics seeking to make the environment intelligent could pass, not by a systematic integration of computing power within each object, but rather by a more reasoned and mutualized use of the possibilities of our devices. Moreover, due to the fact that processing can be done at the peripheral level, this solution offers an alternative to cloud computing. It also allows to reduce the energy footprint, since it does not require the internet network or the datacenter, while limiting the leakage of personal data.

5 Conclusion

The current trend is to systematically integrate computing capabilities into each object. However, an alternative would be to propose a more reasoned and mutualised use of the possibilities of our devices. Thanks to an architecture model inspired by the concept of artefact, we propose to virtually put forward the dispositions of our connected devices in order to reduce the redundancies within an environment. We implemented the model on Android which allowed us to highlight the multitude of unused opportunities present in our environments. From the results, we found that a single smartphone or tablet could power many services. This collective power allows us to reduce the number of batteries, screens and computer components (RAM, processor, storage) and thus contribute to a step towards more eco-responsible computing.

References

1. Baldauf, M., Dustdar, S., Rosenberg, F.: A survey on context-aware systems. Int. J. Ad Hoc Ubiquit. Comput. **2**(4), 263–277 (2007)
2. Böhlen, M., Frei, H.: Ambient intelligence in the city overview and new perspectives. In: Nakashima, H., Aghajan, H., Augusto, J.C. (eds.) Handbook of Ambient Intelligence and Smart Environments, pp. 911–938. Springer, Boston (2010). https://doi.org/10.1007/978-0-387-93808-0_34
3. Bordage, F.: Study - The environmental footprint of the digital world (2019)
4. Cailloce, L.: Numérique: le grand gâchis énergétique (2018)
5. Cetnarowicz, K.: From algorithm to agent. In: Allen, G., Nabrzyski, J., Seidel, E., van Albada, G.D., Dongarra, J., Sloot, P.M.A. (eds.) ICCS 2009. LNCS, vol. 5545, pp. 825–834. Springer, Heidelberg (2009). https://doi.org/10.1007/978-3-642-01973-9_92
6. European Commission: EU commission, critical raw materials, internal market, industry, entrepreneurship and SMES, May 2020. https://ec.europa.eu/growth/sectors/raw-materials/specific-interest/critical_en
7. DeLoach, S.A.: Multiagent systems engineering: a methodology and language for designing agent systems. Technical report, Department of Electrical and Computer Engineering of Air Force Institute of Technology (1999)
8. Denis, P.: Skuad, software kit for ubiquitous agent development. http://skuad.onover.top/ (2018). http://skuad.onover.top/
9. Ferber, J.: Les systèmes multi-agents: vers une intelligence collective. I.I.A. Informatique intelligence artificielle, InterEditions, France (1995). https://books.google.com/books?id=jlpDOwAACAAJ
10. Fontaine, R., Aky, N., Courdier, R., Payet, D.: Vers une utilisation éco responsable des objets connectés par la mutualisation de leurs composants physiques: Une approche basée sur le concept d'artefact. In: Actes de la conférence nationale en intelligence artificielle CNIA - PFIA 2020, Angers, vol. 23, p. 38 (2020)

11. Gateau, B., Naudet, Y., Rykowski, J.: Ontology-based smart IOT engine for personal comfort management. In: 2016 11th International Workshop on Semantic and Social Media Adaptation and Personalization (SMAP), pp. 35–40. IEEE, Thessaloniki (2016)
12. IEEE: Middleware and application adaptation requirements and their support in pervasive computing. IEEE Computer Society, Los Alamitos (2003)
13. Jennings, N.R.: On agent-based software engineering. Artif. Intell. **117**(2), 277–296 (2000)
14. Kjær, K.E.: A survey of context-aware middleware. In: Proceedings of the 25th Conference on IASTED International Multi-Conference: Software Engineering, pp. 148–155. SE 2007. ACTA Press, Anaheim (2007)
15. Kwan, J., Gangat, Y., Payet, D., Courdier, R.: A agentified use of the internet of things. In: Full Paper in 9th IEEE International Conference on Internet of Things (iThings 2016). IEEE CS (2016). http://hal.univ-reunion.fr/hal-01478263
16. Laleci, G.B., Dogac, A., Olduz, M., Tasyurt, I., Yuksel, M., Okcan, A.: Saphire: a multi-agent system for remote healthcare monitoring through computerized clinical guidelines. In: Annicchiarico, R., Cortés, U., Urdiales, C. (eds.) Agent Technology and e-Health, pp. 25–44. Birkhäuser Basel, Basel (2008). https://doi.org/10.1007/978-3-7643-8547-7_3
17. Maamar, Z., et al.: How to agentify the internet-of-things? In: 2018 12th International Conference on Research Challenges in Information Science (RCIS), pp. 1–6. IEEE (2018)
18. Mohamed, N., Al-Jaroodi, J., Jawhar, I.: Middleware for robotics: a survey. In: RAM. pp. 736–742. IEEE, Chengdu (2008)
19. Omicini, A., Ricci, A., Viroli, M.: Artifacts in the A&A meta-model for multi-agent systems. Auton. Agents Multi-agent Syst. **17**(3), 432–456 (2008)
20. Pantoja, C.E., Soares, H.D., Viterbo, J., El Fallah-Seghrouchni, A.: An architecture for the development of ambient intelligence systems managed by embedded agents. In: SEKE, pp. 215–214 (2018)
21. Ramos, C., Marreiros, G., Santos, R., Freitas, C.F.: Smart offices and intelligent decision rooms. In: Nakashima, H., Aghajan, H., Augusto, J.C. (eds.) Handbook of Ambient Intelligence and Smart Environments, pp. 851–880. Springer, Boston (2010). https://doi.org/10.1007/978-0-387-93808-0_32
22. Russell, S.J.: Rationality and intelligence. Artif. Intell. **1**(94), 57–77 (1997)
23. Seinturier, L., Merle, P., Rouvoy, R., Romero, D., Schiavoni, V., Stefani, J.B.: A component-based middleware platform for reconfigurable service-oriented architectures. Softw. Pract. Experience **42**(5), 559–583 (2012). https://doi.org/10.1002/spe.1077, https://hal.inria.fr/inria-00567442
24. Weiser, M.: Some computer science issues in ubiquitous computing. Commun. ACM **36**(7), 75–84 (1993)
25. Wooldridge, M.: Agent-based software engineering. IEE Proc. Softw. **144**(1), 26–37 (1997)

Analysis of Distance Sensor in Lego Mindstorm

Wasana Leithe[1], Tor-Morten Grønli[1(✉)], and Muhammad Younas[2]

[1] Mobile Technology Laboratory, Department of Information Technology,
Kristiania University College, Oslo, Norway
Tor-Morten.Gronli@kristiania.no
[2] School of Engineering, Computing and Mathematics, Oxford Brookes University, Oxford, UK

Abstract. Internet of Things is a concept that many physical devices can connect and share information. IoT development in mobile apps aimed to control connected devices. This paper describes the form of an application-led project by building a smart application system using the Lego Mindstorm kit. It decides on and simulates scenarios for the IoT solutions and the design and develop a proof-of-concept mobile and IoT application with emphasis on the technical implementations, architectural considerations, and interoperability. It demonstrates through graphical programming environment the configuring, implement and evaluation of distance sensor technologies in a mobile application.

Keywords: Internet of Things · Mobile computing · Lego Mindstorm

1 Introduction

At present, smart network sensors open new opportunities for designing control systems. Automotive and industrial automation systems, sensors are connected to field busses for distributed control. Mobile application systems such as robots and smart vehicles take spontaneously exploit sensor information provided by an instrumented environment is becoming increasingly powerful [1]. The IoT is a network that connects uniquely identifiable "things" to the Internet. The things have sensing/actuation and potential programmability capabilities. Through the exploitation of unique identification and sensing, information about the thing can be collected. It can change the state of the thing from anywhere, anytime, by anything. There is consensus that the IoT is one of the most important revolutions in technology in decades at present. It has attracted a lot of attention from both industry and academia [2].

Moreover, the integration between the IoT with the cloud (IoT-Cloud or sensor-cloud) has received significant interest from academia and industry. Based on mobile user location tracking, the IoT cloud plays a role as a controller, which makes schedules for physical sensor networks on-demand [3]. The IoT has many benefits that should be considered. It is expected that by 2025, the IoT nodes will connect most of the objects, and many of them are essential in our day to day life. Many people in the world have a smart mobile at present. Most of the people will be interconnected with the internet and they will be online all the time in the future. The main purpose of the IoT is to uniquely

© Springer Nature Switzerland AG 2021
J. Bentahar et al. (Eds.): MobiWIS 2021, LNCS 12814, pp. 185–194, 2021.
https://doi.org/10.1007/978-3-030-83164-6_15

identify, signify and access things of our day to day life anytime and anywhere through the internet, and allow them to be controlled as far as possible [4].

This paper describes the form of an application-led project by building a smart application system using the Lego Mindstorm kit. The background is described in Sect. 2. The detail of the design and implementation includes prototype architecture and three different scenarios with state machines describes in Sect. 3. Section 4 is a result of design and implementation. Section 5 is a discussion about the overall research. Plus, a conclusion in Sect. 6. Moreover, Appendix on the latest of the paper presents the mobile dashboard with the distance sensor information of all three scenarios.

2 Background

Lego Mindstorms kit is a simple robot with a programming environment for constructing an autonomous robot like block composition [5]. There are many applications of robots, which are useful in industrial, medical, and domestic environment [6]. It is very widely to use the Lego in academic scenarios for mobile robot platforms with sensors for vision and color recognition. Its use to teach programming languages, robotics, and embedded systems. Also, its use in teaching is a good way to motivate engineering students, which is fundamental to successful teaching [7, 8]. It makes a very convenient framework for course projects that integrate mobile application systems for color recognition, line-following, obstacle detection, and vehicle interaction, among the most common cause [9].

Even though the Lego Mindstorms kit was initially designed as a toy for children over 12 years of age, its use in university courses is increasing yearly. It gets the attention of people working in many areas. These are including artificial intelligence, embedded systems, control systems, robotics, and operating systems. The Lego Mindstorms kit is inexpensive, easily reconfigurable, reprogrammable, versatile, and robust. Therefore, it is well suited for use in teaching in education scenarios [10]. The Lego modularity makes the rapid prototyping of different robot configurations easier. This easiness presents itself as extra motivation for the persons who take their first steps in the world of mobile robotics [11].

It will be able to build the robot from the Lego Mindstorm kit. Then, download the Lego Mindstorms kit coding application that can run both mobile or tablet. Lego Mindstorms kit makes it possible to build embedded systems without any prerequisite knowledge of programming language. It can solve real problems with constraints such as sensors. This application allows the programming scenario to make programs. It runs programs that control the robot's behavior, for example, moving, picking up, throwing, and seeing. It can program the robot by using the Mindstorms application via block graphical programming. It easy to scratch programming environment using blocks, which will connect blocks and the program flow from top to bottom. The application connects Lego robots via Bluetooth, which has sensors to control the robot.

Lego Mindstorms kit has four medium motors. It has two sensors that are distance sensor and color sensor. It can also touch, sound, ultrasound, and light.

3   Design and Development

Figure 1 presents the prototype architecture that application on smartphone or tablet connects hub via Bluetooth. Hub has two different sensors. The first sensor is a distance sensor that the robot can move at different distances. Another sensor is a color sensor that can distinguish colors. It will control the robot, for example, throwing a ball when a color is green.

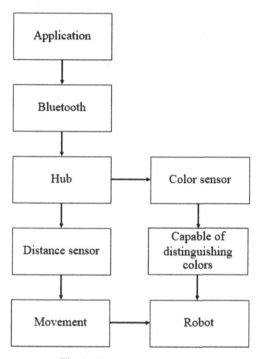

Fig. 1. Prototype architecture

Figure 2 explains the detail of the Lego robot that its name Tricky. It has two different sensors, which color sensor and a distance sensor. It has three motors that are A, B, and C, which can behave as actuators. Motor A and B control movement. Motor C controls two arms. It is a two-wheeled robot that can move forward, backward, turn right and turn left. It can pick up the object, for example, a ball or something in scenario A. Furthermore, it can play bowling in scenario B as the same components of Lego in this picture.

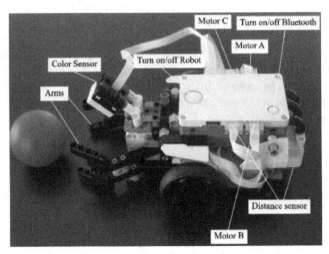

Fig. 2. Components of bowling Lego robot

The ways are long 90 cm in two different directions ways which are straight road and swing road. Each distance moves 10% and 100% of speed as the states Speed 10% and Speed 100%. That means it has four different cases in this scenario which, speed 10% at the straight road, speed 10% at the swing road, speed 100% at the straight road, and speed 100% at the swing road. Each case will try ten times. The result will calculate in percent of the robot that can lift and hold the object in the air.

Figure 3 presents the scenario that the robot can move and play bowling using the distance sensor. The component of the robot is the same in scenario A. It starts at the Idle state that is the beginning of the state when the application connects to the robot as the robot will pick the object up. Also, the states, which Hub off, Hub on, Bluetooth on, and Wait 3 s are the same. The motor controls the robot's arm. The robot throws the ball on pins. It will stop moving forwards, reducing its movement, and then stop and exit the program. The robot will play bowling at two different distances between the robot and all pins, which are 10 cm and 20 cm. Each distance moves 50% and 100% of speed. That means it has four various cases in this scenario, speed 50% at distance 10 cm, speed 50% at distance 20 cm, speed 100% at distance 10 cm, and speed 100% at distance 20 cm. Each case will try ten times. The result will calculate in percent of the robot that can knock down each pin.

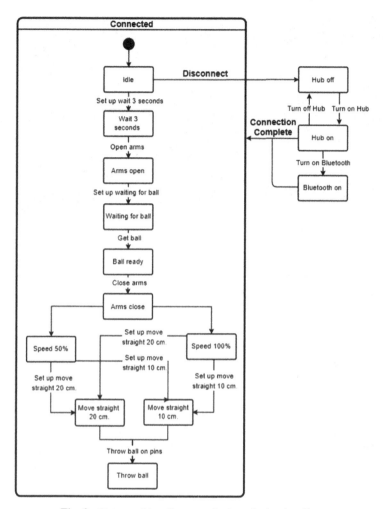

Fig. 3. State machine diagram of robot playing bowling

Figure 4 explains the detail of the Lego robot that is almost the same Fig. 2. However, the distance sensor is in front of it, and the color sensor is in the back.

It has three motors as same Fig. 2 and the motor C controls two lang arms, which can score a slam dunk in the basketball. When it can throw the ball in the correct position, the two targets will come out. Figure 5 presents the scenario that the robot can move and play basketball using the distance sensor. It starts at the Idle state that is the beginning of the state when the application connects to the robot as the robot will pick up the object.

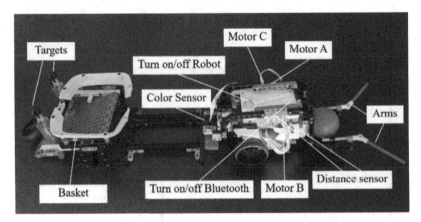

Fig. 4. Components of basketball slam dunk Lego robot

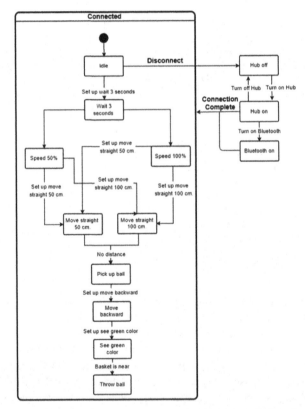

Fig. 5. State machine diagram of the robot in basketball slam dunk

4   Results

Figure 6 explains that the robot could pick up the object at speeding 10% better than 100%. It was better at straight road than swing road. Furthermore, it was the best when the robot moved slowly at the straight road. Therefore, speeding 10% at the straight road is the best case in this scenario.

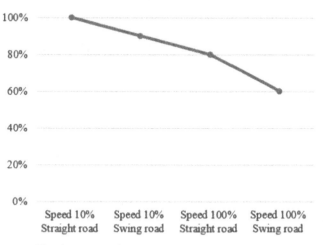

Fig. 6. Percent of the robot could pick up the object

Figure 7 explains that the robot played bowling and could knock down the pins at speeding 100% better than 50%. It was better when the robot was near to the pin 10 cm than 20 cm. Furthermore, it was best when the robot moved fast and near the pins. Therefore, speeding 100% in the distance of 10 cm is the best case in this scenario.

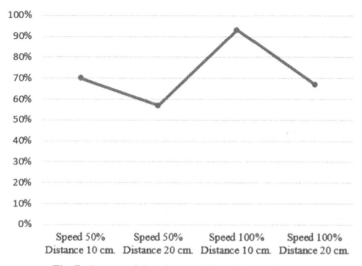

Fig. 7. Percent of the robot could knock down the pins

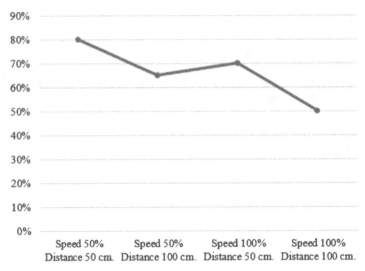

Fig. 8. Percent of the robot got to score a slam dunk

Figure 8 explains that the robot got to score a slam dunk in basketball at speeding of 50% and distance from the ball 50 cm is the best score. In contrast, 100% speeding and distance from the ball 100 cm is the worst score.

5 Discussion

We designed the IoT application scenarios, build the Lego Mindstorm kit system, and implement a block-based visual programming language. As the result of scenario A. It programmed the robot to move, pick up, hold the objects in the air at different speeds, and directions way. Speeding affected how the robot picked up the object. The distance sensor is used to control the robot's arms motor when picking up. Moving slower could pick up better. Swing road made it moved in the wrong direction. Both speeding and swing road can affect it. Sometimes it moved very fast as maximum speed. It moved not straight and stopped the incorrect position as it should be. Therefore, it could not pick up the object. It is always a good idea to reduce the speed for motors that require precision. If it moves too fast, it cannot pick up the objects effectively. In the real world, it is the same when driving vehicles. When driving is so fast at swing the road, maybe they can move out of the road and out of control.

In scenario B, the robot played bowling and could knock down the pins. The distance sensor in front of it controlled itself to moved forward. The distance between it and the pins was near 10 cm and a maximum speed of 100% was the best result. It could knock down the pins very well. In contradiction, the result was not so good when speeding slower and far from the pins. Sometimes it could not knock down any pins because it moved slowly at 50% of speed. The ball moved not straight, stopped in the incorrect position as it should be. Therefore, the ball was far away from the pins. Slowing speed was not knock down all the pins occasionally because it did not have enough energy.

There is a particular floor or slide that is the same in the real world when playing bowling. It is easier to knock down the pins when throwing the ball very fast with energy and close them.

In scenario C, the robot got to score a slam dunk. The color sensor in front of it controlled itself to score a slam dunk when the robot could see green color on the floor in front of the basket. The best score for this experiment was speed 50% and moved forward 50 cm as backward. The robot moved both forward and backward slowly in the correct direction way. It could pick up the ball and come back to the basket correct position at the green color in front of the basket. Therefore, it could get more score than another case. In opposite, when speeding 100% and moved forward 100 cm was the worst case. The robot moved too fast and could not come back to the correct position. Sometimes it moved not straight and stopped in the wrong position. Also, it was not enough energy to make the two targets jumped out from the basket. Therefore, it could not score or only one score a slam dunk. It is the same when persons throw a ball in a basket or something a target. They should stand at the appropriate position and throw a ball with suitable energy. Thus, they will get a score. Speed and distance that control by distance sensor is significant in this experiment.

Moreover, we think about the real-world in a self-driving smart car. It can operate its own by measuring the distance of various objects beside roadsides and with other vehicles running on roads [12]. However, there are many difficulties in a self-driving field because of the dynamic environment and the fast and complex movement. Different tasks are needed in a self-driving field such as vehicle distance measurement, vehicle detection, and obstacle detection [13]. Sensor controls cars, which can drive on asphalt, sand, or another. Plus, the robots in all three scenarios in this paper moved on the tree floor. It is smoother than asphalt on the real road. Additionally, the robot's wheels are smooth plastics. Therefore, many variables make robots move in different as to need.

6 Conclusion

In this paper, we presented an analysis of a distance sensor in the Lego Mindstorm kit. In all three scenarios, the distance sensor controlled the robot's movement. The distance and speeding affect how the robots picked up the object, played bowling, and scored a slam dunk in basketball. Moving slower could pick up the object better. Swing road made the robot moved in the wrong direction. However, when the robot played bowling, it could knock down the pins better when closed to them. In the scenario of scored a slam dunk in basketball, it lowered speeding and closed the basket to help it get more score. That means both distance and speeding could affect the robot's movement.

Additionally, in these three scenarios, blocking path encoding or the next function controls the robots about moving, action, and doing something. It identified the problem as step by step for the robots to reach its destination. It is the same as real-world programming that programmers must change their algorithms to control the robot's behavior and situations. It plans to write the coding of what happens before, present, and future. Sometimes it should use a condition, for example, if-else, switch-case. It is essential to design sequence, speed, distance that the robots can move slower or faster. We have learned the thought process behind creating a program, programming functions, and how we cloud to control the robots' actions or events. It used block coding programming in the mobile application. There are many different possibilities to design, build on scenarios, and code using the Lego Mindstorm kit. Therefore, this paper described and helped to understand and approaches by which mobile computing, sensors, and Internet of things.

In the future research targets mobile computing, sensors, and Internet of things. It would analyze more different types of roads. It is important where robots drive. Additionally, it can explain cases scenario with more specific detail. The result may be different.

References

1. Brade, T., Kaiser, J., Zug, S.: Expressing validity estimates in smart sensor applications. In: 26th International Conference on Architecture of Computing Systems, Prague, Czech Republic, pp. 1–8 (2013)
2. Liu, X., Baiocchi, O.: A comparison of the definitions for smart sensors, smart objects and things in IoT. In: 2016 IEEE 7th Annual Information Technology, Electronics and Mobile Communication Conference (IEMCON), Vancouver, BC, pp. 1–4 (2016)
3. Bachpalle, S.D., Shinde, M.R.: Integration of sensors for location tracking using Internet of Things. In: 2018 International Conference on Information, Communication, Engineering and Technology (ICICET), Pune, pp. 1–4 (2018)
4. Islam, T., Mukhopadhyay, S.C., Suryadevara, N.K.: Smart sensors and Internet of Things: a postgraduate paper. IEEE Sens. J. **17**(3), 577–584 (2017)
5. Tominaga, H., Onishi, Y., Hayashi, T., Yamasaki, T.: LEGO robot programming exercise support for problem solving learning with game strategy planning tools. In: 2007 First IEEE International Workshop on Digital Game and Intelligent Toy Enhanced Learning (DIGITEL 2007), Jhongli City, pp. 81–88 (2007)
6. Trung, P., Afzulpurkar, N., Bodhale, D.: Development of vision service in robotics studio for road signs recognition and control of LEGO MINDSTORMS ROBOT. In: 2008 IEEE International Conference on Robotics and Biomimetics, Bangkok, pp. 1176–1181 (2009)
7. Pinto, M., Moreira, A.P., Matos, A.: Localization of mobile robots using an extended Kalman filter in a LEGO NXT. IEEE Trans. Educ. **55**(1), 135–144 (2012)
8. Padayachee, K., Gouws, P.M., Lemmer, M.: Evaluating the effectiveness of Lego Robots in engaged scholarship. In: 2015 Annual Global Online Conference on Information and Computer Technology (GOCICT), Louisville, KY, pp. 16–20 (2015)
9. Ariza, D.V., Palacio, A.M., Aragón, I.P., Pulido, C.M., Logreira, E.A., McKinley, J.R.: Application of color sensor programming with LEGO-Mindstorms NXT 2.0 to recreate a simplistic plague detection scenario. Scientia et Technica **22**(3), 268–272 (2017)
10. Prieto, S.S., Navarro, T.A., Plaza, M.G., Polo, O.R.: A monoball robot based on LEGO Mindstorms [Focus on Education]. IEEE Control Syst. Mag. **32**(2), 71–83 (2012)
11. Goncales, J., Lima, J., Malheiros, P., Costa, P.: Realistic simulation of a Lego Mindstorms NXT based robot. In: 2009 IEEE Control Applications, (CCA) & Intelligent Control, (ISIC), St. Petersburg, pp. 1242–1247 (2009)
12. Mamun, M.I., Rahman, A., Khaleque, M.A., Mridha, M.F., Hamid, M.A.: Healthcare monitoring system inside self-driving smart car in 5G cellular network. In: 2019 IEEE 17th International Conference on Industrial Informatics (INDIN), Helsinki, Finland, pp. 1515–1520 (2019)
13. Zaarane, A., Slimani, I., Hamdoun, A., Atouf, I.: Vehicle to vehicle distance measurement for self-driving systems. In: 2019 6th International Conference on Control, Decision and Information Technologies (CoDIT), Paris, France, pp. 1587–1591 (2019)

Author Index

Printed in the United States
by Baker & Taylor Publisher Services